Collegescope™

ACADEMIC AND CAREER
SUCCESS STARTS HERE

Kendall Hunt
publishing company

human℮sources®
Your potential. Our passion.

Cover image © shutterstock

publishing company
www.kendallhunt.com
Send all inquiries to:
4050 Westmark Drive
Dubuque, IA 52004-1840

CONTENTS

WELCOME MESSAGE

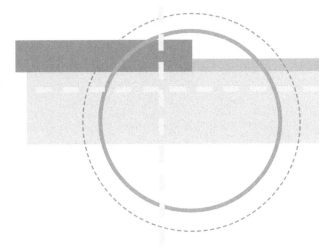

Thank you for taking part in the CollegeScope student success program. The CollegeScope text is enhanced with links to online resources and includes readings, activities, quizzes, videos, journal entries and much more. The goals of the program are to help you find satisfaction and success in school, at work, and in your personal life.

CollegeScope also takes the unique approach of making things personal. How you find success and where you find success is up to you. This program will start by helping you learn about yourself: your strengths and challenges, your values and interests, and your belief in your abilities. Then you will learn to set goals, make decisions, study, work, communicate, and ultimately succeed in your goals – all according to your unique set of traits and characteristics.

©Daniel Dash/Shutterstock.com

©Antonio Guillem/Shutterstock.com

The program is divided into chapters and each chapter begins with a Starting Survey and a Motivation Check. The survey is just to see what you know before you begin, so you can measure how much you learn in each chapter. The Motivation Check is there to get you thinking about the chapter topic in a way that motivates you and sets a positive attitude toward what you will learn. You may be surprised, excited, made curious, frustrated or even shocked by the Motivation Check. The last thing we'd want is to be boring.

We hope you enjoy CollegeScope, learn from it, and provide feedback in one of the many places we make that option available. Just like the people we serve, we hope to improve CollegeScope through what you tell us about it.

1

PERSONAL AWARENESS

PERSONAL AWARENESS

This is a quick survey to measure what you know about this chapter topic, both before and after you complete the chapter. Just be honest and rate how much each of the following statements applies to you now. Give yourself a score of:
1 for Not a bit • 2 for A little • 3 for Some • 4 for Mostly • 5 for Definitely

©arka38/Shutterstock.com

BEFORE CHAPTER

		Not a bit 1	A little 2	Some 3	Mostly 4	Definitely 5
1	I reflect on and clearly understand what motivates me.	○	○	○	○	○
2	I can describe how I benefit from having a clear purpose.	○	○	○	○	○
3	I have a strong sense of purpose and can describe what my purpose is.	○	○	○	○	○
4	I can describe how my education and career relate to my purpose.	○	○	○	○	○
5	I know which values are most important to me and which are less important.	○	○	○	○	○
6	I consider my values when making choices about school, work, and my personal life.	○	○	○	○	○
7	I can explain the benefits of keeping my actions aligned with my values.	○	○	○	○	○

		Not a bit 1	A little 2	Some 3	Mostly 4	Definitely 5
8	I can describe my strengths and challenges according to my personality type.	○	○	○	○	○
9	I understand how to adapt and work with other personality types.	○	○	○	○	○
10	I have a clear understanding of my intelligence profile—my strengths and potential challenges.	○	○	○	○	○
11	I know how to use my intelligence strengths most effectively and how to develop my challenge areas.	○	○	○	○	○
12	I know my top work interest areas.	○	○	○	○	○
13	I can name educational programs and careers that best align with my top work interest areas.	○	○	○	○	○
14	I can explain the benefits of working with people who have similar interests and with those who have different interests.	○	○	○	○	○
15	I can describe what self-efficacy is and how it relates to achievement.	○	○	○	○	○
16	I know my own level of self-efficacy and how to improve it.	○	○	○	○	○

Add up your scores to determine your **Before Chapter** total and write it down here:

PERSONAL AWARENESS: KNOWING MYSELF

Key Questions

1. Motivation Check: Do I Really Know Myself?

2. How can I find purpose in what I do?

3. What do I value most?

4. How does knowing my personality type help me?

5. How can I develop multiple intelligences?

6. How can I find my interests at school and work?

7. What is self-efficacy and will it affect my success?

©studio_chki/Shutterstock.com

Part of knowing yourself is knowing your purpose. Before we ask you to share your purpose, however, we hope to motivate you by sharing ours.

Our Purpose

> **Connect people to opportunities that matter—for learning, working and living.**

Our Strategy

- **Know Yourself**
  Learn more about yourself on a deeper level: your values, personality, interests and abilities. Become aware of your strengths and challenges and what works best for you in learning, working, and in your personal life.
- **Know Your Opportunities**
  Discover a wide variety of learning, work and life opportunities. Build goals and plans around the ones that fit you best.
- **Advance Your Opportunities**
  Provide the strategies and motivation to take action and achieve success.

We believe this three part strategy will lead to you to a happier and more successful life. Therefore, everything we say and ask you to do in *CollegeScope* should fit with that strategy. In fact, we want you to actively think about that strategy as much as possible. Connect as many ideas and activities in *CollegeScope* as you can to that strategy. Doing this should help keep you motivated and focused as you work through the program.

Start with Your Purpose

This chapter will focus on the first part of that strategy—know yourself. Knowing yourself starts with knowing your purpose, and that is where we begin below.

"The better you know yourself, the better your relationship with the rest of the world."

– TONI COLLETTE

MOTIVATION CHECK

Do I Really Know Myself?

Think about the following questions. Don't answer them directly, but indicate how confident you are that you could give specific answers to these questions right now.

Are you confident in your answer?
1 = least confident   5 = most confident

		1	2	3	4	5
1	What is your favorite color?	○	○	○	○	○
2	What brings you fulfillment?	○	○	○	○	○
3	What kind of foods do you like to eat?	○	○	○	○	○
4	How do you learn best?	○	○	○	○	○
5	What TV shows or movies do you enjoy?	○	○	○	○	○
6	What are your greatest strengths and challenges?	○	○	○	○	○
7	What are some songs you like and some you dislike?	○	○	○	○	○
8	What are your top values?	○	○	○	○	○
9	Where do you like to shop?	○	○	○	○	○
10	What is your style of communicating and how does that affect others?	○	○	○	○	○

Answering Difficult Questions

Did you notice the difference between the odd-numbered and even-numbered questions? Which questions are harder to answer? Which questions are more important for making decisions that will bring you real happiness and success?

If your confidence was much lower for the even-numbered questions, don't worry. Most people are just like you. It is easy to get caught up in simple, everyday things and forget about the deeper questions we should be asking ourselves—like the even-numbered questions.

Would you like to be better able to answer deeper questions about yourself? If so, great! CollegeScope is designed to help you tackle the tougher questions, to really get to know yourself, and advance toward that real happiness and success.

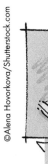

DO I REALLY KNOW MYSELF?

Think about how you answered the different types of questions in the Do I Really Know Myself activity above. Was there a big difference between the surface-level (odd) and the deeper (even) questions? Record what you think this means about how well you really know yourself, and what you plan to do about it.

SECTION 1-1 FINDING PURPOSE

Learning Objectives

- Describe what purpose is and see examples of purpose in others
- Begin to form or strengthen your own sense of purpose
- Understand the benefits of having purpose

What Is Purpose?

A definition of purpose to consider:

A general goal or direction with an outcome that has significant meaning for you and the world beyond you.

Purpose is not simply about what makes you happy. Eating chocolate or relaxing on a warm beach may make you happy, but it does not provide fulfillment. Working towards a purpose is usually a long-term

©Ollyy/Shutterstock.com

endeavor that takes effort and persistence, and will make you feel good about what you accomplish.

©Sofi photo/Shutterstock.com

SOMEONE I KNOW WITH PURPOSE

Can you think of someone you know who seems to live with purpose? What is it that makes you think this person has purpose?

To help you think about purpose, look at the following examples of purpose statements.

Examples of Purpose

- To chase dreams
- To make history
- To live as long as possible
- To seek wisdom and knowledge
- To challenge oppression
- To eat, drink, and be merry
- To reduce suffering
- To make the world a better place to live
- To love

- To seek beauty in all its forms
- To understand the mysteries of the universe
- To strive for power and superiority
- To build wealth and prosperity
- To follow a higher being
- To help others
- To raise a happy and healthy family
- To face fears
- To attain enlightenment

Do any of these connect with you? Some should be more appealing than others. Knowing what appeals to you and what does not should help you gain a sense of your desired purpose.

Video Discovery

Below are weblinks to videos about people working toward a specific purpose. View at least one that looks interesting to you and think about whether it inspires you.

- Accomplish Big Things (see Link 1-1)
- Inspire Others (see Link 1-2)
- Help Others (see Link 1-3)

- Start a Movement (see Link 1-4)
- Be Successful (see Link 1-5)
- Be Extraordinary (see Link 1-6)

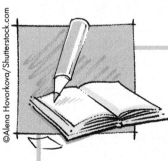

SELECT A PURPOSE STATEMENT

Out of all the purpose statements above (video titles and list of examples), which connects with you the most? Why?

"Every choice before you represents the universe inviting you to remember who you are and what you want."

– ALAN COHEN

Why Purpose?

Your purpose is a reflection of who you are and what motivates you. From your purpose you can identify more specific goals that you will be motivated to attempt and feel rewarded by accomplishing. Also, making choices that lose sight of your purpose can conflict with your values and cause you to lose motivation. Without developing a clear purpose, you can become frustrated and unsatisfied with your life. Having a purpose and acting according to that purpose has many positive effects.

Having purpose can help you be successful in what you want to accomplish. Consider the following quotations from some very successful people.

Quotations from Successful People

AREA	AUTHOR	QUOTATION
Politics	John F. Kennedy	Efforts and courage are not enough without purpose and direction.
Business	Mary Kay Ash	We must have a theme, a goal, a purpose in our lives. If you don't know where you are aiming, you don't have a goal.
Design	Frank Lloyd Wright	The thing always happens that you really believe in; and the belief in a thing makes it happen.
Science	Albert Einstein	Nothing truly valuable arises from ambition or from a mere sense of duty; it stems rather from love and devotion towards men and towards objective things.
Social Cause	Helen Keller	Many persons have a wrong idea of what constitutes true happiness. It is not attained through self-gratification but through fidelity to a worthy purpose.
Art	Michelangelo	I saw the angel in the marble and carved until I set him free.
Writing	Washington Irving	Great minds have purposes, others have wishes.
Music	Alanis Morissette	I started playing piano when I was 6. And I knew that I wanted to be involved in that form of expression, whether it was through music, or acting, or dancing, or painting, or writing.
Sports	Andy Roddick	At some point in your life you either have the thing you want or the reasons why you don't.

QUOTATION ABOUT PURPOSE

Find your own favorite quote about purpose from BrainyQuote using Link 1-7. Copy the quote and record it here.

The Importance of Purpose

Not only is purpose an important part of success, it can be an important part of basic survival.

Consider the story of Viktor Frankl, an influential neurologist, psychiatrist, author, and Holocaust survivor:

The Greatest Motivating Force

Viktor Frankl grew up in Austria with a strong fascination for psychology. While in medical school he organized a program that provided free counseling to high school students. The program focused on students at a time when they received report cards, a time when the student suicide rate usually peaked. In 1931, while the program was active, the student suicide rate in Vienna dropped to zero for the entire year.

When the Nazi takeover occurred in 1938, Frankl, a Jew, began to lose access and privileges in medical facilities. Eventually he was sent to the Jewish "Ghettos," but was able to continue his work in psychiatry helping the people in the ghetto with the psychological stresses of living there. He spent two years in that ghetto helping people and even hosted a series of public lectures that promoted good mental health. Then, he was sent to Dachau concentration camp to work as a slave laborer. He toiled there for 5 months until the camp was liberated by the Americans.

During his time in the ghetto and the concentration camps, Frankl's wife, mother, father, and brother all died either in the gas chambers or as a result of the brutal conditions imposed by the Nazis. He credits his own perseverance to finding meaning and purpose in his life, despite the horrific circumstances around him. He also observed this perseverance in some of his fellow prisoners. He found that having purpose and meaning in life was a significant factor in determining whether someone survived the Nazi concentration camps.[1]

His medical education combined with his experience in the Holocaust helped Frankl develop Logotherapy, which is based on the idea that the most powerful motivating and driving force in humans is finding meaning or purpose in one's life. This idea differed from other theories that claim human motivation derives from a desire to gain power or to seek pleasure.

Frankl's career remained focused on his purpose of helping others through an understanding of human psychology. In that endeavor, he also led a very successful career. Frankl authored 32 books, including Man's Search for Meaning, which is listed by the U.S. Library of Congress as one of the "Ten Most Influential Books in America." He has 29 honorary doctorates from universities around the world and received 19 national and international awards and medals for his work.

The story of Viktor Frankl is an extreme example of the role purpose can play. However, purpose has significant effects on a smaller scale and under more typical circumstances. The following are some effects of having and living according to purpose. These points are all based on research that examines large groups of people.

Positive Effects of Purpose

1. Improves overall life satisfaction[2]

2. Lowers stress[3]

3. Protects the mind from the effects of age[4]

4. Protects against heart disease[5]

5. Improves sense of identity and self-esteem[6]

MY PURPOSE

Time to think of a purpose for yourself.

1 Record what you think your purpose might be. Be as general or specific as you want. If you are unsure, just record some ideas you picked up in this chapter so far.

2 Describe one thing you have done (or are doing) that is most closely aligned with your purpose. Don't worry, it doesn't have to be something big—anything you can think of. How did you feel at the time?

Act on Your Purpose

While many people can tell you about their purpose when asked, many of us forget to consider our purpose when making important choices. We also get caught up in daily routines: cleaning, running errands, or watching TV. In other words, we know our purpose, but we often neglect to act on it.

"Many men go fishing all of their lives without knowing that it is not fish they are after."

— HENRY DAVID THOREAU

How to Achieve Purpose

So, what is the first step to achieving your purpose? The first step is to relax and realize that achieving your purpose is a lifelong journey. Becoming anxious because you don't have a clear purpose yet will only make things harder. Breathe. Everybody realizes their purpose at different times in their life. Your purpose will come in time, if you work towards it.

OK, step one is done. See, you are already on your way!

What is step two, you ask? Look for inspiration from others. We have already started you on step two by showing you quotes, videos and the story of Viktor Frankl. Be sure to look for inspiration elsewhere in your life—friends, relatives, or even stories of complete strangers. Also, look for opportunity. Some people achieve their purpose by recognizing a problem and dedicating themselves to fixing it. Ever hear of Mother Theresa, Gandhi or Martin Luther King?

As you look for inspiration, it is important to think about your traits—what makes you *you*. You may find inspiration in some things, but not necessarily find a purpose that fits you. To better understand what purpose fits you, consider the following questions.

- What are my *values* – what I consider worthy and important?
- What is my *personality* – my natural tendencies and viewpoints?
- What are my *abilities* – the things I do well?
- What are my *interests* – the things I enjoy?

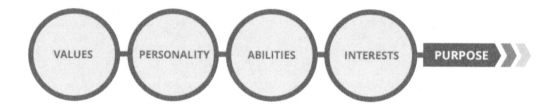

The next sections will help you determine exactly what your values, personality, abilities, and interests are.

SECTION 1-2: PRIORITIZING VALUES

Learning Objectives

- Describe your personal values and learn how to prioritize them
- Be able to explain and carry out behavior according to values
- Relate personal values to education, career, and life choices

The previous section mentioned that values, along with some other factors, can help clarify our purpose and define our path in life.

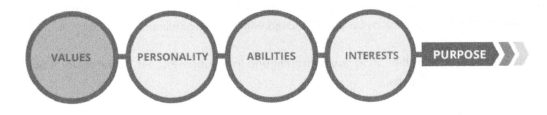

VALUES

Do you remember how we described values? Select what you think describes values best, then check your answer.
- what is considered important
- natural behaviors and tendencies
- what is enjoyed
- what can be done well

Answer: Values are our core beliefs—what we consider most worthy or important.
There is a close relationship between values and purpose. Like purpose, acting according to your values brings fulfillment and psychological well-being. Betraying your values causes distress.

People can value things such as relationships and personal achievement. A person may value both of those things, but there are times when those two values can be in conflict.

Career or Relationship?

Imagine two close friends who have to compete for the same spot on a team or for the same job. One friend may decide to withdraw to allow the other to gain the spot rather than jeopardize the relationship. Or, one may decide to compete aggressively because it is an important opportunity for career advancement which should not affect the friendship. In both cases, one value holds more importance than the other.

Education or Family?

Picture a student who is accepted to a prestigious college far from home, but decides to attend a less prestigious, local college to stay close and help out family. Neither choice is right or wrong. Instead, the choice is a matter of which values are most important to the individual making the choice.

Do Values Change?

Our values come from multiple sources, like our parents, teachers, coaches, friends, media, religion and culture. Once formed, values tend to be stable. However, certain factors can cause priorities to shift over time. These shifts usually occur slowly as we experience and learn from different life stages. Drastic changes may occur in response to dramatic life events such as being diagnosed with cancer or winning the lottery.

In order to help make decisions that bring you fulfillment and true happiness, it is important to remain aware of your values throughout your lifetime.

"Happiness is that state of consciousness which proceeds from the achievement of one's values."

– AYN RAND

Values and Careers

You may already have an idea of some of your values, but it always helps to reflect on and prioritize them. Prioritizing can be difficult because it means putting some values ahead of others. However, prioritizing is important because many of life's decisions involve sacrificing one value for another. For example, many careers naturally favor certain values over others.

* A police officer is expected to uphold laws, sometimes at the expense of forgiveness and kindness.
* A corporate executive is often expected to optimize efficiency and profit, sometimes at the expense of helping others.
* A care worker for the sick or elderly is expected to help others, usually while sacrificing a higher level of pay.

While some occupations may favor certain values over others, many occupations have the flexibility to support multiple values. Within occupations, there are other factors that affect the priorities of different values. Consider the difference between a doctor who works in a private clinic versus one in a refugee camp versus one who is a consultant for a pharmaceutical company.

VALUES ALIGN OR CONFLICT

Imagine two people. One person has a job that is closely aligned with his or her values. The other person has a job that conflicts with his or her values. How do you think each person would feel about his or her job? What do you think would be each person's general happiness in life?

A Moral Dilemma

When making career decisions it is a good idea to reflect on the priority of your values. An effective and interesting way to challenge your priorities is to consider a moral or ethical dilemma. An ethical dilemma is a choice with no clear right or wrong answer. How each person would choose depends on his or her values.

Consider the following dilemma adapted from the story of Les Misérables.

What is Right?

Jean Valjean is a young peasant in France in the early 1800s. He steals a loaf of bread to feed his sister's starving children and is arrested and put into prison. His stay in prison is extended for many years after he makes several attempts to escape. He is finally released after almost 20 years. At this point Valjean is left to sleep in the streets, bitter toward the system that imprisoned him and the society that now rejects him for his past.

He encounters a kind bishop who shows him mercy and convinces Valjean to turn his life around by working hard to provide for others. As he considers this life-changing moment, out of habit, he steals a dropped coin from a boy. Soon after the boy runs away scared, Valjean repents and searches for the boy to return the coin and beg forgiveness. However, the police have already been informed and are now searching for Valjean. He realizes that if caught, he will be locked away for life as a repeat offender. So, he flees to another small town and changes his identity.

Six years pass and Valjean, remembering the bishop's words, has worked hard and become a factory owner employing many of the townspeople. He also wins the respect of the townspeople through good deeds and generous acts. In fact, many of the less fortunate townspeople become dependent on his generosity. He is eventually named mayor because of his popularity.

One day, Valjean hears of the capture of a thief. The police think it is Valjean! He is torn. He knows the thief will be punished more severely because the police believe it is him. However, he feels that he has redeemed himself and now many good people are dependent on him for basic needs. The thief is a criminal who is not helping anybody. Valjean wants to turn himself in because it is the right thing to do for his own redemption. But, perhaps continuing to help good, innocent people, as he is doing now, is the more selfless act. The police will probably not show any leniency toward Valjean despite his rehabilitation.

A MORAL DILEMMA

The questions that follow relate to the story you've just read about Jean Valjean.

1 What do you think Valjean should do: turn himself in or keep his real identity secret?

2 Provide your reasons by describing why one choice is better than the other.

3 Think about a situation when you had to make a choice that forced you to consider your priorities – a time when you had to sacrifice one value for another. Did you consider your core values? How do you feel about that decision now? Explain.

Work Values

Now that you have reflected a little, it is a good time to take a survey of your values—specifically, your work values. Don't worry if you have had little work experience; you can reflect on what you value as a student and in your personal life. Ask yourself, "What is most important in keeping me happy and productive?"

WORK VALUES SURVEY

Instructions: Compare all of the following statements and rate how important each is to you. Assign a rating of 1 to 10 points for each statement, with 1 point being the least important and 10 points being the most important.

NOTE: avoid rating everything the same or saying that everything has high importance. This exercise is about *ranking* your values from most important to least important. Therefore, you should rate some items lower, some in the middle, and some higher.

1   Have opportunities to advance my position or status

     1   2   3   4   5   6   7   8   9   10

2   Be able to work free of supervision

     1   2   3   4   5   6   7   8   9   10

3   Direct or instruct others

     1   2   3   4   5   6   7   8   9   10

4   Act with strong ethics and morals

     1   2   3   4   5   6   7   8   9   10

5   Have the trust and support of superiors

     1   2   3   4   5   6   7   8   9   10

6   Have security and stability

     1   2   3   4   5   6   7   8   9   10

7   Be well paid for the work I do

     1   2   3   4   5   6   7   8   9   10

8   Perform well and achieve at a superior level

     1   2   3   4   5   6   7   8   9   10

9   Make my own decisions
        1   2   3   4   5   6   7   8   9   10

10   Be admired and respected by others
        1   2   3   4   5   6   7   8   9   10

11   Have good relationships with my peers
        1   2   3   4   5   6   7   8   9   10

12   Get clear instructions and training in what I have to do
        1   2   3   4   5   6   7   8   9   10

13   Have the opportunity to work alone
        1   2   3   4   5   6   7   8   9   10

14   Get benefits in addition to my pay
        1   2   3   4   5   6   7   8   9   10

15   Make use of my specific talents or abilities
        1   2   3   4   5   6   7   8   9   10

16   Try out my own unique ideas
        1   2   3   4   5   6   7   8   9   10

17   Get recognition—have my work noticed
        1   2   3   4   5   6   7   8   9   10

18   Help others
        1   2   3   4   5   6   7   8   9   10

19   Be treated fairly and have clear rules
        1   2   3   4   5   6   7   8   9   10

20   Feel active and busy most of the time
        1   2   3   4   5   6   7   8   9   10

21   Have a level of physical comfort and convenience
        1   2   3   4   5   6   7   8   9   10

Each of the statements you rated for the work values survey belongs to one of the seven topics described below. Your score for each topic can range from 3 (minimum) to 30 (maximum). To determine your scores, add up the points for each topic, as indicated.

Topic	Scores
Achievement: Using your particular skills and talents and performing at a superior level	Total points for statements 1, 8 and 15:
Independence: A combination of creativity, ownership, and working without supervision	Total points for statements 2, 9 and 16:
Recognition: Getting promoted, having authority, and getting recognition and admiration	Total points for statements 3, 10 and 17:
Relationships: Having good relationships, strong ethics, and the chance to help others	Total points for statements 4, 11 and 18:
Support: Encouraged by superiors, and receiving clear direction and fair treatment	Total points for statements 5, 12 and 19:
Traditional Work Ethic: Having plenty of activity and variety, while feeling stable in the role and being able to work alone	Total points for statements 6, 13 and 20:
Benefits: Being rewarded for work done, with money or other forms of compensation, and having material comforts and conveniences	Total points for statements 7, 14 and 21:

Remember that there is nothing good or bad about the priority of your values. Like your physical traits, they are simply part of who you are. The words used to describe the seven areas have neutral meaning here. So avoid passing judgment and ignore any positive or negative connotations these words may have for you. For example, some people may think that "achievement" sounds like a more admirable value than "support." But all values are equally worthy. They are just different for different people.

If your results surprised you, it may be because you haven't yet been forced to place some values ahead of others. In many of our decisions and actions, we don't have to worry about prioritizing our values. But there are usually important times in our lives when we do.

Some Key Times to Consider Values

- Choosing your education
- Choosing your career
- In relationships
- Major purchases
- Whether to have kids
- How to raise kids

Reflecting on and knowing your priorities before these events occur can help you make decisions that promote your long-term happiness. Important events often catch us by surprise and you feel like you haven't had time to think about your decision. It is better to have considered your values beforehand. It is similar to knowing in advance what few things you would save if your house suddenly caught fire—preparation is key.

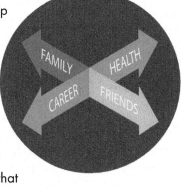

©Mr Bachinsky/Shutterstock.com

Think again about your results from the work values survey. Are you headed in a direction that supports your top values? In other words, do the school courses or programs you are taking, or plan to take, support a career path that aligns with your top values? Complete the following activity to help you consider those questions.

Work Values Activity

Use the U.S. Department of Labor's O*NET website to identify which values are best supported by different careers. Choose **one** option below based on your situation.

Option 1

You have clear future plans for your education and career.

1. Visit the O*NET site at Link 1-8. Use any of the search methods available to find your top two career choices.
2. On the summary report screen for each career, go to the "Work Values" section.
3. Compare the values listed for those careers with the values in the results of your work values survey. Record your two career choices and the values listed for those careers in the journal below.

Option 2

Your career and education plans are not yet clear.

1. Go to the work values search on the O*NET site at Link 1-9.
2. In the first two selectors, choose the top two values from the results of your work values survey and click Go. (see Note below for "Working Conditions")
3. A list of careers organized by Job Zone (education and training) will be displayed. Feel free to use the other options, such as Job Zone, to filter the list of careers.
4. The goal here is not to finalize your future career, but rather to get a sense of which careers align with your values. Choose two careers that you favor from the matching list and record their titles and listed values in the journal below.

NOTE: The last two values on our work values survey, Traditional Work Ethic and Benefits, are combined into one value called Working Conditions on the O*NET site. We felt that separating the concepts and renaming them in this program made it easier to understand what is being measured. Calculate the average between traditional work values and benefits to get your score for working conditions.

WORK VALUES ACTIVITY JOURNAL

From the activity above, you should have identified two careers, each with its top values. Record those careers and their values below, then respond to either option A or B at the bottom.

Career choice 1 and its top values:

Career choice 2 and its top values:

For this next question, you have two options. Choose one and respond to it in the space below.

Option A

You would prefer to think and reflect on your values and plans for the future.

Using what you have learned about careers and your values, explain how your planned career can support your values. Describe specific activities and outcomes from your planned education and career that align with your top values.

Option B

You would prefer to talk to others about values and plans for the future.

Find someone who is happy and satisfied in their career and is willing to do a short interview about work and work values. Record a summary of your interview below, including both the questions and answers. You can create your own interview questions or use the sample questions below. For privacy, please do not identify your interviewee in this entry.

Sample Questions

- Do you feel that your most important values are supported by your work?
- Can you provide some examples of how your work supports your values? Or, what it is about your work that keeps you happy and satisfied?
- Do you do things outside of work that support your values? Explain.

Enter your response from either Option A or B. Title your response with the option you chose.

SECTION 1-3: PERSONALITY TYPE

This section explores how personality type plays a role in helping to define our path and purpose in life.

> *"Your vision will become clear only when you can look into your own heart. Who looks outside, dreams; who looks inside, awakes."*
>
> – CARL JUNG

PERSONALITY

Do you remember how we described personality? Select the definition that you think describes personality best, then check your answer.

- what is considered important
- natural behaviors and tendencies
- what is enjoyed
- what can be done well

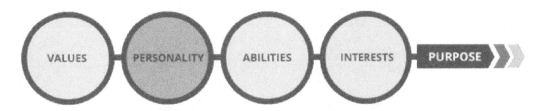

Answer: Personality refers to our natural behaviors—how we understand and interact with the world around us.

Of the four attributes shown in the graphic above, personality is likely the most stable over our lifetime.

Personality and Purpose

There is a close relationship between personality and purpose. Your personality has certain areas of strength and areas of challenge. For example, one aspect of personality is how extraverted or introverted you are.

- An **extravert**'s strength is interacting with many people and in busy environments. That same extravert may find it difficult to sit quietly and reflect on their own thoughts.
- An **introvert**, of course, would be the opposite. Therefore, certain educational programs, careers, and other life situations may be better suited to one personality type than the other.

In this section you will be taking the *Do What You Are®* personality assessment. In it you will be shown pairs of descriptions and asked to select which is most like you. Try to be as honest as possible about your true self. You may be tempted to answer in a way that seems more socially acceptable, or with what feels like the "better" answer. However, there are no better answers, only the way you truly are.

To help you understand a little more about personality type and how each type has value, we'd like you to watch a video about one dimension of personality type. We hope the video puts you in a frame of mind to get the most accurate results possible from the *Do What You Are* assessment. You can view the video with Link 1-10.

VIDEO FOLLOW-UP

Whether you are an introvert or extravert, what is the main message you get from the video?

Did you like this video? From 1 (not helpful at all) to 10 (extremely helpful), rate what you think of the video.

| 1 | 2 | 3 | 4 | 5 | 6 | 7 | 8 | 9 | 10 |

Ready to take the assessment? To get started, open a browser and go to www.humanesources.com. Click the Login link at the top of the page. If you have not already registered, follow the instructions to register with your Access Key. In your portfolio, select the link for *Do What You Are®* to begin the assessment.

Review your results from the Do What You Are® assessment online, located in your portfolio. Make a note of your personality type here, so you can refer to it later: _____

Use the links below for each letter combination to learn about the different personality types.

Table of All 16 Personality Types

ENFJ (Link 1-11)	ENFP (Link 1-15)	ENTJ (Link 1-19)	ENTP (Link 1-23)
ESFJ (Link 1-12)	ESFP (Link 1-16)	ESTJ (Link 1-20)	ESTP (Link 1-24)
INFJ (Link 1-13)	INFP (Link 1-17)	INTJ (Link 1-21)	INTP (Link 1-25)
ISFJ (Link 1-14)	ISFP (Link 1-18)	ISTJ (Link 1-22)	ISTP (Link 1-26)

ACTION PLAN FOR MY PERSONALITY

Let's apply your personality type to something more immediate—college. Look through your *Do What You Are* report one more time and focus on the sections labeled, "College Satisfiers" and "Your Preferred Learning Style." Choose one bullet point from each section that you want to address. Think of actions you can take as a student within the next week to apply the ideas in those two points. Based on the two points from your *Do What You Are* report, record the specific actions you plan to take below.

Be sure to complete all your responses before you finish this chapter.

For my college experience to be satisfying, I plan to...

To accommodate my preferred learning style, I plan to...

PERSONALITY RELATED TO CAREERS

For this question, read all of the instructions first, then review your *Do What You Are* report in your portfolio. Return to this page to respond to the questions.

Instructions:

View the list of suggested careers and majors in your *Do What You Are* report. These careers and majors are most likely to result in satisfaction and success based on your personality type and the career areas in which you expressed an interest. Not every item on the list will be ideal, but it should provide some good options and narrow your focus if you are still undecided.

1. Select two possible careers from the list that you think are reasonable options.
2. Read the two career profiles focusing on the sections titled Knowledge and Skills and Tasks and Activities. You can print the pages that you need.
3. Review your personality description and describe how your personality type matches the two careers you select.

Two careers that match my personality type and that I consider reasonable options are:

These careers match my personality in the following ways:

©Sofi photo/Shutterstock.com

Talk to Someone

Share your *Do What You Are* report with someone you know well. Focus on the section titled Your Interpersonal Negotiating Style. Talk about how misunderstandings with others may have occurred because of your personality type. The person you talk to is there to provide a more objective view of yourself. Be sure to listen carefully—you will be recording a summary of your discussion in the journal activity below.

DISCUSSING DIFFERENT PERSONALITIES

Refer to the previous page with the links to the table of 16 personality types. With the help of that table, guess the personality type of the person with whom you shared your *Do What You Are* report. Compare your two personality types and think of ways you can avoid misunderstandings by considering the other person's viewpoint.

Explain how you and another person can consider each other's personality types and avoid misunderstandings.

SECTION 1-4: MULTIPLE INTELLIGENCES

This section is about how our abilities help shape our purpose.

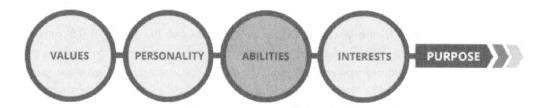

ABILITIES

Do you remember how we described abilities? Select the definition that you think describes abilities best.
- what is considered important
- natural behaviors and tendencies
- what is enjoyed
- what can be done well

Answer: Abilities are what can be done well—our talents and skills in accomplishing specific tasks.

There are two important things to remember about abilities:

1. Abilities are a result of natural talent **AND** the degree to which we develop them.

2. Different abilities can be used to accomplish the same goal.

You may be wondering why the title of this section refers to intelligences, when so far we have just been describing abilities. This section will focus on the similarities between "intelligences" and "abilities."

What is Intelligence?

People usually associate *intelligence* with knowledge and under-standing, and think it applies only to subjects like science, math and languages. On the other hand, we tend to think of *abilities* as applying more broadly to areas such as sports, music, humor, self-control and helping others. So, on the surface, intelligence and abilities appear to be different. However, carrying out any action correctly requires knowledge and understanding. And a narrow definition of intelligence does not recognize the special talents of people with great abilities.

We feel that a new definition of intelligence is more useful, and that is:

Intelligence is the capacity to do and create things that are valued in the current culture.

Different Intelligences

This is a more inclusive definition—it allows us to identify a wider range of abilities as "intelligence." An educator and researcher named Howard Gardner proposed a new theory of multiple intelligences that fits nicely with that definition. His research provides evidence that our brains use nine different intelligences. So, rather than just having intelligence or not, you have a unique set of intelligences with different strengths and challenges.

> *"Everybody is a genius. But if you judge a fish by its ability to climb a tree, it will live its whole life believing that it is stupid."*
>
> – ALBERT EINSTEIN

Next, you will be taking an assessment called *MI Advantage*. It measures your multiple intelligences, gives you a profile of your intelligence strengths and challenges, and shows you careers that match your intelligence profile.

Ready to take the assessment? To get started, open a browser and go to www.humanesources.com. Click the Login link at the top of the page. If you have not already registered, follow the instructions to register with your Access Key. In your portfolio, select the link for **MI Advantage** to begin the assessment.

Thank you for completing *MI Advantage*. You can view your full report online at any time in your portfolio. Remember that this report shows you where your intelligence strengths and challenges are. It does **not** determine how "smart" you are.

You will need to refer to the full report for some of the activities that follow.

USE YOUR STRENGTHS

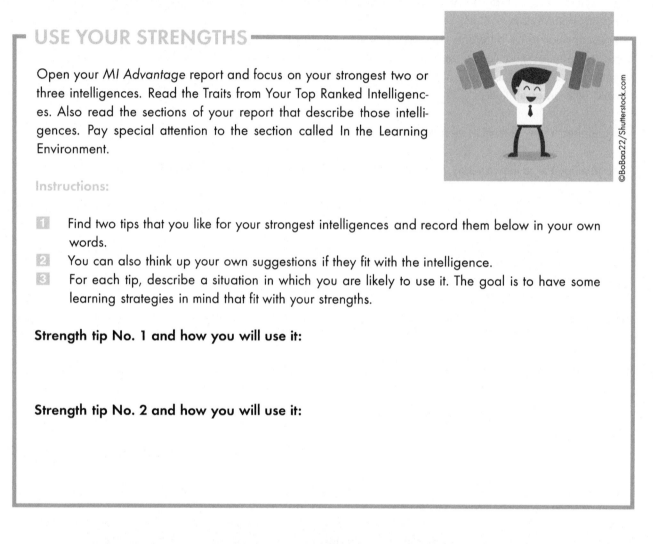

Open your *MI Advantage* report and focus on your strongest two or three intelligences. Read the Traits from Your Top Ranked Intelligences. Also read the sections of your report that describe those intelligences. Pay special attention to the section called In the Learning Environment.

Instructions:

1. Find two tips that you like for your strongest intelligences and record them below in your own words.
2. You can also think up your own suggestions if they fit with the intelligence.
3. For each tip, describe a situation in which you are likely to use it. The goal is to have some learning strategies in mind that fit with your strengths.

Strength tip No. 1 and how you will use it:

Strength tip No. 2 and how you will use it:

Over the next few weeks, apply the strategies in various learning situations and see what works. Feel free to try other strategies from your *MI Advantage* report as you see fit.

Know Your Challenges

It is also important to be aware of areas that may be a challenge for you—for two reasons.

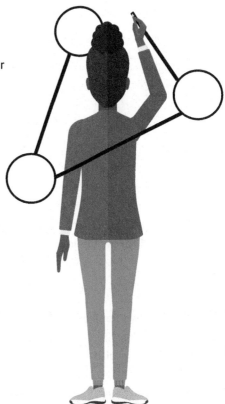

1   **Knowing your challenges helps you know when to use alternate strategies that cater to your strengths.**

For example, it is probably not a good idea to study for tests by reading and re-reading textbooks if linguistic intelligence is not your strength. If spatial intelligence is a greater strength for you, it would be a good idea to create mind maps and seek out visuals like diagrams and charts that represent the information.

2   **Knowing your challenges allows you to focus on what you can work on and how to work on it.**

We often shy away from our challenge areas and may neglect developing them when working on them can really help.

"The ultimate measure of a man is not where he stands in moments of comfort and convenience, but where he stands at times of challenge and controversy."

— MARTIN LUTHER KING, JR.

A Strategy for Challenges

While some students do not like reading, a lot of reading and writing is typically required throughout school and work. At times you will be able to use alternate strategies that take advantage of strengths other than linguistic intelligence. Sometimes, however, alternatives just won't be practical, and you will have to use your linguistic intelligence. While you do not need to develop all your intelligences to a high level, it is a good idea to develop all of them to some degree. Having more working "tools" available can help you be more successful in a variety of tasks and situations.

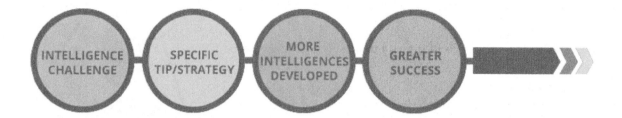

OVERCOME YOUR CHALLENGES

Look again at your *MI Advantage* report. Find your lowest rated intelligence type, read that section, and follow the instructions below.

Instructions:

1. Find two tips that you like for your lowest intelligence and record them below in your own words.

2. You can also think up your own suggestions if they fit with the intelligence.

3. For each tip, describe a situation in which you are likely to use it. The goal is to have some learning strategies in mind that fit with your challenges.

Challenge tip No. 1 and how you will use it:

Challenge tip No. 2 and how you will use it:

INTELLIGENCES MATCHING ACTIVITY

Now that you have examined your intelligence strengths and challenges, let's review all the intelligences. Look through your full *MI Advantage* report (in your online portfolio) using the tabs for the nine different intelligences. Focus on the first three sections for each intelligence titled: Description, Famous People and Intelligence and You. Those sections will help you understand what each intelligence is all about. Then, complete the following activity to test what you have learned.

Read the descriptions and then match them to each of the multiple intelligence labels below.

A.   pitch, rhythm, and melody
B.   shapes, visual patterns, space, and distance
C.   movement and coordination
D.   self, personal strengths and limitations
E.   understanding and expression of language
F.   the physical environment
G.   reasoning, sequences, and patterns in information
H.   how different ideas connect into a broader concept
I.   people, relationships, and communication

1   Bodily-Kinesthetic

2   Existential

3   Interpersonal

4   Intrapersonal

5   Linguistic

6   Logical-Mathematical

7   Musical

8   Naturalist

9   Spatial

SECTION 1-5: WORK INTERESTS

Learning Objectives

- Learn about work interests and complete a survey to determine your top interest areas
- Compare work interests with education and career options to make better decisions for current and future plans
- Consider multiple factors in education and career planning
- Learn how interacting with others who are similar and those who are different can benefit you

Interests and Purpose

This section explores how interests play a role in helping to define our path and purpose in life.

People have varied interests and interests can shift over time. However, people usually settle on a few of their strongest interests as they enter into adulthood.

Also, while people may enjoy many different activities, we can group those activities into a few interest areas. The interest areas that you settle on are usually related to your personality type, because you tend to enjoy what comes naturally to you.

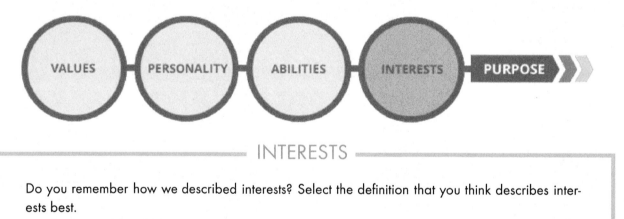

INTERESTS

Do you remember how we described interests? Select the definition that you think describes interests best.
- what is considered important
- natural behaviors and tendencies
- what is enjoyed
- what can be done well

Answer: Interests refer to what we enjoy—what brings us happiness or what we are drawn toward.

Matching Your Interests

The first step in matching up your interests to your work is learning what your interests are. As you did with values, personality and abilities, it is useful to learn about your interests through an assessment. Remember, assessments should help you determine your true preferences, with minimal influence from social expectations. You want to learn what your preferences are, not what you think other people would like you to prefer. Also, an assessment categorizes your interests in a way that can be useful for determining your ideal study strategies, program options, and career paths.

Complete the following work-interest assessment. Think carefully before you respond to each question and try to answer as honestly as possible.

WORK INTERESTS SURVEY

Vary your ratings throughout this survey—not everything can be your *top* interest. Give yourself a score of:

5 for Not at all
10 for Very little
15 for Some
20 for Mostly
25 for Definitely

		Not at all	Very Little	Some	Mostly	Definitely
1	I am better at making and fixing things than helping people with their problems.	5	10	15	20	25
2	I prefer to read and learn about things first before I ask or talk about them.	5	10	15	20	25
3	Others would describe me as artistic and creative, rather than logical and organized.	5	10	15	20	25
4	I am better at working with people than with tools, computers, or other objects.	5	10	15	20	25
5	I am more assertive and confident than curious and thoughtful.	5	10	15	20	25
6	I am better with numbers or organized information than with creative or abstract ideas.	5	10	15	20	25
7	I prefer sports and athletics to activities like writing, art, film, and design.	5	10	15	20	25
8	Others would probably describe me as more of a rational thinker than an energetic speaker.	5	10	15	20	25

9	I tend to go with my intuition or feelings rather than concern myself with facts and details.	5	10	15	20	25
10	I prefer helping or teaching to being competitive or in charge of others.	5	10	15	20	25
11	I enjoy competition or debate more than mystery or investigation.	5	10	15	20	25
12	I tend to be more concerned with being detailed and accurate than artistic or tactful.	5	10	15	20	25
13	I prefer to do a task or activity myself, rather than organize it or get others to do it.	5	10	15	20	25
14	I like learning new information, figuring out how things work or reading about recent discoveries.	5	10	15	20	25
15	I like to create and do things because I'm inspired, not to gain recognition or be competitive.	5	10	15	20	25
16	Others would probably describe me as more kind and caring than rational and logical.	5	10	15	20	25
17	I am more of a risk-taker than someone who goes with what has worked before.	5	10	15	20	25
18	I prefer specific directions or steps to follow rather than try to solve complex problems on my own.	5	10	15	20	25
19	In school, I prefer physical education, technology and trades courses more than math and language arts courses.	5	10	15	20	25
20	In school I prefer investigative subjects like science over practical courses like accounting and technology.	5	10	15	20	25
21	In school I prefer subjects like art, music, poetry, and design over math and technical subjects.	5	10	15	20	25
22	I am involved with outreach, volunteering, or other community service activities.	5	10	15	20	25
23	I am drawn to activities such as leadership, entrepreneurship, student government, or public speaking.	5	10	15	20	25
24	In school, I am better at math or technical subjects than at art, music, or creative writing.	5	10	15	20	25

Your work interests survey scores can range from 20 (minimum) to 100 (maximum) and represent your level of interest in six defined interest areas. Each interest area is further explained below. There are four statements for each interest area. To determine your scores, add up the points for each topic, as indicated.

Take note of your top two or three interest areas. They will be used in an activity later.

Topic	Scores
Realistic: Realistic occupations frequently involve work activities that include practical, hands-on problems and solutions. They often deal with plants, animals, and real-world materials like wood, tools, and machinery. Many of the occupations require working outside, and do not involve a lot of paperwork or working closely with others.	Total points for statements 1, 7, 13 and 19:
Investigative: Investigative occupations frequently involve working with ideas, and require an extensive amount of thinking. These occupations can involve searching for facts and figuring out problems mentally.	Total points for statements 2, 8, 14 and 20:
Artistic: Artistic occupations frequently involve working with forms, designs and patterns. They often require self-expression and the work can be done without following a clear set of rules.	Total points for statements 3, 9, 15 and 21:
Social: Social occupations frequently involve working with, communicating with, and teaching people. These occupations often involve helping or providing service to others.	Total points for statements 4, 10, 16 and 22:
Enterprising: Enterprising occupations frequently involve starting up and carrying out projects. These occupations can involve leading people and making many decisions. Sometimes they require risk taking and often deal with business.	Total points for statement 5, 11, 17 and 23:
Conventional: Conventional occupations frequently involve following set procedures and routines. These occupations can include working with data and details more than with ideas. Usually there is a clear line of authority to follow.	Total points for statements 6, 12, 18 and 24:

The survey you just completed is based on the Holland Codes, named after psychologist John Holland. According to Holland's theory, both people and work environments are oriented toward two or three out of six possible work-interest areas. When a person's interest areas are similar to the interest areas associated with their career, that person tends to be happier and more successful. Read the following descriptions and examples to better understand the six interest areas.

Realistic people like:
- practical, hands-on problems and solutions
- work outside and often deal with plants and animals
- work with real-world materials like wood, tools, and machinery
- minimal paperwork
- working independently

Typical occupations: technicians, pilots, trainers, civil engineers, and first responders

Investigative people like:
- working with ideas
- a significant amount of thinking
- searching for facts and figuring out problems mentally

Typical occupations: scientists, doctors, engineers, marketing specialists, and IT professionals

Artistic people like:
- working with forms, designs, and patterns
- using self-expression and work that can be done without following a clear set of rules

Typical occupations: architects, artistic or creative directors, designers, writers, and media professionals

Social people like:
- working with, communicating with, and teaching people
- helping or providing service to others

Typical occupations: counselors, therapists, educators, correctional specialists, and training professionals

Enterprising people like:
- starting up and carrying out projects
- leading people and making many decisions
- taking risks at times
- dealing with business (typically)

Typical occupations: lawyers, managers, administrators, sales agents, detectives, and special agents

Conventional people like:
- following set procedures and routines
- working with data and details more than with ideas
- having a clear line of authority to follow

Typical occupations: archivists, librarians, treasurers and controllers, analysts, inspectors, and paralegals

Source: National Center for O*NET Development. Interests. O*NET Online.

All Interests Are Equal

Before judging these interest areas, remember that no one area is better than another. They are just different. For some people, words like "enterprising" or "artistic" can sound appealing even if those interest areas do not truly match their own. All of us are influenced by media, friends, authority figures and others. It can be difficult to remain true to yourself and your own interests. A good assessment will help to reveal your true interests. Please consider your results from the assessment carefully before answering the question below.

MY INTERESTS

How do your assessment results in the table compare to what you thought your interests were before? Do they surprise you, or are they what you expected? Explain.

Provide examples of things you do that match your interests.

Matching Multiple Interests

The previous page listed occupations matching each interest area. However, when searching for careers that will hold interest for you, it is usually a good idea to try to match your top *two* or *three* interest areas. A useful tool to match multiple interest areas to a potential career is on the O*NET website. The activity below will help you use the website effectively.

MATCHING INTERESTS TO CAREERS

Use the U.S. Department of Labor's O*NET website to identify which interests best match different careers. Choose **one** option below based on your situation.

Option A
You have clear future plans for your education and career.
1. Find your top two career choices on the O*NET site (see Link 1-27).
2. On the summary report screen for each career, go to the "Interests" section.
3. Compare the interests listed for the career to the interests you identified in the Work Interests Results Table. Below, record your two career choices and the interests listed for them.

Option B
Your career and education plans are not yet clear.
1. Go to the search by interests (see Link 1-28) section of the O*NET site.
2. Select your top interest.
3. On the next screen, select your second and third interests and click Go to narrow the results further.
4. A list of careers organized by Job Zone (education and training) will display. Feel free to filter your results by Job Zone (see Link 1-29).
5. The goal here is *not* to finalize your future career, but rather to get a sense of which careers align with your interests. Choose two careers that you favor from the matching list and record their titles and listed interests below.

Career No. 1 and its top interests:

Career No. 2 and its top interests:

MATCHING INTERESTS TO EDUCATION

Complete the journal using either option A or B.

Option A

You would prefer to think and reflect on your interests and plans for the future.

Using what you have learned about your interests, describe how your education plans can support your interests. Describe specific activities related to your educational and career paths that align with your top interests.

Option B

You would prefer to talk to others about interests and plans for the future.

Find a person who really enjoys their education program and is willing to do a short interview about their interests. Record a summary of your interview below, including both the questions and answers. You can create your own interview questions or use the sample questions. For privacy, please do not identify your interviewee in this entry.

Sample Questions:

- Do you feel that what you are taking in school matches your interests?
- Can you provide some examples of how your program matches your interests, or describe what it is about school that keeps you engaged and motivated?
- Do you do things outside of school that match your interests? Explain.

Enter your response from either Option A or B. Title your response with the option you chose.

Working with Others

Whether in school, in your job, or in other circumstances, you often have to work with others on different tasks. Some people you work with will have similar interests to yours and some will have different interests. There are advantages to both situations.

Partners with Similar Interests

Having similar interests to your working partner can be beneficial in determining an overall direction or strategy for your work. For example, if you are enterprising and your working partner is too, you will both feel comfortable taking risks together, such as creating an unusual new ad campaign.

Partners with Different Interests

When your partners have different interests, it can be beneficial to divide work tasks according to interests. Imagine you are working on an ad campaign with a conventional partner and you are artistic. As the artistic one, you could work on the creative ideas and designs while your conventional partner handles the detail work and organizational tasks. The trick is to make sure you agree on the overall strategy first. That may take some compromise if your interests are very different.

"Diversity: the art of thinking independently together."

– MALCOLM FORBES

WORKING EFFECTIVELY WITH OTHERS

Think of a task or project on which you can work with a partner. It can be a task you have already done or one you will likely do in the future. Answer the following questions with that task in mind.

Briefly identify the project and a few of the key tasks that you and your partner will need to do to complete the project.

Describe how you might approach the project and its tasks with a partner who has interests similar to yours. You can return to the O*NET site (see Link 1-30) to review the types of tasks that match your interests.

Describe how you might approach the project and its tasks with a partner who has interests **different** from yours. You can return to the O*NET site (see Link 1-31) to review the types of tasks that match various interests.

SECTION 1-6: SELF-EFFICACY

Self-Efficacy and Purpose

This section is about how self-efficacy helps determine whether we succeed in our purpose.

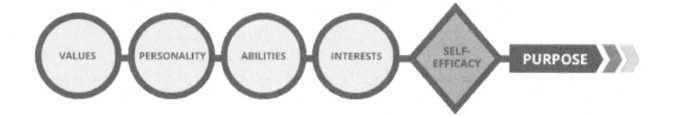

Self-efficacy is the degree to which you believe you can perform an action or behavior. It is similar to confidence. However, confidence is just a general belief in yourself, while self-efficacy is the belief that you can do what it takes to complete certain tasks and goals.

As the diagram above indicates, self-efficacy can be the filter through which you achieve success or not. You can have all the right attributes to achieve success in your purpose, but without the right amount of belief that you can do it, you may never get there. Research shows that self-efficacy is a predictor of success in school, work, and areas of personal life such as maintaining health and relationships.

ACADEMIC SELF-EFFICACY SURVEY

Instructions: Complete the following survey to measure the level of your academic self-efficacy. There are no right or wrong, or good or bad, answers. Just *be honest* with your responses.

Rate your level of confidence in the statements as they apply to you.
1 = no confidence 10 = complete confidence

I CAN...

Find ways to remember and master the things I need to learn.

   1   2   3   4   5   6   7   8   9   10

Maintain a strong effort in all my courses, not just the ones that I find most interesting.

   1   2   3   4   5   6   7   8   9   10

Make time for studying and complete all my assignments on time.

   1   2   3   4   5   6   7   8   9   10

Work effectively with my peers, instructors and other school staff, even those who may be difficult to get along with.

   1   2   3   4   5   6   7   8   9   10

Find people and resources that will help me when I need help.

   1   2   3   4   5   6   7   8   9   10

Understand lectures, reading material, and take effective notes.

   1   2   3   4   5   6   7   8   9   10

Produce high quality writing when it is required.

   1   2   3   4   5   6   7   8   9   10

Study effectively for and score well on tests.

   1   2   3   4   5   6   7   8   9   10

Complete activity-based assignments, such as labs and projects.

   1   2   3   4   5   6   7   8   9   10

Continue to perform well in school when there are other pressures and responsibilities in my life.

   1   2   3   4   5   6   7   8   9   10

Please enter your most recent cumulative grade point average (GPA). Enter it either on the standard 0.00-4.00 scale or as a percentage on a 0-100 scale. This is just for comparison purposes – so you can compare your self-efficacy to your GPA.

©arka38/Shutterstock.com

Specific Tasks and Outcomes

Generally, it is good to have high self-efficacy. However, it is important to remember the definition of self-efficacy. It is about believing you can complete specific tasks. It is not about believing you can simply accomplish anything. Self-efficacy also includes the belief that your actions *will* affect the outcome of a situation, and that outcomes are *not* beyond your control.

For example, academic self-efficacy, which was measured in the survey you just completed, is about believing that you can study effectively and learn all the material necessary to achieve high grades, even when things get challenging. It is not about succeeding just because you think you are smart and it will be easy. It is about believing that your efforts in school will result in good grades.

If you have too little self-efficacy, you may think you can't handle difficult tasks. You may shy away from challenges and give up on your goals. If you avoid challenges, you will miss out on developing yourself and achieving something meaningful.

Self-efficacy and Choosing a Major

Research shows that self-efficacy can also affect how you choose your college major. If you think a college major is challenging, a low self-efficacy may cause you to take a major that is not right for you just because it appears easier.

Creativity

A common area in which people often have low self-efficacy is creativity. Many people believe creativity is something you either have or you don't. They forget that creativity is something you can develop through hard work and a little self- efficacy.

Watch the video at Link 1-32 on how to build your creative confidence. It should provide some inspiration and help you respond to the journal questions that follow.

SELF-EFFICACY REFLECTION

Reflect on occasions when you had low and high self-efficacy.

Describe a situation when you had low self-efficacy for a certain task or activity and the impact that your low self-efficacy had. In your description, show that you have a good understanding of the definition of self-efficacy.

Describe a situation when you had high self-efficacy for a certain task or activity and the impact or outcome that your high self-efficacy had. In your description, show that you have a good understanding of the definition of self-efficacy.

Developing Self-Efficacy

So, the important question is, how do you develop self-efficacy? There are several ways to develop self-efficacy, and it is best to take advantage of every possible approach.

Task Splitting

Large tasks can seem daunting—studying for a big exam, for example. Identify a small unit or section that will be part of the exam, preferably the section you find easiest or most interesting. Focus on that section for a while and then test yourself, or ask someone to test you on just that section. If you are successful, start on other sections, one at a time, in order of increasing difficulty. If the first section is too difficult, break the task down into even smaller pieces.

The point is to organize tasks to let you achieve early success. This will build your self-efficacy, and you will be better able to handle the longer, more difficult pieces later on.

Mentor or Model

When you identify with someone who succeeds in school, you are more willing to believe that you can succeed too.

You can also learn from observation some of the behaviors and techniques needed to achieve success. More than that, you can just ask! This is why mentorship programs are so popular and effective. The key is to choose someone with whom you feel a connection. You need to believe that you can do the things that your mentor can do if given enough time and practice.

Feedback and Reinforcement

It is always a good idea to get feedback if you want to improve. You certainly want to get feedback from your mentor, if you can. But you should also seek and listen to feedback from experts like your instructors.

A good way to approach getting feedback is to seek it until it is positive. Initially feedback may be instructive, explaining how to improve. Don't take it as criticism – learn from it. As you learn from the feedback, you should improve in what you are doing, and the feedback should shift to positive reinforcement to reflect your improvement.

Ideally, you want both kinds of feedback. Getting all instructive feedback can make you feel like you aren't doing anything right. If you are getting all positive reinforcement, you are probably not learning anything new. Seek feedback from different sources and aim for a balance between instructive feedback and positive reinforcement.

Mood and Attitude

Avoid difficult tasks while in a negative mood. Use techniques to improve your mood before attempting tasks. You can listen to music, do light exercise, watch

a short comedy, or get out into nature for a time. All of those things have been proven to enhance mood.

For a positive attitude, start tasks with the idea that if you carry out the proper steps, you will eventually be successful. There may be some failures along the way, but failures are really learning opportunities that lead to success.

"Success consists of going from failure to failure
without loss of enthusiasm."

– WINSTON CHURCHILL

DEVELOPING SELF-EFFICACY

To finish this section on self-efficacy, let's make some specific plans to develop your self-efficacy. For each of the four development methods we've described, think of a way you can apply that method to *what you do* in school. Be specific and describe strategies you can actually try. Record your strategies in the spaces below.

Task Splitting

Mentor or Model

Feedback and Reinforcement

Mood and Attitude

CHAPTER 1 QUIZ

Personal Awareness

Select the best answer for each question.

1. Logotherapy is based on the idea that the most powerful motivating force in people is to:
   a. survive
   b. be happy
   c. seek money or power
   d. find purpose or meaning
   e. live according to their values

2. *Personality type* is best described as:
   a. what is enjoyed
   b. what can be done well
   c. what is considered important
   d. natural behaviors and tendencies
   e. a general direction in life

3. *Values* are best described as:
   a. what is enjoyed
   b. what can be done well
   c. what is considered important
   d. natural behaviors and tendencies
   e. a general direction in life

4. *Interests* are best described as:
   a. what is enjoyed
   b. what can be done well
   c. what is considered important
   d. natural behaviors and tendencies
   e. a general direction in life

5. *Abilities* are best described as:
   a. what is enjoyed
   b. what can be done well
   c. what is considered important
   d. natural behaviors and tendencies
   e. a general direction in life

6. Which of the following is NOT true about having *purpose*?
   a. You will have better physical health
   b. You will gain self-esteem
   c. You will have lower stress
   d. You should have a clear purpose early in life
   e. You should consider your purpose in all important decisions

7. Which of the following is NOT true about *personality type*?
   a. Some personality types are better than others
   b. Personality type is related to purpose
   c. It is an effective way to narrow your career search
   d. Knowing your type helps realize your strengths
   e. Knowing your type helps realize your challenges

8. Which of the following is NOT true about *values*?
   a. You should prioritize your values
   b. You are born with certain values that don't change
   c. It is an effective way to narrow your career search
   d. Living according to your values brings fulfillment
   e. Betraying your values causes distress

9. Which of the following is NOT true about *self-efficacy*?
   a. It includes believing your actions will affect the outcome of a situation
   b. Your level of self-efficacy affects what college major you choose
   c. To improve it, complete large projects all at once
   d. To improve it, seek both instructive and positive feedback
   e. To improve it, follow a mentor or model for what you want to accomplish

10. Which of the following is NOT true about *interests*?
   a. Working with people who have similar interests is beneficial
   b. Working with people who have different interests is beneficial
   c. It is an effective way to narrow your career search
   d. People orient toward two or three out of six possible Holland interests
   e. A good interest assessment is strongly influenced by social expectations

Congratulations on completing Chapter 1—almost!

Each chapter in *CollegeScope* will conclude with a brief summary and a completion survey. Your results on the completion survey will be compared to the starting survey so you can measure what you have learned from the chapter.

Key Ideas In This Chapter

- Deep personal awareness involves knowing your values, personality, interests, abilities, and self-efficacy.
- Increasing your personal awareness helps you find and achieve purpose.
- Having and following your purpose brings health, happiness, and success.

Making Connections

We also connected these ideas to your current education and future career path. The more things in your life you can connect to your purpose, the more you will have health, happiness, and success.

Now that you know yourself a little better, you should be able to more easily connect *your* values, personality, interests, and abilities to the things you do at school and work.

Looking Outward

This first chapter focused on looking inward, at yourself. The remaining chapters focus outward on topics such as college awareness, career planning, communication, learning, and productivity. Learning about these topics will give you more places to look for connections and more tools to be successful in your purpose.

We can help show you how to find purpose and be happy and successful, but it is up to you to *pursue* that happiness and success. The key is to pay attention and take advantage of opportunities when you see them.

We would say "good luck," but because it is more about pursuit than luck, we'll say, **good pursuit!**

CHAPTER 1 SURVEY

Personal Awareness

This is a quick survey to measure what you know about this chapter topic, both before and after you complete the chapter. Just be honest and rate how much each of the following statements applies to you now. Give yourself a score of:
1 for Not a bit • 2 for A little • 3 for Some • 4 for Mostly • 5 for Definitely

AFTER CHAPTER

		Not a bit 1	A little 2	Some 3	Mostly 4	Definitely 5
1	I reflect on and clearly understand what motivates me.	○	○	○	○	○
2	I can describe how I benefit from having a clear purpose.	○	○	○	○	○
3	I have a strong sense of purpose and can describe what my purpose is.	○	○	○	○	○
4	I can describe how my education and career relate to my purpose.	○	○	○	○	○
5	I know which values are most important to me and which are less important.	○	○	○	○	○
6	I consider my values when making choices about school, work, and my personal life.	○	○	○	○	○
7	I can explain the benefits of keeping my actions aligned with my values.	○	○	○	○	○
8	I can describe my strengths and challenges according to my personality type.	○	○	○	○	○
9	I understand how to adapt and work with other personality types.	○	○	○	○	○

10	I have a clear understanding of my intelligence profile – my strengths and potential challenges.	○	○	○	○	○
11	I know how to use my intelligence strengths most effectively and how to develop my challenge areas.	○	○	○	○	○
12	I know my top work interest areas.	○	○	○	○	○
13	I can name educational programs and careers that best align with my top work interest areas.	○	○	○	○	○
14	I can explain the benefits of working with people who have similar interests and with those who have different interests.	○	○	○	○	○
15	I can describe what self-efficacy is and how it relates to achievement.	○	○	○	○	○
16	I know my own level of self-efficacy and how to improve it.	○	○	○	○	○

Add up your scores to determine your **After Chapter** total and write it down here:

Write your **Before Chapter** total here:

Compare your Before and After scores to see how your knowledge of this chapter topic has changed.

"Do stuff. Be clenched, curious, not waiting for inspiration's shove or society's kiss on your forehead. Pay attention. It's all about paying attention. Attention is vitality. It connects you with others. It makes you eager. Stay eager."

– SUSAN SONTAG

Congratulations, you've completed Chapter 1! To conclude your learning in this chapter, consider and note the following:

What parts of this chapter were most helpful to you?

How would you improve this chapter?

COLLEGE AWARENESS

This is a quick survey to measure your college awareness before and after the chapter. There are no right or wrong answers. Just be honest and rate how much each of the following statements applies to you. Give yourself a score of:
1 for Not a bit • 2 for A little • 3 for Some • 4 for Mostly • 5 for Definitely

BEFORE CHAPTER

		Not a bit 1	A little 2	Some 3	Mostly 4	Definitely 5
1	I know some good strategies for planning my courses.	○	○	○	○	○
2	I have budgeted my time using a time management exercise.	○	○	○	○	○
3	I understand the difference between high school teachers and college professors.	○	○	○	○	○
4	I can describe at least 10 habits of highly effective college students.	○	○	○	○	○
5	I can describe the connection between majors, minors and careers.	○	○	○	○	○
6	I have researched different majors to see if they fit me.	○	○	○	○	○
7	I know what extracurricular activities are offered on my campus.	○	○	○	○	○

©arka38/Shutterstock.com

8	I know three extracurricular activities that suit me and will help with my career plans.	○	○	○	○	○
9	I have a plan on how to get involved outside of my school in a way that will help my future.	○	○	○	○	○
10	I know how my school can help me with financial aid, health or other services, and how to contact those service providers.	○	○	○	○	○
11	I know what my own strengths and blindspots as a student are.	○	○	○	○	○
12	I can explain the difference between a fixed and a growth mindset.	○	○	○	○	○
13	I know the schedule of a typical college year and what to expect in different months.	○	○	○	○	○
14	I understand why frustration can be good, and I feel comfortable asking for help.	○	○	○	○	○
15	I know several strategies to make the most of my time in class.	○	○	○	○	○
16	I know strategies for choosing a major that will work best for me.	○	○	○	○	○

Add up your scores to determine your **Before Chapter** total and write it down here:

COLLEGE READINESS: HOW TO THRIVE ON CAMPUS

Key Questions

1. Motivation Check: What can I gain from college?
2. How can I thrive on a college schedule?
3. What can I expect in class, in a course, and from my instructors?
4. What do I need to know about programs and majors?
5. What extracurricular activities are available?
6. Where do I go if I have questions or need help?

©michaeljung/Shutterstock.com

MOTIVATION CHECK

One of the most important determining factors of whether you will merely survive or thrive in college is your **mindset**.

"Thriving, that's fighting. Surviving is barely getting by."

– JILLIAN MICHAELS

The activity below is called a concept formation activity. Instead of having the concept explained, you "form" the concept yourself by working through the activity. The concept, in this case , is a **growth versus fixed mindset**. The only information you have to begin with are the labels of "growth," "fixed," and "mindset." In this case, "fixed" means unchanging or still.

Growth versus Fixed Mindset

For each statement below, choose whether you think it is part of a **growth** or **fixed** mindset. In this case, the definition of "fixed" is unchanging. You may have to read through several statements before you begin to make your selections. Also, feel free to take guesses and make mistakes. You can change your answers as many times as you like before checking your answers. After all, learning from mistakes is part of a good growth mindset—that is your first clue!

		growth	fixed
1	Believe our futures are mostly based on the choices we make	○	○
2	Avoid challenges that might reveal a "weakness"	○	○
3	Learn from and use criticism	○	○
4	Feel that praise is deserved according to status or position	○	○
5	Welcome challenges as opportunities to improve	○	○
6	Ignore or avoid criticism	○	○
7	View setbacks and failures as a normal part of progress	○	○
8	Think that we are born with specific abilities and talents	○	○
9	Constantly seek to achieve at higher and higher levels	○	○
10	See others' success as a threat to personal status	○	○
11	Feel complete with my current level of achievement	○	○

12	Believe our futures are mostly pre-determined	○	○
13	Think that our abilities and talents change and grow with effort	○	○
14	Feel praise needs to be earned through hard work	○	○
15	Appreciate and learn from others' successes	○	○
16	Give up after experiencing setbacks or failures	○	○

Answer: Growth statements are numbers 1, 3, 5, 7, 9, 13, 14, 15. All the others are Fixed statements.

The concepts of fixed and growth mindsets came out of the research of psychology professor Carol Dweck. Learn more about Dweck's work by visiting Link 2-1. She discovered that when students have a growth mindset, they perform much better in school than with a fixed mindset.[1]

WHAT IS YOUR MINDSET?

Look again at the statements for each type of mindset. Which one do you lean toward? Be honest. Everyone would like to think they have a perfect growth mindset, but not everyone does. And, even people who do can sometimes slip into a fixed mindset. However, everyone can develop a consistent growth mindset. Knowing your current mindset will help you develop a better growth mindset.

What kind of mindset do you have? Describe some actions you have taken that support how you describe your mindset.

Whatever your mindset is now, you can always benefit from developing a stronger growth mindset. Here are some websites that provide advice for doing just that. Check out Link 2-2 to learn how you can change from a fixed to a growth mindset. You can also view Link 2-3 to learn about how mindset connects to success.

SECTION 2-1: COLLEGE SCHEDULES

High School versus College

A recent college graduate reflects on the biggest difference between high school and college:

> "...the freedom and ability to do what you want, when you want (in college). For someone who can manage their time, college is a great time to have fun, meet people, and do new things. But for those that lack time management, they will find their time is gone all too soon."[2]

The goal of this chapter, and this section in particular, is to help you make the most of your time while you are in school so that you can reach your goals, pursue potential interest areas, and have fun along the way.

©Sofi photo/Shutterstock.com

HIGH SCHOOL REFLECTION

Respond to the opening quote. Based on your experiences, do you agree with what it says? What was a typical day like in high school? What time of year was most challenging and why?

We realize the word "typical" may be misleading—yet we are going to talk about "typical" days, semesters and years. We know you are unique and are likely anything but typical. So, we aim to help you with strategies that will help you make the most of your time. Before we do, consider the following questions:

- Are you at a two-year, four-year, or other type of school?
- Do you live on campus, travel to school, or take classes online?
- Are you a part-time or full-time student?

While movies and other media often portray college as an on-campus four-year experience, research indicates that the largest percentage of students (36%) are enrolled at a public two-year school. Wherever you are, we want to help you make the most of it!

Enrollment at U.S. Colleges[3]

Institution Type	Percent Enrollment
Two-year public	36
Four-year public	34
Four-year private	25
Two-year private	2.5
Less than two years	2.5

Typical Day

While each day will vary, here is a "typical" day at college:

AM

- **6:45** Wake up and get ready for class
- **8:00** First class
- **9:00** Class ends, quick review of material and notes before next class
- **10:00** Second class
- **11:00** Class ends, quick review of material and notes
- **11:30** Lunch and maybe some socializing with friends

PM

- **1:00** Third class
- **2:00** Class ends, quick review of material and notes
- **3:30** Volunteer, work, internship, team practice, or workout
- **6:30** Dinner and socializing with friends
- **8:00** Study time or sometimes attend an event such as a basketball game
- **10:30** Wind down by organizing notes, and prepping for next day by reviewing syllabus
- **11:00** Sleep

Times will vary widely of course. You may have to take back-to-back classes. You may have only one morning class and two afternoon classes, or even have a night class. Some days, you may have only one class or up to four classes. For back-to-back classes, you will have to double up on the review when you actually do get a break. Also, some students are natural night owls and can schedule their first class to start later in the day. In that case, just shift all the times a few hours later.

Whatever variations you may have, the key points are to do quick reviews right after each class, and to schedule some time later in the day to do the more intensive studying and assignment work. It is also important to have some balance, which is why physical exercise and socializing with friends was included. Lastly, remember that preparing for the next day really helps. When you know what is coming next in your classes, your brain will better absorb the information and you will feel more confident about your day.

The weekend for a student like this would probably include a work shift or a team competition on Saturday. Saturday might also be a good day for a group study session as the social aspect can increase the fun factor. Sunday is a good day to make an organizational day, for catching up on laundry, groceries and other errands. If it's hard to find time for exercise during the week, it is a good idea to get some form of exercise on Sunday, along with friends if it helps. Play some team sports, run with a partner, or just go to the gym with a friend. Exercise can be a great stress reliever at the end of a long week. And it's a great way to save time when you combine social interaction with the things you need to do.

SECTION 2-1: COLLEGE SCHEDULES

Typical Semester—Class Schedule

A semester in college depends on the class schedule you choose at the start. When making up your schedule, keep the following in mind:[4]

Course load: Are you planning to be a full-time or part-time student? Do you also plan to work part time? Make sure that your course load is only as full as you can manage with your work schedule. If you feel you can handle more classes, add them in the second semester when you are more adjusted to college life.

Time of day: This one seems obvious, but many students forget to try to schedule classes around the time of day that they work best. Sometimes you don't have much choice and the class you need is only offered at a time outside what works best. It is always possible to adjust your internal clock. Travelers and shift workers do it all the time. The key is going to bed and waking up at a consistent time each day. It may take a week or two before it feels normal, but it will eventually if you keep at it.

Location: Depending on the size of the school campus, you may need to schedule your classes so they are not back-to-back, allowing you time to get from point A to point B on the other side of the campus. Large schools often have trams or encourage bicycle riding for this purpose.

Other class schedule considerations: Some classes may have labs or discussion components that require different time commitments. Students involved in honors programs will also need time to schedule special meetings.

Typical Year

No two days, months, or years are really ever the same at college, and each school's schedule varies. Yet, you can arm yourself with information that can help you.

The annual academic calendar can be found at your school's website. Be sure to check the calendar for specific information regarding exam schedules, registration deadlines, term start and end dates, and other important events.

A 'Typical' Flow to the Year

While your school's calendar will be useful for guiding your expectations and planning, there are some things that you will not see in a typical academic calendar. The table below[5] outlines common transitions, school events, and responses or feelings students may experience. Of course, every school and every student is different.

August/September
- Classes begin
- Excitement
- Testing newfound freedom
- Anxiety about professors and classes
- If living in residence hall, potential homesickness and frequent visits

October
- Students question: "Do I fit in here?"
- First test grades returned
- Midterm exams
- Consequences of decision making experienced
- If residential, roommate problems may surface

November
- Midterm grades returned
- Many exams and papers due before holidays
- Roommate challenges become clearer
- Excitement or anxiety regarding visits

December
- Anxiety over preparations for finals
- Excitement or anxiety regarding going home for the holidays
- Sadness about leaving new friendships or relationships

- New semester transition
- Starting new routine
- Feelings of cabin fever and depression of winter, especially in northern states
- Relationship challenges, influenced by Valentine's Day

March

- Midterm exam stress
- Anxiety regarding planning for next year
- Excitement or disappointments regarding Spring Break plans
- Consequences of decision making experienced
- Concern over summer employment

April

- Concern over declaring major
- End of semester pressure
- Excitement with arrival of spring

May

- Final exam anxiety
- Apprehension about returning home for the summer
- Sadness over leaving new friendships or relationships at school

Time Management 101

Now that you have a sense of what a typical day, semester and year look like, it is important to think about how YOU are using YOUR time. The first step to managing your time effectively is being aware of how you are currently using it. Please walk through the exercise below.

Instructions: In a typical weekday, how many hours should you spend in each of the areas listed below? Record the hours for each on a separate sheet (for example: commute = 0.5 hrs.; sleep = 8 hrs.). There may be activities that would fit in more than one area below—just record it under one area of your choice. Don't worry about adding up to 24 hours yet. Just focus on the number of hours it would take to be successful in college and to remain happy and healthy.

- Class time
- Studying
- Job or work
- Sleep
- Commuting or transportation
- Athletics or fitness
- Co-curricular activities (clubs, councils, etc.)
- Family responsibilities
- Social life
- Eating
- Personal hygiene

Now, add up the number of hours.

If it's more than 24, you are overcommitted—you will have to reduce the number of hours for one or more areas. This means you will have to think carefully about your priorities.

If it's less than 24, you are under committed—you need to add hours to one or more areas, and you will also have to think about your priorities.

If it's exactly 24, nice work! However, you should still look at each area and ensure you are committing your time appropriately.

Take a look at Link 2-4 for some great tips on how to spend your time wisely.

TIME MANAGEMENT

Reflect on what you learned as you went through the time management exercise. Do you have a realistic schedule? Are you trying to pack too much in? Or could you better utilize some "extra" hours you have? Describe a few things you could adjust starting tomorrow.

SECTION 2-2: COLLEGE INSTRUCTORS AND CLASS TIME

REVIEW QUESTION

In college, how is a course schedule typically determined?

- I tell my advisors and they create a schedule for me.
- I wait for the school to email me with my schedule.
- I build a schedule myself.
- My parents send in a request.

Answer: I build a schedule myself. Also, remember to consider your major, career goals, and strengths and challenges when choosing your courses.

Learning Objectives

- Understand the increased expectations of college versus high school
- Apply strategies for effective classroom learning
- Develop positive habits for success in college—based on personal strengths and challenges

In this section, we will help you understand what's expected and equip you with some tools to help you do your best in class studying, and with your professors. Just as your high school teachers likely varied in style, personality and expectations, so will your college professors. One very important distinction between high school teachers and college professors is that college profs typically expect much more independence and initiative on the part of the student. They are not likely to assign nightly homework or check to see that you have finished it. More typically, they will give you a syllabus, expect YOU to read it and expect YOU to complete things on time—whether they remind you or not.

> *"A professor is someone who talks in someone else's sleep."*
>
> – W. H. AUDEN

The following quotations are tips from college students that were included in the book, *How to Survive Your Freshman Year*.[1] When you've finished reading them, be prepared to write your own quote based on what has worked well for you.

- "Wake up early and study. Even if you're not a morning person, make yourself one. It's the quietest time in the dorm and you'll be so productive."
- "Get involved with people who are taking classes with you. When you have friends who are doing the same things with the same goals, it's easy to work together and you can build off each other."
- "After a lecture, I would always go back and go through my notes and rewrite them. If the professor says something more than once, that is a strong clue that it is important."
- "In high school, I could get away with cramming the night before; that changes in college."

Check out the video at Link 2-5 of college students comparing their high school experience to college.

©Alena Hovorkova/Shutterstock.com

QUOTE FOR A COLLEGE FRESHMAN

If you were to submit a quote for this program, what would you say?

SECTION 2-2: COLLEGE INSTRUCTORS AND CLASS TIME

Class Expectations

As difficult as it was in the last section to accurately depict a typical day, it may be even more challenging to describe a typical class. Much of this depends on the size of the school, your major and the courses you take. It is not uncommon for freshmen to be in a large lecture hall with hundreds of other students listening to the professor. If you are in a science class or technical program, there may be smaller lab or hands-on sessions.

Writing classes often come in smaller groups. You might have some classes that are completed online and require an even higher level of independence. Regardless, college tends to emphasize lecturing and discussion over activities and movies. Be prepared to focus and adapt to each unique class setting.

What about what you should do DURING class?

Your In-class Plan

Think about the following to help you be successful in your classes.

- **Know What to Bring**
  Most of the time, you will not need your textbook. More often, you will be taking notes. Bring plenty of pens, multiple colors if you use them, and a notebook. Of course some classes such as labs, fine arts, and others may require you to bring special supplies. Your syllabus is usually a good source of info regarding the materials you'll need. Note: Using electronic devices (laptops and tablets) for note taking has been shown to be less effective than writing your notes.[2]

- **Sit Front and Center**
  OK, sitting at the front may not have the "cool" factor, and it may feel like everyone is staring at the back of your head. However, it has been shown time and again that students who sit at the front and center of class achieve higher grades.[3] Not only are you able to see and hear the professor better, but you also have fewer distractions (other students) in front of you.

  > **Keys to In-class Success**
  > - Know what to bring
  > - Sit front and center
  > - Read ahead
  > - Have a study routine
  > - Use the syllabus
  > - Talk to your professor

- **Read Ahead**
  So, you have all your materials and you are sitting in the right place to absorb all that information. But is your brain ready? If you walk into a lecture with no background information, you will have a much more difficult time understanding the lecture than if you had read a little ahead of time. Check the syllabus or even ask the instructor to find out what is being covered in the next class. Then skim through any reading related to that topic. Even if you only spend 10 minutes skimming and end up with a partial understanding of the topic before the lecture, you will have a much easier time during the lecture. You will also have better questions, and your notes from the lecture will be much better.

- **Have a Study Routine**

  Some schools and some instructors tell students how many hours of studying are expected for each hour of class. If you can't find this information, a general rule of thumb is about two hours of study per hour of class time. You will probably also have to put in additional hours to study for major tests. While this may seem like a lot, it will be much easier if you break it up with a daily routine of reading ahead, reviewing and revising notes, and completing other assigned readings.

  A regular study routine is what your high school teachers were trying to teach you. They assigned daily homework to help you establish good study habits. The biggest mistake college students make is waiting until exams to do any real studying. Typically, you will have four to five weeks of classes before your first exam. That is about 14 hours of class time and at least 28 hours of study needed to prepare for the test. Imagine trying to cram 28 hours of study into a few days! You will be a lot less stressed and more successful if you establish a regular study routine.

- **Use the Syllabus**

  Perhaps even more important than your assigned text is the course syllabus. Ordinarily a professor will provide a syllabus, which serves as a course outline, provides important expectations, describes outcomes, and usually includes required materials and important deadlines and dates. Another common mistake students make is to look over the syllabus once when they get it, and then ignore it for the rest of the course. Protect it in a plastic sleeve at the front of your notebook. Treat the syllabus like a daily study guide or to-do list for the course. Make notes on your progress, check off assignments you complete, and use it to record important updates you get from the instructor.

- **Professors**

  Professors are typically considered experts in their field and may be more—or less—approachable. Either way, talking to them can help you significantly. Because they are passionate about the subject they teach, they are usually happy to talk about it. You can even ask questions about material you're already familiar with, just to get a sense of what the professor thinks is most important and, therefore, what's likely to be on the exam.

Remember Who You Are

While knowing what to expect and hearing about successful habits are important, as with everything you are learning, it will be even MORE helpful to know what you have learned about YOU. Make sure, at some point, that you examine your full *Do What You Are*® report located in your portfolio. You can also use the links below to learn about other personality types.

Table of All 16 Personality Types
Click on the letter combinations to see the different profiles.

ENFJ (Link 2-6)	ENFP (Link 2-10)	ENTJ (Link 2-14)	ENTP (Link 2-18)
ESFJ (Link 2-7)	ESFP (Link 2-11)	ESTJ (Link 2-15)	ESTP (Link 2-19)
ESFJ (Link 2-7)	INFP (Link 2-12)	INTJ (Link 2-16)	INTP (Link 2-20)
ISFJ (Link 2-9)	ISFP (Link 2-13)	ISTJ (Link 2-17)	ISTP (Link 2-21)

Your personality type report has a section called *Your College Satisfiers*. Knowing them can help you identify the courses, activities and projects that will be the most natural fit for you and which may be challenging. Your report also has a section called *Your Preferred Learning Style*, which will further define your classroom strengths and challenges. Open a browser and review these sections of your *Do What You Are* report. Then, return to this page and answer the journal questions below.

©Alena Hovorkova/Shutterstock.com

STRENGTHS AND CHALLENGES IN CLASS

1. Thinking about the college satisfiers described in your *Do What You Are* report and the tips in this section, describe one thing you can do in the next few days to improve your chances for classroom success.

2. Thinking about your preferred learning style in your *Do What You Are* report and the tips in this section describe another thing you can do in the next few days to improve your chances for classroom success.

How to Do Your Best: 15 Habits of Highly Successful College Students

Professors Lynn Jacobs and Jeremy Hyman, who write for *U.S. News and World Report*, have identified 15 habits of highly successful college students. We have modified them slightly. When you've finished reading them, we'll ask you to reflect on which ones are most helpful.

The 15 Habits of Top College Students[4]

What makes some college students successful? One of the most important things to develop in college is a collection of good habits—things you do on a regular basis that set you aside from the hordes of other, more scattered students. Here are 15 very important habits of successful college students.

1. **Plan ahead.**
   Not only do they know where the tests and papers fall in the semester, but these students have a pretty good sense of what work needs to be done each week. Nice and balanced: no panic attacks or all-nighters before turning in papers or taking tests.

2. **Divide up the tasks.**
   Readings are divided into manageable chunks (not 200 pages in one sitting). Studying for quizzes and tests is done over the course of a week (not at 3 a.m. the night before). And paper ideas begin developing when the assignment is handed out (not two days before it's due).

3. **Manage their surroundings.**
   It's hard to do any real work without the tools for the job: a working computer with the right software, a printer, and even ink and paper to go with it. Not to mention the materials of the course: a full set of lecture notes, the textbooks and articles, and course handouts and assignments. Likewise, hanging out with friends who value school can be a positive influence (and the opposite can be negative).

4. **Don't kid themselves.**
   For instance, when you think you're studying but you're really tweeting about how you barely survived your bonfire-jumping last night. Or when you're alternating between reading the online article and checking out your friend's Facebook page every eight seconds or so. Or when the only thing being studied in your study group is the other members of your study group. You're the easiest person you know to deceive. Don't.

5. **Manage their feelings.**
   It's difficult to excel in a course if you're feeling inadequate, bummed out or doomed to fail. Students who know how to focus on their own positive achievements—rather than on what they got on the quiz that counts for about two percent of the course grade—have a leg up on the rest.

6. **Challenge themselves.**
   Successful students are intellectually energetic. So when they read, they think actively about what they are reading. When they go to class, they don't zone out or text (at least most of the time). On tests and papers,

they pounce on the questions and answer them directly and fully. This distinguishes their work from that of cohorts who try to BS their way through the question.

7 Are persistent.

In some courses, some of the work is tough. Maybe it's a problem set that requires really hard thinking or a paper that has to go through a number of painful drafts, or a presentation that has to be rehearsed repeatedly. The successful student doesn't flinch at the extra effort needed or the uncertainty of the result. His or her motto is: I'll get this right if it kills me. (Don't worry, it won't.)

8 Don't cut corners.

Tired? Stayed out too late socializing or studying? "Like the owl, I do my best work at night." Three-hour final? "I'll stay to the bitter end. Maybe I can touch up my essay and collect a few extra points."

9 Are open to feedback.

While it's easy and more fun to throw away your graded papers and exams or conveniently forget to pick them up, the best students carefully study the comments and go over any mistakes they've made. And then when the next graded piece of work rolls around, they take another look at the previous set of comments to see if there are any mistakes they can correct on the new piece of work.

10 Engage the prof.

Demonstrate a genuine interest in learning the material that the professor has devoted a lifetime to mastering. They might go to an office hour, talk to the professor before or after class, or even send a short email asking some erudite question. People like a person who shares their interests.

11 Keep themselves in tip-top shape.

Never underestimate the value of sleeping and eating right. As basic as it may sound, staying healthy is a crucial part of a successful semester. For some reason, being sick as a dog just isn't conducive to mastering topology, Russian history or international finance.

12 Look out for yourself.

While some students are willing to blow off school to satisfy the needs of others—for example, a demanding boss during busy season or an extended family event during finals—successful students know that college is their job and make doing well their highest priority. Be especially mindful of this during the last month of the semester when those big-ticket items (like term papers and final exams) roll around and two-thirds of the grade is won or lost.

13 Visualize success.

It always helps you reach a goal if you devote some time to visualizing yourself achieving it. Not just vaguely daydreaming, but seeing your "successful self" and experiencing the feelings that go with success. This will give you the motivation to go out and do what you have to do to make it happen.

14 Learn from experience.

Instead of coming unglued if something goes wrong in a course—say, bombing a test or paper—the best students view any setbacks as learning experiences that, in the end, teach them what they need to know to do better in this course ... and all their other courses too.

15 **Aim high (or at least to a decent level).**

In college, simple regurgitation of the basics doesn't cut it. Top students know that doing just the minimum gets a B minus, at best. In many courses, a B minus puts you near the bottom of the heap.

CHOOSE YOUR HABITS

It's hard to do everything at once.

1 From the list of habits above, identify one that is a strength you can leverage. Describe a specific situation in which you can apply that habit and how you will apply it.

2 From the list of habits above, identify one that is likely to be a challenge for you. Describe some things you can do to overcome that challenge.

"Motivation is what gets you started.
Habit is what keeps you going."

– JIM RYUN

SECTION 2-3: PROGRAMS AND MAJORS

═══ REVIEW QUESTION ═══

Which of the following best describes what to expect in class and from instructors?

- Professors will provide lots of reminders.
- Professors do not like to meet with students during office hours.
- Professors are more likely to take an interest in supporting students who reach out and engage them.
- Professors are a lot like high school teachers, just older.

Answer: Professors are more likely to take an interest in supporting students who reach out and engage them. Find out your professors' office hours or even take a few minutes after class, if appropriate, to talk to your professors.

Learning Objectives

- Understand the concepts of majors, minors, and programs
- Research available majors
- Assess fit of a major based on strengths, interests, and goals

It may seem like the question, "What do you want to do when you grow up?" was more fun when you were five years old and you could pick something like professional athlete, teacher, police officer or famous singer. That question can feel a bit more intimidating now that you've hit college and have to pick a major. Career paths don't seem as clear and simple any more. Don't worry, you will have plenty of options.

"Nothing that means anything happens quickly—we only think it does. The motion of drawing back a bow and sending an arrow straight into a target takes only a split second, but it is a skill many years in the making. So it is with a life, anyone's life."

– JOSEPH BRUCHAC

What is a Program of Study?

A program of study, or just "program," is a series of courses that prepare you for a specific career or category of careers. Examples include dental hygiene, business, computer science, fine arts or carpentry. There are many possible programs and you can be taking a program of study in high school or college. In four-year colleges and universities, a program is often called a degree program, or just "degree."

Programs can range in length from six months to six years or more if you include professional programs and apprenticeships. Some programs have very specific requirements, with a limited choice of courses available. Other, more general programs can be completed through many different course combinations. However, general programs usually require you to choose a major or specialization within the program to narrow your focus.

What is a Major?

A major is a specific focus a student takes within a program of study. Not all programs require a major. Typically, you are required to "declare" a major when you take a four-year degree program. For example, you can take a business degree with a major in accounting. Between one-third and one-half of the courses you'll take in college will be in your major or related to it. In some colleges, you can...

* Major in two fields
* Have a major and a minor (a specialization that requires fewer courses than a major)
* Create your own major

If you attend a liberal arts college, ordinarily you will select a focus (your major) but also take a broad range of classes called general education requirements. If you attend a technical college, you may take fewer general education requirements and focus more on your major.

Choosing a Major

If you're earning a two-year degree, you'll probably select a major right from the start because the program is much shorter. If you are attending (or plan to attend) a four-year college, you may not have to pick a major until the end of your sophomore year. This gives you plenty of time to check out various subjects and see which ones interest you. Some majors—like areas of engineering—are exceptions to this rule. You have to commit to these fields of study early so you have time to take all the required courses.

Here are a couple of student quotes about the "sweet spot" of when to pick a major.[1]

Not too early

Don't take classes that are super important for your major in the first quarter. I entered school as a chemistry major, so I took a chemistry class right away and it totally kicked my butt. It's fine to have a major in mind, but know it might change. You need time to adjust to college life. If I could do it over again, I'd only take GEs for a quarter or two.

– UCLA student

Not too late

Don't wait too long to choose a major. I didn't declare until my third year and I ended up needing to take four classes per quarter. It was intense, and not very fun when you're nearing the end of college and you want to have a good time with your friends.

– Anonymous student

How to Research and Choose a Major

1 The Catch-22 of Choosing a Major

Like many important decisions you make in life, it is important to think about the end first. You should know your goal before you make plans to get there. If you know your career goal, then it becomes easy to choose the major that will prepare you for that career. However, this can feel like a "catch-22" situation. Don't know what means? Read a description with Link 2-22.

How do you know which career to choose if you haven't experienced the courses related to that career? How do you know which courses to choose if you don't know which career you want? Some students are lucky and know exactly what career they want, but this is often not the case.

So, what should students do if they are not sure of their career plans?

Know Yourself

The first chapter in this program certainly helps by getting you to learn more about yourself. In that chapter, we used assessments and reflection to help you think about careers related to your personality, intelligences, interests, and more.

Narrow Your Options Over Time

Another approach is to start with many options and slowly narrow your options over time. This means choosing very general courses in your first year at school. These are typically labeled as General Education Requirements. Examples include English, math, and social science courses. You can also choose some elective courses that would be useful in just about any career. Some examples are computer science, communication, and psychology. Because they count toward completion of nearly all programs and majors, you can still choose from many majors after you complete general education courses. And you will have had more time to experience different courses, volunteer opportunities, and internships to help you select a major.

Within your elective options, take courses in areas that appeal to you and then think about which subject truly motivates you. A class you never planned to take could end up helping you choose your major.

Learn the Graduation Requirements

Once you are ready to choose your major, find out what is required to graduate or complete that major. You want to make sure you can complete the program with a reasonable course load and within a reasonable time frame.

Research Programs and Majors at Your School

- Check your school's website or admissions office for more information about **associate degree programs**
- Check your school's website or admissions office for more information about **undergraduate degree programs**
- Check your school's website or admissions office for more information about **graduate degree programs**
- Check your school's website or admissions office for more information about **degree and transfer requirements**

MY COURSE PLAN

Look up your major or program of study, whether you have already chosen it or are considering it. Look at the course options and any of the completion or degree requirements. Create a course plan for this year and the next, if you haven't already.

Your plan should have a mostly even course load each semester. Also, if you can spread out your more difficult courses, it helps. If all your difficult courses are taken at the same time, it will be a tough semester. That said, it can be useful to load some more difficult courses in your last few semesters when you are a more experienced college student.

Do you have a plan that seems to balance your courses? Briefly describe your strategy for choosing the courses in your plan.

Connect Majors to Careers

Your *Do What You Are* report can help you see the connections between majors and careers.

Keep in mind that many career and major resources only show typical career paths for each major and do not provide a complete list. Often one major can prepare you for several careers. Be sure to investigate all career options so you can choose the one that is best for you. Many employers prefer candidates with some experience outside the specific field for which they're applying. Having a well-rounded education can be useful in some cases.

The Occupational Outlook Handbook, published by the U.S. Bureau of Labor Statistics, is another great source of information about connecting careers with education programs.

ARE YOU ON THE RIGHT PATH?

Use the instructions below to guide you through the Occupational Outlook Handbook (OOH) and complete the activity. Keep this page open to make sure you can still see the instructions while you navigate the OOH website.

Instructions:

1. Go to the Occupational Outlook Handbook, using Link 2-23
2. From the Occupation Groups list on the left, click on the group that best fits your (planned) major.
3. From the resulting list, click on the occupation that best fits your major.
4. Click on the How to Become One tab near the top of the profile.
5. Read the page to learn about different paths and requirements to achieve the career.

Note: You may need to check out a few different groups and careers to find the one you are looking for.

Based on the description of "how to become one" for the career you selected, are you on the right path for your career goals? Describe some of the options you have in regards to your major or other educational choices you can make to prepare for your career.

Can I Change My Mind?

If you're not sure about your college major early on in the process, don't worry. Most students switch their majors during college. Some even switch programs. Even students who think they are sure about what they want to major in often change their minds.

Studies show that most students change majors at least once and many switch several times. So it might not be a good idea to pick a college only for its program in one major. Instead, consider colleges that offer a range of options that interest you. That way, changing majors won't necessarily require changing colleges too.

Remember, you're not alone when choosing a major. Ask academic and peer advisors for help.

What is a Pre-professional Program?

It might surprise you to know that pre-med, pre-law, pre-pharmacy, and pre-veterinary are not majors. They are special college programs that guide students through the process of preparing for and applying to professional schools, such as medical or law school.

While pre-professional programs do not have required courses (therefore, they are not majors), students wishing to pursue particular careers are encouraged to follow a recommended curriculum that will best prepare them for graduate school.

If you choose to participate in one of these programs, you'll still have to declare a major. Many pre-med students, for example, major in biology or chemistry. As long as you fulfill the admission requirements of the professional school, you can major in just about anything. Be sure to check with your professional school of interest to make sure you are meeting requirements.[2]

SECTION 2-4: EXTRACURRICULAR ACTIVITIES

Be Committed

College is the perfect time to explore interests and get involved—and sometimes these activities can be used to develop your career. For example, someone interested in mental health could volunteer on a psychiatric ward in a hospital. A future teacher could volunteer at a community-based program teaching English language learners how to read. You can participate in activities like these to have fun, meet people, explore options and be part of the campus. But it is also more than that. Being involved by just "showing up" will only yield minimum returns. You need to be *committed* to the activities you choose. Put everything into what you do, and you will get much more in return.

> *"The difference between involvement and commitment is like ham and eggs. The chicken is involved; the pig is committed."*
>
> – MARTINA NAVRATILOVA

MY PAST ACTIVITIES

Think about extracurricular activities you have done before. Describe at least one activity that makes you particularly proud and gives you a sense of accomplishment. Then, explain why.

Pace Yourself and Remember to Sleep!

Before we encourage you to go overboard with extracurricular activities, let's remember the basics, such as the importance of sleep. Watch the video at Link 2-24 to learn how getting enough sleep will lead to a more productive, inspired, and joyful life.

Once you've carved out enough time to sleep, you can figure out how much time you have to get involved.

Why Commit to Extracurricular Activities?

Extracurricular activities tend to be highly emphasized in high school, when they're viewed as a way to help students get into the "right" college. But there are lots of reasons to commit to them, besides developing a good resume. Extracurricular activities can help you:

- Discover interests
- Develop skills and knowledge
- Help others
- Expand your network
- Stay healthy
- And boost your resumé

An assistant provost at Richard Stockton College of New Jersey says,

> "Whatever your choice (of majors), be sure that you develop the skills that graduate schools and employers need, want and expect when you graduate. These include writing, speaking ... and skills students often underestimate, including demonstrating leadership, responsibility, collaboration, a strong work ethic, and integrity. These can be developed in your college experiences both in and out of the classroom through student clubs and organizations, service learning, internships, volunteerism, work experiences. These skills can be learned in any and all majors, if you choose your related options strategically and wisely."[1]

Hopefully that last sentence helps take the pressure off the major decision and makes it clear that what you do *outside* of class can be as important as what you do *in* the classroom.

What is Available?

Some people wonder what the difference is between extracurricular and co-curricular activities.

Co-curricular activities complement what you are learning in your courses, but are usually not graded or for credit. A co-curricular example is writing for the school newspaper to complement a communications or journalism degree. You could also write on different topics to complement other degrees—science articles for a science degree, or even help with technical support for an online paper to complement a computer science degree.

Extracurricular activities are not specifically connected to your degree or major. These are often done purely for fun or interest's sake.

Whether an activity is extra- or co-curricular depends on whether you can connect the activity to your major, rather than the nature of the activity itself. A business student who volunteers at the hospital may be doing extracurricular work, but a student in health sciences would be engaging in a co-curricular activity. As you would expect, it is usually better to seek co-curricular activities that have the added benefit of experience in your academic focus area.

On Campus

All of the following activities have the potential to be either a college-related extra- or co-curricular activity.

- **Clubs and Organizations**
  These can cover just about any topic. Just a few examples are music, accounting, astronomy, video games, politics, the environment, journalism, and dancing. You may be able to find some information about student clubs and organizations on your school's website.

- **Athletics**
  This is not just varsity teams. Most campuses also organize club teams, intramurals, and other athletic pursuits. For some examples, check out the websites of the NCAA (Link 2-25) and NAIA (Link 2-26).

- **Honor Societies**
  One of the oldest and most popular honor societies is Phi Beta Kappa. But there are many societies and at least one at every campus. Your school probably has some on-campus honor societies. You can also check out the website of the Association of College Honor Societies at Link 2-27.

- **Career Services**
  Just about every campus in the U.S. and around the world has some form of career services. They can help with finding a career after graduation, a job while in college, co-ops, internships, or even just help with your resumé. All students should visit their local career center at least once while they are in college. You can also check out the website of CareerOneStop at Link 2-28.

- **Student Government and Leadership**

  Most schools have a form of student government, which can help develop organizational, leadership, and communication skills. Some schools have an independent leadership program as well. Getting involved in this area can really help develop your resumé. For more information, see Link 2-29 to learn about the American Student Government Association.

- **Residential Life**

  Not all schools offer campus residences, but if yours does, it usually comes with activities and leadership opportunities in the dorm.

- **Study Abroad**

  Many schools provide programs that allow you to explore the world, and often for tuition exchange, so primary costs are for travel. For more information, check out the website of StudyAbroad.com at Link 2-30.

- **Work Study**

  Need to earn some extra cash but want to stay on campus? Some students qualify for work-study programs offered at many campuses, often in conjunction with state or federal programs. Another bonus is that these programs typically provide opportunities for students to work in a field related to their academic focus. For a look at one program, see Link 2-31 for information about the Federal Work Study program.

Off Campus

The opportunities are endless. Don't forget about community organizations that serve the homeless, children, immigrants or others. There may be a strong fine and performing arts community. Find a library, a business or a community theater where you can offer your time or even find a job. Most cities have a visitor's center or chamber of commerce. Stop by or check out their websites to learn more about what is available in your community.

BRAINSTORM ACTIVITIES

Brainstorm seven extracurricular activities you might like to try this year.

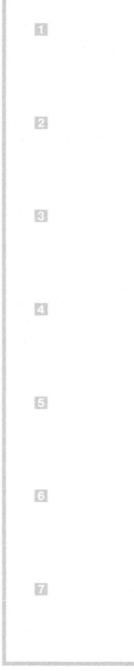

1

2

3

4

5

6

7

Narrow Your Focus and Commit

You might or might not get to do all seven of the activities you've listed. Here are some ideas on how to narrow your list and get started:

1 **Choose a Focus**

If you don't already know what career you're interested in pursuing, start by asking yourself some basic questions. What was your favorite subject in high school? What subjects did you do well in? The answers to these questions are likely to coincide and give you an idea about where you want to focus.

2 **Find Relevant Clubs that Boost Your Resumé**

In college you can find a club for just about anything. Even if something seems a little bit interesting, check it out! You've got nothing to lose and it might just turn out to be your favorite extracurricular activity in college. You'll meet people and add to your resumé at the same time. For more information about activities that may help your resumé, check out the site at Link 2-32.

3 **Consider Other Options: Volunteering and Internships**

Clubs aren't the only extracurricular activities in college worth trying. Internships and volunteer programs are other options that are highly regarded by employers—as well as being a lot of fun.

4 **Narrow Your Choices**

Remember how we talked about the importance of sleep? There are so many options and you want to try all of them. But it's important not to overload yourself in the end. Choose only a few extracurricular activities to be truly involved in at any one time. Between your course load and a couple of extracurricular activities in college, you'll be swamped!

5 **Make Your Own!**

If you have tried at your school and still haven't found the right extracurricular activities, here is another option. Most colleges allow students to form new clubs! If you have a unique hobby or interest that hasn't yet been turned into a club, take the initiative.

Finding your passion is what college is all about, and extracurricular activities can help. It is important to choose a direction and follow through. Extracurricular activities in college can help you find your calling and spruce up your resume for the job you're looking for.[2]

NARROW YOUR FOCUS

Narrow the list you brainstormed on the previous page to the top three activities you might try this year. Write your top three in the spaces below.

1.

2.

3.

College "To Do" List

So far in this section we have put the focus on organized activities. However, there are many other ways to be committed to your school and get the payoffs that commitment can bring. Sometimes it is a simple act that you do on your own. The following is a sample list of things a student might have as their "to do" list—things you feel you should do to make your college experience count.

Sample top 10 list of things to do in your first or second year of school.

1. Write and submit an article for the campus publication.
2. Get involved with a varsity sports team or in an intramural sport.
3. Declare a major or specialization.
4. Try out for the college mascot.
5. Meet with a professor to discuss a course topic or opportunities in his or her field of study.
6. Attend a campus event—a play, a game, a performance.
7. Organize a study group and meet regularly to compare notes and quiz each other.
8. Create your resumé (don't forget that the career office can help).
9. Start at least two new healthy habits (sleep, food, fitness) and stick with them the rest of the year.
10. Start building a network of contacts that might help you in school and your career, and keep in touch.

TOP 5 "TO DO" LIST

Create your own Top 5 To Do List. Choose things that are meaningful to you and will get you more committed to being successful in college. Write your top five in the spaces below.

1

2

3

4

5

SECTION 2-5: COLLEGE SERVICES AND HELP

Learning Objectives

- Know your strengths and blindspots as a student
- Know where to go on campus for help with financial aid, health, or other services
- Know the difference between a fixed and a growth mindset

First Step in Learning

The first step in learning, before you get any information, is having the attitude that you can learn something. That attitude comes from having the confidence that you are able to learn, but also the humility to admit you don't know something.

> *"Take the attitude of a student, never be too big to ask questions,*
> *never know too much to learn something new."*
>
> – OG MANDINO

A Little Frustration is Good

Frustration can be a natural part of learning and growing. It means you are being challenged. Remember the motivation check for this chapter, where we focused on mindset? One of the best things to remember as you face challenges in college is that they are NORMAL and you can work through them.

The same idea can be applied to problem solving in life in general. We encourage you to adopt a growth mindset rather than a fixed mindset.

- Fixed mindset—means you believe you are born a certain way and that you either "get it" or you don't
- Growth mindset—means you believe that you can adapt, learn and grow if you put in the effort

Applied to problem solving, a growth mindset would see things as an opportunity to learn, grow and seek out support. It would be reflected in statements like, "I will look back on this situation and learn from it."

A fixed mindset would be reflected in statements like, "I can't adjust to college life" or "I am just not cut out for college."

In addition to believing you can develop your abilities, it is important to know your strengths and challenges so you can build on strengths and seek support for and overcome your challenges.

Remember the *Do What You Are* personality inventory you completed earlier? There is a section of the report titled *Strengths and Blindspots*. Reviewing your blindspots will help you determine which situations might require a little support or extra help. Before you review your blindspots, let's take a look at a definition:

Blind spot: *A tendency to ignore something especially because it is difficult or unpleasant.1*

For example, if one of your blindspots is "not being totally accurate with facts" or "not following through on important details and deadlines," you may want to be extra sure to check out the help of your student tutoring center.

©Sofi photo/Shutterstock.com

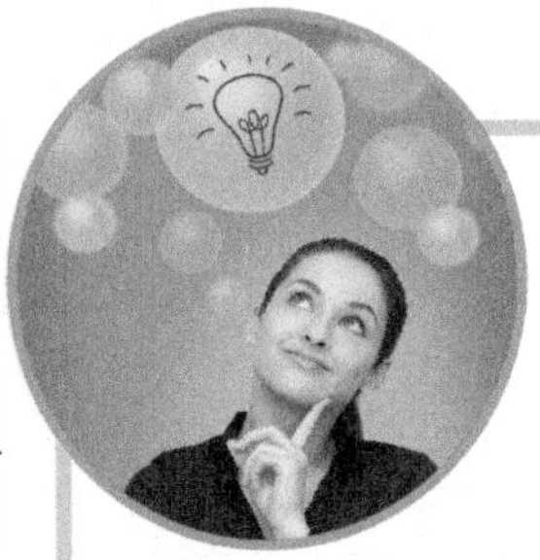

KNOW YOUR BLINDSPOTS

Now, review your blindspots as identified in your online *Do What You Are* report, and describe two for which you might ask for help.

1

2

The next step in learning is to know where and how to get information. In other words, you should ask the right questions of the right people. Yes, we said "people"! We know that nowadays everyone seems to type their questions into a keyboard, or sometimes even ask a digital voice. That can be useful, but it is hard to replace the value of a conversation when learning new information, especially when colleges are staffed with so many people intent on helping students succeed. Besides, we will cover proper research methods—typing good questions—in a later chapter.

> *"Sometimes you have to disconnect to stay connected. Remember the old days when you had eye contact during a conversation? When everyone wasn't looking down at a device in their hands? We've become so focused on that tiny screen that we forget the big picture, the people right in front of us."*
>
> – REGINA BRETT

Help Request and Response Examples

Student:

I'm having a few problems, and not just with my classes. It's not like I can't handle it, but it would be nice to just talk to someone and not have them tell me all the things I should be doing differently.

Frances Northcutt, editor of *How to Survive Your Freshman Year*, responds:

The staff at the counseling center are trained to listen and not to tell you what to do. You are an adult and can make your own decisions, but sometimes it helps to talk through your experiences with someone objective. Counseling sessions are confidential, so you can be upfront and honest about whatever's on your mind without worrying about it getting back to your professors, your friends, your family.[2]

Get to Know Your Campus Services

Now that you know how a growth mindset can help you, and you know your blindspots, it's time to practice seeking out help.

As the title of this lesson suggests, we want to help you know where to go if you have questions or need something. While every school's services may look different, and the names of those services may differ from school to school, there are many common themes. For example, the name "wellness" may be used on one campus while "health and safety" may be the title elsewhere, but in both instances the concept is the same.

Services You Might Seek

Your campus has a lot of resources available to you and most, if not all, of them are covered by your tuition fees. Here's a look at some examples and what they typically offer:

- **Advising center or academic support** – help with all things academic, such as course selection, transfers, degree requirements, writing papers, studying, and more. Some colleges use the counseling center for these things. You may be able to find information about academic advisement services on your school's website.
- **Campus security or police** – if you have any safety concerns or an issue that would involve police, depending on the severity of the issue, you can contact your campus safety or police office. You may be able to find information about the campus public safety office on your school's website.
- **Career center** – provides guidance and services related to career exploration, planning, and the job search process.
- **Counseling center** – helps with personal development and personal, relationship, social or academic difficulties. You may be able to find information about counseling services on your school's website.
- **Disability services** – many students have specific individual needs that can be addressed by disability services. You may be able to find information about disability services on your school's website.
- **Financial services** – deal with everything from financial aid, tuition and fees, scholarships, and more. You may be able to find information about financial aid programs on your school's website.
- **Health and wellness** – anything to do with health; sickness, injury, sleep, mental health, or even if you are healthy already but are looking for some tips to optimize your health. You may be able to find health office information on your school's website. You can also find some general health and wellness information on the National Institutes of Health website (Link 2-33) and on healthfinder.gov (Link 2-34).
- **Military outreach** – deal with all things related to military and services for veterans. You may be able to find information about veteran services on your school's website.
- **Substance abuse** – while a regular health office can be a big help in this area, some schools offer intervention and education services over and above the regular health office. Your school wants all students to visit the alcohol awareness site at Link 2-35.
- **Orientation or First-Year Experience** – just as the name says, this office can help students new to college. Please check out Link 2-36 to learn how to make the most of your orientation.
- **Registrar** – for help with registration and transcripts. This will be important as you apply for graduate school, jobs and certificates. You may be able to find information about the registrar or admissions office on your school's website.
- **Residential life** – relates to living environments, dorm rooms and more. Applies to schools with on-campus residences.
- **Technology services or support desk** – everyone at one time or another needs help with technology. You may be able to find information about technical help or the IT desk on your school's website.

Note that, just as there were off-campus activities and opportunities in which to get involved, you can also access many of the helpful services provided to people living in the community.

CHAPTER 2 QUIZ

College Awareness

This quiz covers all of the topics from this chapter on college awareness. Before you answer any questions, scan them and review any pages necessary in order to be confident in your answers.

1. Who is primarily responsible for selecting a college student's course schedule?
   a. the student
   b. the parent
   c. the advisor
   d. the college registrar

2. What types of things should be considered when scheduling courses?
   a. course load
   b. course location
   c. time of day
   d. other class or employment considerations
   e. all of the above

3. What is typical of college professors (and likely different from high school teachers)?
   a. assign daily homework
   b. expect students to monitor syllabus requirements
   c. provide reminders of assignments
   d. call your parents if you aren't doing well
   e. all of the above

4. What is NOT considered a habit of a highly successful college student?
   a. be persistent
   b. study the way you did in high school
   c. engage professors
   d. plan ahead
   e. all of the above

5. Which of the following are good ideas for planning your college courses?
   a. take more general courses early on and your major-specific courses later
   b. take all your difficult courses in your last semester when you are more mature
   c. you should always declare your major before you start taking any courses
   d. don't select courses according to a planned career—develop all your career skills later
   e. all of the above

6. Which of the following is true about pre-professional programs, such as law school?
   a. there is only one major to pick
   b. there may be classes that I need to take in addition to my major
   c. majors and pre-professional programs are the same thing
   d. as long as I get 'A's, I will get in
   e. all of the above

7. Which of these items is NOT an example of an extracurricular activity?
   a. theater
   b. athletics
   c. internships
   d. history class
   e. volunteer work

©Piotr Marcinski/Shutterstock.com

8. Which of the following are good reasons to try a variety of activities while in college?
   a. provide a service to others
   b. feel more connected to your school
   c. develop additional skills
   d. build a network of contacts
   e. all of the above

9. What best describes a "blindspot"?
   a. a tendency to ignore something that is diffi cult or unpleasant
   b. a place on campus where you can't see the rest of campus

c. something that can never change
d. the part on your application that others could not view

10. Which of the following is an example of a growth mindset?
   a. believing that praise is deserved for status or position
   b. ignoring criticism or failure
   c. enjoying and appreciating the success of others
   d. avoiding difficult challenges
   e. all of the above

CHAPTER 2 SURVEY

College Awareness

This is a quick survey to measure your college awareness before and after the chapter. There are no right or wrong answers.
Just be honest and rate how much each of the following statements applies to you now. Give yourself a score of:
1 for Not a bit • 2 for A little • 3 for Some • 4 for Mostly • 5 for Definitely

AFTER CHAPTER

	Not a bit 1	A little 2	Some 3	Mostly 4	Definitely 5
1. I know some good strategies for planning my courses.	○	○	○	○	○
2. I have budgeted my time using a time management exercise.	○	○	○	○	○
3. I understand the difference between high school teachers and college professors.	○	○	○	○	○

4	I can describe at least 10 habits of highly effective college students.	○	○	○	○	○
5	I can describe the connection between majors, minors and careers.	○	○	○	○	○
6	I have researched different majors to see if they fit me.	○	○	○	○	○
7	I know what extracurricular activities are offered on my campus.	○	○	○	○	○
8	I know three extracurricular activities that suit me and will help with my career plans.	○	○	○	○	○
9	I have a plan on how to get involved outside of my school in a way that will help my future.	○	○	○	○	○
10	I know how my school can help me with financial aid, health or other services, and how to contact those service providers.	○	○	○	○	○
11	I know what my own strengths and blindspots as a student are.	○	○	○	○	○
12	I can explain the difference between a fixed and a growth mindset.	○	○	○	○	○
13	I know the schedule of a typical college year and what to expect in different months.	○	○	○	○	○
14	I understand why frustration can be good, and I feel comfortable asking for help.	○	○	○	○	○
15	I know several strategies to make the most of my time in class.	○	○	○	○	○
16	I know strategies for choosing a major that will work best for me.	○	○	○	○	○

Add up your scores to determine your **After Chapter** total and write it down here:

Write your **Before Chapter** total here:

Compare your Before and After scores to see how your knowledge of this chapter topic has changed.

CHAPTER SUMMARY

The goal of this chapter was to help you make the most of your college experience by increasing your overall college awareness. You need to know what to expect from your classes, your instructors, the campus and the people on it. You also need to make sure that you are benefiting from all these factors in the right ways. A great summary of the "right ways" to benefit from college is delivered in the video at Link 2-37. Some of the video advises on how to select a college. If you are already attending college, translate that advice into advice for selecting courses, activities and other things within the college you are attending.

CHAPTER 2 FEEDBACK

Congratulations, you've completed Chapter 2! To conclude your learning in this chapter, consider and note the following:

What parts of this chapter were most helpful to you?

How would you improve this chapter?

3

CAREER EXPLORATION

CAREER AWARENESS

This is a quick survey to measure what you know about this chapter topic, both before and after you complete the chapter. Just be honest and rate how much each of the following statements applies to you now. Give yourself a score of:
1 for Not a bit • 2 for A little • 3 for Some • 4 for Mostly • 5 for Definitely

BEFORE CHAPTER

		Not a bit 1	A little 2	Some 3	Mostly 4	Definitely 5
1	I can describe how I might express myself through my work.	○	○	○	○	○
2	I know where to find useful career information online.	○	○	○	○	○
3	I have personal contacts who can help me with my career path.	○	○	○	○	○
4	I know services in my school and community that can help me with my career path.	○	○	○	○	○
5	I can describe at least two career clusters that interest me.	○	○	○	○	○
6	I can explain different ways to categorize careers.	○	○	○	○	○
7	I have used career groupings to explore options I hadn't considered before.	○	○	○	○	○

©arka38/Shutterstock.com

8	I know how to look up the job outlook for my career choices.	○	○	○	○	○
9	I can describe lifestyle factors that are important to me and might be influenced by work.	○	○	○	○	○
10	I can explain why preparing for one career may not be enough.	○	○	○	○	○
11	I can describe why career transitions happen and what to do when I transition.	○	○	○	○	○
12	I understand what can be gained by exploring different career groups.	○	○	○	○	○
13	I know which career information is most important in helping me choose a career.	○	○	○	○	○
14	I can describe how much impact different levels of education have on unemployment and earnings.	○	○	○	○	○
15	I know of several important industry trends and why they might be happening.	○	○	○	○	○
16	I can describe the career expectations of different generations.	○	○	○	○	○

CAREER EXPLORATION: IT'S MORE THAN A "JOB"

Key Questions

1. Motivation Check: What I can I gain from different careers?

2. Where do I find career information?

3. What do all the different career groups mean?

4. What career information is important and why?

5. What will the world of work look like when I graduate?

6. Is preparing for one career enough?

©kurhan/Shutterstock.com

CHAPTER PREVIEW

This chapter on careers seeks to help you gain awareness not only about what types of careers are out there and how to learn about them, but also what you hope for in your own career journey. The first section will help you learn how to find information about careers, followed by a section on what career groups mean and how you might traverse various groupings over the course of your career. In the third section, we will help you discern what career information is important for you, and will then conclude the chapter with a long-term perspective on your career.

> *"The biggest mistake that you can make is to believe that you are working for somebody else. Job security is gone. The driving force of a career must come from the individual. Remember: Jobs are owned by the company, you own your career!"*
>
> – EARL NIGHTINGALE

MOTIVATION CHECK

Have you signed up on LinkedIn? You can check it out by using Link 3-1. What if you could get inside the head of the founders of LinkedIn, people who have been shaping how we think about careers? We think the following slideshow outlining three secrets of successful college graduates will really get you thinking! We realize you may not be ready to graduate, but knowing the secrets and tips of a graduate helps you to "begin with the end in mind" and have a vision for where you are headed.

The slideshow is based on the book, *The Startup of You: Adapt to the Future, Invest in Yourself, and Transform Your Career*, written by LinkedIn founders Reid Hoffman and Ben Casnocha. It should only take about 10 minutes to go through the slides. To view the slideshow, open a web browser and go to Link 3-2.

WHICH CAREER SECRET DO YOU LIKE?

Which "secret" do you find most useful as you think about what you can gain from different careers? Why, and how will you apply it?

SECTION 3-1: CAREER INFORMATION SOURCES

Learning Objectives

- Become aware of useful career research and information resources
- Make decisions about which career resources work best for you

"'Entrepreneur' just denotes that you recognize that you're doing things across disciplines and that you're blazing your own path."

–PHARRELL WILLIAMS

As you learned in Chapter 1, it is important to understand yourself, your interests, your values, and what motivates you. While this lesson will focus on how to learn more information about careers, it is important to emphasize the importance of viewing this information through the lens of knowing what you know about yourself.

As a reminder, our purpose with this curriculum is to *connect you to opportunities for learning, working, and living that matter to you.* This chapter focuses on helping you understand your work options, so you can make good decisions for YOU that lead to a happier and more successful life. It fits in the context of our strategy of helping you know yourself, discover opportunities, and provide knowledge and skills to choose wisely.

In the book *Startup of You,* Reid Hoffman, founder of LinkedIn, says, "Whether you're a lawyer, businessperson, medical assistant or [something else] ... you need to also think of yourself as an entrepreneur at the helm of at least one living, growing start-up venture: your career."

What is a Career?

In this section, we will look at a definition of career and help you find career related information. Before diving into the information, let's look at the context. Look at the image that associates several words with career.

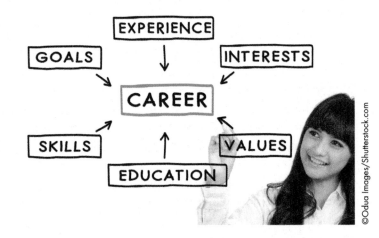

WHAT IS A CAREER TO YOU?

What words do you associate with career and why? Feel free to use words from the image and add your own.

A typical dictionary definition of career is "a job or profession that someone does for a long time." Synonyms may include words like occupation, vocation, and calling. We like to think of career as something that is developed over time.

How Will I Ever Decide on a Career?

As you will see in this chapter, a career is not simply about climbing a ladder. Working towards a meaningful career is usually a long-term endeavor that takes effort and persistence, and hopefully will make you feel good about what you accomplish. The first chapter examined personal awareness and its role in all aspects of your life. This chapter will focus on the work—or career—aspect of your life. In choosing your career, it is wise to revisit some of the questions we asked regarding purpose:

- What are my *values*—and how might they influence my career?
- What is my *personality*—and what career might be a good fit?
- What are my *interests*—and might there be an industry or career that leverages those?
- What are my *abilities*—and where do I differentiate myself from others?

With that as background, we will dive into the focus of this section - finding career information so you CAN make good decisions along the way.

What are the Best Resources for Career Information?

So, where should you go for career information? As you might expect, the Web is a great source of information. But it's not the only one, nor necessarily the best. Don't forget your networks, books and other resources too. They're all excellent information sources. In this section, we will describe and give you experience with all of them.

Online Sources of Career Information

There is a LOT of information about careers on the Web. One of our jobs is to help you understand how to find the information that is best for you. There are two main types of career information:

- **General career information and career profiles** provide background information on a variety of careers, career groupings, industry, education requirements and other general planning information. A career profile is a detailed description of a career which typically includes information about salary, requirements, outlook, related interests, typical work activities and more. A career profile describes what having a job in that career would *typically* be like, but individual jobs may differ.
- **Specific job search information is more tailored to those actively looking for a job.** A great strategy is to read "position descriptions" to learn more about what certain jobs may entail. LinkedIn, Monster, Indeed, and Career Builder are just a few sites of this type. We'll delve into them further in a later section.

The U.S. government has an entire department dedicated to studying general career information—the Department of Labor. Within that department are the Employment and Training Administration ("ETA", see Link 3-3) and the Bureau of Labor Statistics ("BLS", see Link 3-4), which are dedicated to helping people find work and advance their careers. Because they are government sites, they have some very important traits that you should know.

1. They are objective—because they are publicly funded.
2. They are accurate.
3. They are entirely free!

No other career development website can equal those two agencies in regards to those three traits. Visit the websites for each of the two agencies and scan the pages. You will see their mission statements and guiding principles—they are pretty impressive. We highly recommend using these resources for career information. They contain a lot of information to sift through—and we can help guide you through them.

Some online tools created by the ETA and BLS are listed in the activity below. Each tool can help people plan and advance their careers in different ways.

> *"Getting information off the Internet is like taking a drink from a fire hydrant."*
>
> – MITCHELL KAPOR

CAREER INFORMATION WEBSITES

Use the links to BRIEFLY visit each of the five career websites below. Rate your likelihood to visit each site in the future for information. Also list any career-related sites that you like and aren't included here.

1. O*NET Online (Link 3-5)—detailed descriptions of careers and the world of work. Click on Find Occupations to browse careers grouped by different category types. We will look at career clusters more closely in the next section.

2. U.S. Bureau of Labor Statistics (Link 3-6) and USBLSK12 (Link 3-7)—widely used resource for occupational forecasting (such as, number of job openings). The K12 site provides information and activities aimed at students and young adults.

3. My Next Move (Link 3-8)—search for information about hundreds of jobs based on keywords, by industries, or not sure. You can take a 15-minute assessment to obtain a list of potential careers to explore. Click on the section that is appropriate for you.

4. The Occupational Outlook Handbook ("OOH", Link 3-9)—focuses on outlook and trends for careers and career areas. It also has some useful search tools to find jobs according to specific attributes.

5. Major Resource Kits (Link 3-10)—wonder what you can do with a specific major? This site will help you find out. Click a major and get a summary, sample job titles, potential employers, professional associations, and employment resources.

Do you know of any other websites that you would recommend to your peers? Provide details below.

People as a Source of Career Information

Your network is one of the best assets you can use as you prepare to think about your future. A great way to connect with people in your network is LinkedIn, or another network building tool. Online networking tools let you tap into a network with global reach.

Whether you have your own online profile or not (and if not, we strongly encourage you to create one!), you can use it to find people and learn more about their professional role, background and experiences—sort of like a dynamic online resume. Profiles usually include current and past jobs, education background, references and more. You can use these tools to connect with people over email, a conversation, a cup of coffee or whatever. Use the table below to record ideas of people in your network who might be able to give you tips on accessing career information.

Don't forget that you probably also have a career center right on your school's campus. The center will have people who are trained to talk to you about individual careers and your career path in general.

TALK TO SOMEONE: CAREER RESEARCH

Find someone who appears to be satisfied with his or her career. Discuss how that person's career evolved. Often you will find a career path that has not followed a straight line, but has consisted of a series of roles that changed over time. Record the main points of that discussion below.

Books and Experiences as Sources of Career Information

Books are another great source of career information. Rather than jumping directly into factual information about careers, books do a great job of teaching you a method to evaluate the career information you read. The ones we list below also help with inspiration and motivation, so you are more likely to take career research seriously and benefit from it. Here are several popular ones to look for:

1. *Do What You Are: Discover the Perfect Career for You Through the Secrets of Personality Type*, by Paul Tieger (Note: this book is directly related to the *Do What You Are* assessment in this program)
2. *The Start Up of You*, by Reid Hoffman
3. *Frames of Mind: The Theory of Multiple Intelligences*, by Howard Gardner
4. *What Color is Your Parachute? 2014: A Practical Manual for Job-Hunters*, by Richard Bolles
5. *Let Your Life Speak—Listening to the Voice of Vocation*, by Parker Palmer
6. *Big Questions, Worthy Dreams*, by Sharon Daloz Parks

Of course, there are many out there. A librarian or website that reviews books may also help you find one you will enjoy.

Don't forget to access resources that help you learn about yourself. The assessments in these chapters are very good for identifying what to look for in your career research and for narrowing your career list later on.

Lastly, as you prepare to search for career information, we hope you will see it more as a journey or process than a hunt for specific answers. Ultimately, you may choose to pursue a certain job or career, but arriving at that point rarely happens in a "straight line."

> *"Information's pretty thin stuff unless mixed with experience."*
>
> – CLARENCE DAY

How Do I Decide What Information is Best for Me?

Look back at the information sources and think about those you found most interesting. Was it the websites? People? Books or other resources? It may be that you chose those most appealing to you. Or maybe you chose what was easiest for now. Regardless of which ones you favor, don't limit yourself to only one source of information. It's important to use multiple sources of input.

MY CAREER RESOURCE

Which career information resource do you feel is most useful? Explain why and describe how will you use it.

SECTION 3-2: CAREER GROUPS

Which of the following is **least** likely to be a good source of **general** career information for helping to determine a career path?

- a job search site
- O*NET career profiles
- US Bureau of Labor Statistics
- a career services professional

Answer: A job search site is more tailored for those actively looking for a job.

Learning Objectives

- Know the various ways in which occupations can be grouped (such as by job family, industry and education level)
- Know how to sort careers to more easily find desired information

Why Should I Care About Career Groups?

Career groups can help us organize information in a way that makes sense. We do that with things like food groups (grains, proteins, dairy, fruits) and exercise (lifelong sports, extreme sports, endurance events, fitness and so on). Why not with careers? These groups are not intended to limit your options, but rather to help you make sense of all of them and to prepare accordingly.

The goal is to find something you are interested in and see both the differences AND the similarities among the groups. Just be careful not to be limited by them. In many ways the groups are "artificial." They simply help us organize the information. While some people remain in the same career area, others find ways to use their skills across multiple areas (or career groups).

Later you will have the opportunity to listen to a speech by Steve Jobs, founder of Apple. In his speech you will hear how his education, training and career shifted among different industries. You will see how a calligraphy class (which would appear to be part of the Arts career group) in college made a big impact in his career at Apple (which seemingly fits in the Business and Information Technology career groups).

Our hope is that the career groups will help you sort information, think about your interest and skill areas, and see the connections among different careers.

Think of the image on the right as a representation of the career groups. Just because you might be "in" one group doesn't mean you can't cross over or change to another.

©robuart/Shutterstock.com

©Sofi photo/Shutterstock.com

THINKING ACROSS DISCIPLINES

Have you taken an interdisciplinary course in high school or college? For example, some Humanities classes combine language arts and social studies. Another might combine math and science. Or you might come across projects that require different skills in different classes.

Describe a time when you have taken a class or done a project in which you've used information from multiple subject areas.

Many people stay in one career area. But other careers are transferable amongst areas. A person in a sales career may have sold wood products initially, but switched to selling medical devices during an economic downturn. Or, someone may have started by studying biology and applied that learning in the context of law with a career as an environmental lawyer.

What Are Job Families?

Job families are groups of occupations in the same field of work that require similar knowledge and skills. Students, parents and educators can use job families to help build education plans and career paths. A program of study in high school and a degree or major in college usually prepare you for one specific job family. As you narrow your focus in school to certain types of classes, you will be preparing for a smaller group of careers within that job family. And, as you complete higher *levels* of education and gain more experience, you can qualify for a more advanced career in that job family. For example, you may be able to advance from salesperson to sales manager to director of sales and marketing. When you become more familiar with job families and other ways careers are connected, you will better understand the path you need to take to qualify for the job you want to have.

BUILD A CAREER GROUP

Examine the 15 sample careers below. Five of these careers fit together in a career group. Select the five that you think belong together in a career group. Before checking your answer, think about what you would label that career group.

- Farmer/Rancher
- Architect
- Museum Director
- Paramedic
- Botanist

- Nutritionist
- Physician
- Journalist
- Athletic Trainer
- Network Administrator

- City Manager
- Electrical Engineer
- Police Officer
- Veterinarian
- Marketing Analyst

1. Career 1

2. Career 2

3. Career 3

4. Career 4

5. Career 5

Answer: The five that belong together are Paramedic, Nutritionist, Physician, Athletic Trainer, and Veterinarian. Did you think of a label for the career group? The label could be Health Professionals or something similar.

Defining career groups is not an exact science, so you may have selected careers that *could* work together, but just haven't been identified as an official career group. Don't worry if you weren't able to get the correct answer right away. The activity is more about having you think about how careers might be related to one another.

Now that you know the five careers that belong together, can you guess the name of the career group? If you guessed healthcare, health services or something similar, you are right! Notice how the five careers require very similar knowledge and skills—biology and physiology—but would appeal to different personalities and interests. This is why you should consider multiple factors when exploring your career options.

Exploring Job Families

O*NET Online has some great tools for helping you explore job families. Below is an activity that uses these O*NET tools so that you can better prepare for your future career path.

Part 1: Explore one family
Open a browser, go to the Browse by Industry webpage and choose any one of the 23 job families.

Browse by Industry (Link 3-11)
* Choose a job family that best aligns with your academic program and browse the career titles that display. Next to each career is an eight-digit code, 29-1127.00 for example. The first two digits indicate the job family. The remaining digits indicate subgroups within that family.
* Click on the word "code" at the top of the career list to sort the careers by code so that the sub-groups will become more apparent.
* Look for a group of careers near each other that seem to match your career goals. Take note of any careers that you hadn't considered before, and think about how you might advance in your career by starting at one job and then moving to those that require more education and experience.
* When finished, close the browser and return here for Part 2.

Part 2: Move across families
Open the browser again and go to the Related Occupations for a Health Educator webpage. Here you will find a list of occupations that are related to the career of *health educator*.

Related Occupations for a Health Educator (Link 3-12)
* Read the titles, look at the codes (remember, the first two digits indicate the family). Think about how these occupations might belong to different families even though they are all related to that one career.
* Select one of the careers in a different family (not 21-) and follow the link. You will land at the top of the career profile for that career.
* Scroll down and look for the section titled *Related Occupations*. Now look at how many occupations there are from different families.
* Choose a new title and repeat the procedure two or three more times.

A career like health educator might fall into two different focus areas: health and education. Not many people have a background in both areas. Having education and experience in both might set you apart when it comes to landing a job.

Most people find new music they like by searching within a music genre, which is like looking through a job family. Radio stations, satellite channels and digital music services group their music by similar traits. This allows people to more easily find what they might like and explore music they might not have considered before. Think about this as you answer the question below.

Were you able to find any interesting careers you hadn't considered before?
Explain.

Did the activity give you any ideas regarding a career path in which you could advance from career to career? Would you progress through one job family or gain experience in more than one? Explain.

What Other Ways can Careers be Grouped?

We focused on job families in this lesson, but there are lots of other ways to organize careers. They can be grouped by industry, interest area, required education level, "green" economy, STEM (Science, Technology, Engineering and Math disciplines) or by career cluster, for example. When you completed *Do What You Are* earlier, you rated "career interest areas," which are similar to industries.

You might hear a lot about industries. Sometimes words like "sector" and "industry" or "field" are used interchangeably. They may seem very similar to job families as well. Don't worry if it seems confusing. The main purpose at this point is to learn how careers are connected and how that may play a role in your career path over your lifetime.

How Do I Decide What Information is Best for Me and Where Do I Start?

You do not have to remain in one job family or industry your whole life! If you are a biology major, you can use that knowledge in multiple industries. The same goes for many, many other majors. Remember what we said about thinking across disciplines.

Look back at the information sources you selected and think about why you would choose them. It may be that you found those ones most appealing. Or maybe you chose what was easiest for now. Regardless of which ones you favor, don't limit yourself to only one source of information. It's important to use multiple sources of input.

> *"Information is a source of learning. But unless it is organized, processed, and available to the right people in a format for decision making, it is a burden, not a benefit."*

– WILLIAM POLLARD

SECTION 3-3: KEY CAREER INFORMATION

Learning Objectives

- Understand how qualifications (academic performance, personal record, extracurricular, physical requirements, etc.) affect the ability to get a job
- Understand the importance of job outlook and how to look it up for specific careers
- Describe the effect of work on lifestyle (salary, travel, scheduling, physical demands, privacy, etc.)

Finding the Right Information

Did you know that **over 80% of workers in the U.S. report some form of job dissatisfaction**?[1] Do you want to be among them? It's more likely you would prefer to be part of the nearly 20% who genuinely feel satisfied with their role. Armed with the right information about yourself and careers, and the willingness to act on that information, you can find satisfaction!

HOW DID YOU RESEARCH SCHOOLS?

Before we talk about how to find the right information about careers, let's get in the right mindset with a question about how you learned about the colleges. How did you research schools to attend? How did you decide what was important and what wasn't? In the end, what were the top one to three factors that helped you make your decision?

"We are drowning in information, while starving for wisdom. The world henceforth will be run by synthesizers, people able to put together the right information at the right time, think critically about it, and make important choices wisely."

– E. O. WILSON

As you learned with the section on career groups, there is a LOT of information to digest when considering careers. As you think about them, it is essential to take in that information through the lens of YOU. To determine what is important, consider the following factors, always checking them against your interests, skills, personality and values. You completed assessments of these in the first chapter. Be sure to revisit those on occasion to remind yourself of the results. Often we imagine ourselves to be one way, sometimes depending on our mood at the time, but assessments help us see our true selves a little better.

What to Look for in Career Information

The following items are probably the most important factors to consider when choosing and preparing for your career. There are some exceptions, but for most situations these are the ones that will have the biggest impact on whether you get a job and your job satisfaction.

- **Tasks, Activities and Skills** – The main traits of the career and what you will be doing in that job on a regular basis. You need to ask yourself how well they align with your traits—your personality, interests and skills.
- **Requirements and Qualifications** – This is what you need to have in order to get a job in that career. Examples include type and level of education, certification, and apprenticeship training. It is also a good idea to look into whether there are any issues of access or equity in that area.
- **Job Outlook** – Will there be jobs available? How stable is this field?

Most job websites have information about these three factors—and they are very important! Chapter 1 helped you learn more about yourself and allowed you to compare your traits to the traits of various careers. The rest of this section will focus on the other two factors of outlook and requirements.

©FuzzBones/Shutterstock.com

Most of the time you hear about job requirements and qualifications it is really about education. What degrees do you have? What courses have you taken? What were your grades? What training have you completed and what certifications do you have?

As a general rule, the more education and training you have, the more careers you qualify for. You also become more desirable to employers. That old myth of being "overqualified" is quickly being forgotten. Just take a look at the article at Link 3-13 on the benefits of being overqualified. Ultimately, this means that more education equals greater pay and lower unemployment.

Check out these statistics from the Census Bureau that show the effect of education on employment and income.[2]

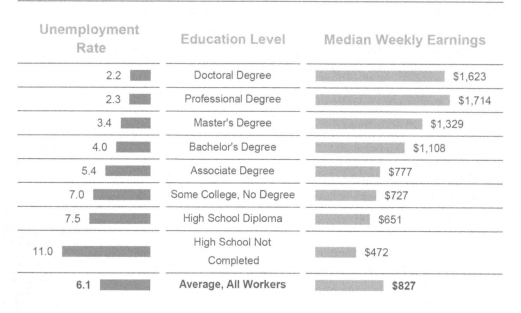

Effect of Education on Unemployment and Earnings in 2013

Unemployment Rate	Education Level	Median Weekly Earnings
2.2	Doctoral Degree	$1,623
2.3	Professional Degree	$1,714
3.4	Master's Degree	$1,329
4.0	Bachelor's Degree	$1,108
5.4	Associate Degree	$777
7.0	Some College, No Degree	$727
7.5	High School Diploma	$651
11.0	High School Not Completed	$472
6.1	Average, All Workers	$827

Based on the above data, we calculated the following lifetime earnings numbers for the different education levels. "Lifetime" assumes 30 years at the average salaries listed above.

Lifetime Earnings Based on Education Level

EDUCATION	LIFETIME INCOME
High school not completed	$736,320
High school graduate	$1,015,560
Some college, no degree	$1,134,120
Associate degree	$1,212,120
Bachelor's degree	$1,728,480
Master's degree	$2,073,240
Professional degree	$2,673,840
Doctoral degree	$2,531,880

So, what does this mean for looking at career information? Look at the range for recommended education and training and aim for the maximum amount required. You can find the recommended education and training for careers in the Occupational Outlook Handbook (OOH)—online version. The activity below will walk you through how to use it.

FINDING CAREER REQUIREMENTS

Follow the steps below to determine what the education requirements are for two different careers. The first career you choose should be one that you are preparing for with your current educational program. Your second career choice should be one that is an alternate choice for you—one that would either be your ideal career (if it is not your current path), or simply a second choice compared to your current path.

©arka38/Shutterstock.com

Link 3-14 will take you to a search tool for the online version of the Occupational Outlook Handbook (OOH). It is a good idea to read through all of the following steps first. Then open a browser, go to the website and complete the steps.

1. At the top right of the OOH you will see a search bar—make sure you use the one labeled "Search Handbook" as there are two search bars. Type in the name of your first career choice. The wording you use may differ slightly from what the OOH uses, so you may need to try a few different search terms to find what you are looking for.
2. Careers and articles will show in a list. Careers have a picture to the left of them. Select the career that best matches your search.
3. For the career profile that displays, click on the tab that says "How to Become One" and read the page. There are other information tabs you are welcome to read as well, but focus on the "How to Become One" tab.
4. Repeat steps 1-3 with your second career choice, then answer the questions below.

What is your first career choice and what are the educational requirements for it?

Are the requirements part of your current educational path? Explain.

What is your second career choice and what are the educational requirements for it?

If you completed all the education and training for your first career, what, if any, additional education and training would you need to complete to be ready for your second career?

Job Outlook

Job outlook refers to how many jobs will be available for a particular career in the future. Outlook is affected by the number of positions available and whether that number is increasing, decreasing or staying the same. If the number of jobs is increasing, the outlook is said to be good because more positions are opening up and becoming available. Another factor is the age of the workforce. If there are many people near retirement age in a career, there should be many positions opening up as well.

Job Outlook by Major Occupational Group[3]

Occupational Group	Projected Percent Change for 2012-2022
Healthcare support	28%
Healthcare practitioners and technical	22%
Construction and extraction	21%
Personal care and service	21%
Computer and mathematical	18%
Community and social service	17%
Business and financial operations	13%
Building and grounds cleaning and maintenance	13%
Education, training, and library	11%
Legal	11%
Life, physical, and social science	10%
Installation, maintenance, and repair	10%
Food preparation and serving related	9%
Transportation and material moving	9%
Protective service	8%
Sales and related	7%
Architecture and engineering	7%
Management	7%
Arts, design, entertainment, sports, and media	7%
Office and administrative support	7%
Production	1%
Farming, fishing, and forestry	-3%
Overall growth, all occupations	11%

As you may have figured out, the green bars indicate areas where growth will be above average. Blue bars indicate career areas where growth will be about average. Red bars show areas that will be below average in growth. It is important to remember that these statistics represent the number of jobs, but not the number of people who are applying to those positions. So, even if the number of jobs available is increasing, the number of people applying may also be increasing, making it just as competitive to get a job. The areas where growth is greatest are most likely to have positions available as education and training programs try to keep up with demand for a labor pool in that area.

Be Guided, Not Governed

Remember, these are overall trends and represent the career areas, not individual jobs. You, as an individual, may experience things quite differently. For example, you may have a passion for the forestry industry and end up finding a dream job as a conservation scientist (Link 3-15), a career in the worst-ranking area of the chart. Don't give up on your dreams because of the statistics. Instead, use them as a guide for your dreams. One way to do that is by following that link for conservation scientist and looking at the tab for "Similar Occupations." There you would find environmental science and protection technicians (Link 3-16), a career that is projected to grow 19%!

Use outlook information to help you find jobs that will be available, but don't forget to also look for careers for which you qualify and that match your traits. By considering multiple factors in your career search, you really improve your chances of finding that dream job. You can find more information on job outlook in the Charting the Projections: 2012-2022 (Link 3-17) issue of Occupational Outlook Quarterly from the U.S. Department of Labor.

OTHER CAREER FACTORS

While qualifications are like "prerequisites" and should be considered by everyone, and outlook is prudent to consider, there are other factors in choosing a career that will be uniquely important to you. Another way to look at this is to consider a career's overall FIT with your values and your preferred lifestyle.

"It's not hard to make decisions once you know what your values are."

– ROY E. DISNEY

Values

As discussed in an earlier chapter, it is important to know what you value. We think this is so important that we are including values here, as a factor to consider when making career decisions. Why? Because you are more likely to be satisfied with your career selection—and your life!—when your work is aligned with your values.

It's one thing to find work that matches your values, but what about when you create the work yourself? When you are in a leadership position, you have the opportunity to influence the values of your work environment. Take a look at the article at Link 3-18 on values-based leadership.

Do you think influencing values is limited to your workplace? In what other places and situations could you have an influence on the values of a group?

Lifestyle Factors

Many people don't realize how much impact a job, especially a career-type job, can have on their lifestyle. The following factors are ways in which your life can be affected by the type of job you choose for yourself.

Finances

Obviously, the amount of money a job pays will have a big impact on everything from your ability to pay bills, buy necessities like food and shelter, purchase other material goods, buy some experiences (vacations, for example), and leisure activities. What many people forget is that your time in the job and the satisfaction that you get directly from it needs to be considered as well. If you are miserable in your job just so you can pay for a few luxury items, is it worth it? Keeping that in mind, everyone's financial goals are different. For some people this is a very important factor, while for others it is not as important.

Each person decides their own financial goals. Before you do, consider this: research shows that people over-rate the happiness they think they will get from material items, and underrate the value of their experiences.[4] You can read more about this in the article at Link 3-19. While you can buy some experiences (vacations for example), your job is something you will experience almost every day!

Questions: What is your ideal salary? What are your long-term financial goals? Can your financial goals be adapted to what your ideal career would support?

Work-life Balance

This relates to how much time and energy you will need to put into your job. Often this can depend more on the individual than the job—you can choose how much time you put in. Sometimes, however, certain jobs demand more time and energy than others. You need to consider how much time and energy you are willing to put into your job versus your family, health, leisure activities, community involvement and more.

Questions: What are your ideal work hours? Is travel an option for you? What family interests and demands do you have? What do you like to do in your free time?

Geography

Some careers are location-bound. For example, jobs in the film industry tend to be located in Los Angeles and New York. Work as a ski instructor inevitably takes place in the mountains, and a career in the military requires going wherever you are required to be. Other careers—such as teacher, doctor or professions in the service industry—are transferable.

Questions: Where do you want to live? Do you prefer a large city? A rural setting? Are you willing to move?

Some careers offer lots of opportunity for advancement (like business, for example,) while others may require staying in the same role (such as teaching or nursing). There is usually a trade-off between opportunity for advancement and stability. Nursing and teaching, for example, tend to be very stable and secure jobs. Going through many progressions means changing your role and having to learn new knowledge and skills. In addition to more rewards, it may also mean more responsibility and commitment. Some people enjoy change more than others. Luckily, you have completed several assessments that reveal this type of information. Pay special attention to the values assessment you completed. The values of "achievement" and "recognition" are closely related to career progression.

This does *not* mean that stable jobs are "dead-end" jobs. You can progress in just about any job, albeit some more slowly than others. And, stability, in part, comes from keeping your skills well-developed and up-to-date. If the work that you do is valuable, whether you are self-employed or working for an employer, you should be able to find work and progress in what you do.

Questions: Is a quick progression from one level to another important to you? Are you a risk-taker or is stability more important?

Remember the statistic at the beginning of this section—that 80% of people report some dissatisfaction with their work? The most common reasons for job dissatisfaction are salary, work-life balance, commute, and other lifestyle concerns. Imagine if that 80% had seriously considered these factors while early in their career development. We know that everyone's situation is different, and that some have fewer options than others. However, the sooner you take control of your career path, the more options you usually have, and the more satisfied you are with your career. The next time you start thinking about how dissatisfied you are with your circumstances, consider the quote below.

"This life is not for complaint, but for satisfaction."

– HENRY DAVID THOREAU

PRIORITIZE YOUR CAREER FACTORS

Though it would be nice to land a dream job in which every factor mentioned in this chapter is satisfied perfectly, it is not likely. A more reasonable expectation is to satisfy the factors you consider most important. Compromises are often necessary, so take some time and think about what is most important to you. For example, if you want to have predictable hours and "leave your work at work," you may have to trade off quick progression or higher pay. Overall work satisfaction comes from finding the "sweet spot"—a combination of the factors you deem most important.

Consider the nine factors we have covered and rank them from 1-9, from most important to least important for you.

1   Job Outlook – I want plenty of job positions to be available

2   Required Qualifications – I want the qualifications to be easy for me

3   Skills and Duties – I want the daily activities to match my interests and personality type

4   Overall Values Alignment – It is important that I do something that aligns with my values

5   Financial Goals/Salary – Financial gain is important to me

6   Geography/Location – Where I live really matters

7   Work-Life Balance – I want a job with flexible hours and other freedoms

8   Progression/Advancement – I want to advance quickly

9   Economic Stability – I want a job that is stable

Here are a couple of scenarios that show how the factors interact with values:

A business executive usually has a high salary but also has demanding hours, frequent travel, and geographically may be required to live in a big city. There is also opportunity for quick advancement and it satisfies the value of achievement. However, these lifestyle factors might conflict with the value of relationships and it might not have the stability or flexibility of other jobs.

A nurse might have a lower salary but has flexibility with hours, which might help balance family and work. A job like this would satisfy those who value relationships. Also, the outlook and economic stability for the nursing profession are quite good.

©Alena Hovorkova/Shutterstock.com

YOUR IDEAL FUTURE JOB

Like the examples above, do your best to imagine your own scenario 10-15 years from now. You are successful and happy. You have a good job, good friends, perhaps a family, and interests you enjoy.

Describe what that job is and how it satisfies the factors you said were most important to you. Also describe the factors you have compromised on because they were less important.

QUESTION GENERATION

We've asked you a lot of questions. Time to ask some questions of your own. What questions do you have about the topics in this section? One example of a question you might have is, "Does every lifestyle factor have to match?" or "What if my priorities change during my career?" You are required to enter at least one question.

Write down at least one question below.

SECTION 3-4: FOLLOWING A CAREER PATH

"There is nothing permanent except change."

- HERACLITUS

Learning Objectives

- Understand why a "career" follows a path that may include many transitions
- Understand that the changing workplace requires lifelong learning and acquiring new skills

Is Preparing for One Career Enough?

How would you answer that question? Think carefully about your answer before you begin this section.

Most likely you said no. But if you said yes, that's OK too. Because for now, preparing for one career is enough. However, odds are, your career will change significantly over time.

Consider the statistics. Members of the baby boom generation—that is, people born between 1946 and 1964—held an average of **11 different jobs between the ages of 18 and 42**. That trend has continued to grow with each new generation of workers. Those most likely to succeed in this ever-changing world of work are students who have been provided with a good foundation of college- and career-ready knowledge and skills in high school. Their education equips them with the flexibility to move between multiple career paths.[1]

The first job decision you make may feel a bit like the picture below on the left—asking yourself, which way should I go? (as if there's only one "right" way). We hope you take a long-term perspective and realize that developing a career may be more like connecting dots—like the picture on the right—than choosing a single path. Your overall career direction and first job decision are important. But they are only the first of many decisions and, likely, many job or career changes, you will make in the course of your working life.

©Ollyy/Shutterstock.com

©jaroslava V/Shutterstock.com

Being Ready for Career Change

We believe a few guiding principles can help you prepare for career change:

- **Do What You Love:** We will illustrate this with a video from a famous college graduation speech
- **Be Aware of Trends:** The world is constantly changing and that affects opportunities
- **Be a Lifelong Learner:** When you are constantly growing and learning, you can view change as opportunity

Do What You Love

Watch a famous Stanford graduation speech from Steve Jobs at Link 3-20. The video is 14 minutes long and has been watched millions of times. Be prepared to comment on what you heard and what you learned.

Here's one quote from the speech:

> *"You've got to find what you love. Your work is going to fill a large part of your life, and the only way to be truly satisfied is to do what you believe is great work. And the only way to do great work is to love what you do. If you haven't found it yet, keep looking. Don't settle. As with all matters of the heart, you'll know when you find it. And, like any great relationship, it just gets better and better as the years roll on. So keep looking until you find it."*

©Alena Hovorkova/Shutterstock.com

FIND WHAT YOU LOVE

Question: Reflect on the quote above—how did Steve Jobs apply it in his life? How do you think you will apply it in your own life? Do you believe it is realistic to do what you love?

One of the notions we hope you take with you from this speech is to seek what you love and what you are good at, but without the pressure of having to "get it right" all at once. As you can see, if Steve Jobs had written a career plan when he was 18, it would have looked very different from how his career actually turned out. It is good to have a plan and a general direction, and equally important to know that life changes. So remember to stay grounded in who you are and what you love along the way. We will come back to this notion at the end of the lesson.

Another way to get a career you'll love is to simply pursue that career from the start. You will likely have to jump a few hurdles to get there, but you can figure out the path knowing what your goal is from the start. This method takes a lot of motivation and determination because sometimes those hurdles are not easy nor enjoyable. To help you build that motivation, check out the website at Link 3-21. On the site you will find videos of people who are in their dream jobs talking about their paths and what they think it takes to get your dream job. Take a look and see if you can find some useful advice and perhaps a little inspiration too.

Be Aware of Trends

As stated throughout this curriculum, it is important to know who you are, to "do what you are" and find what you love. Additionally, you will need to know about the world of work and trends that will impact your future employment opportunities. The world is changing quickly and these changes will affect your career. Steve Jobs took advantage of trends to build a successful business and career. Some say he even created trends. To assure your future success you will need to be aware of, observe, and adapt to trends. This requires forward thinking.

Let's consider the role of desktop publisher as an example. This is a job in which the worker prepares material for physical printing—and it is rapidly being eliminated because print is very quickly being replaced with material that can be accessed digitally. Even when materials are being printed, software makes it easier for non-print professionals to handle the task themselves. So, how are you supposed to spot trends like this? Think about it. Look around. If you use public transportation, do you see more people reading print publications or using digital materials?

Trust your own critical thinking processes. You can also learn about trends by keeping up with news, policy changes and business events. It can be helpful to know why trends occur. Oftentimes it's due to technological innovation (as in the case of the desktop publisher), a drive to reduce costs or efforts to improve safety. It can also be helpful to think about what starts trends—think about motivators such as saving time, saving money, improving safety, innovating (as in case of desktop publishing), decreasing the impact on the environment or finding ways to make things easier.

These can affect the strength or weakness of an industry and be caused by factors such as technology and global competition. The table shows an example of "dying industries"—that is, industries that are gradually vanishing.

10 Key Dying Industries[2]

INDUSTRY NAME	REVENUE 2010 ($MILLIONS)	DECLINE 2000-10 %	FORECAST DECLINE 2010-16 %
Wired Telecommunications Carriers	154,096	-55	-37
Mills	54,645	-55	-10
Newspaper Publishing	40,726	-36	-19
Apparel Manufacturing	12,800	-77	-9
DVD, Game, and Video Rental	7,839	-36	-19
Manufactured Home Dealers	4,538	-74	-62
Video Postproduction Services	4,276	-25	-11
Record Stores	1,804	-76	-40
Photo Finishing	1,603	-69	-39
Formal Wear and Costume Rental	736	-35	-15

REASONS FOR TRENDS

Some trends can be difficult to predict and other times the cause is more obvious. For all of the industries in the table above, choose a reason for the decline in that industry. You will be able to choose one of three reasons. When a **new technology** is released, very often the older technology it replaces sees a rapid decline. As more countries gain the ability for advanced manufacturing, **foreign competition** increases and local industries can decline if they don't stay competitive. People's spending habits change significantly under different **economic conditions**—both corporate and consumer spending habits. How people spend their money can boost or decimate an entire industry.

Choose one of those three reasons for the recent declines in each of the following industries:

1   Wired Telecommunications Carriers

2   Mills

3   Newspaper Publishing

4   Apparel Manufacturing

5   DVD, Game, and Video Rental

6   Manufactured Home Dealers

7   Video Post-production Services

8   Record Stores

9   Photo Finishing

10   Formal Wear and Costume Rental

Answer: New technology (1, 3, 5, 7, 8, 9), foreign competition (2, 4), economic conditions (6, 10).

Generational Trends

About every 20 years, sociologists begin to describe a new generation with similar characteristics. Each generation is typified not only by different historical experiences, fashion preferences and music trends, but also by different opportunities and challenges in the workplace. The trends of one generation influence future generations, and that can be both positive and challenging. Here are a few examples:

- **Baby boomers:** Born between the years 1946 and 1964, this group has changed jobs more often than any previously recorded generation—a sign of things to come. As the largest living generation, they exert enormous influence and are driving demand in fields such as health care, recreation and travel as they retire and age.
- **Generation X:** This group, born between the mid-1960s and the early 1980s, has been greatly affected by unemployment and student loans during difficult economic times. People of this generation tend to place more value on job security than on salary and workplace flexibility.[3]
- **Millennials (also known as Generation Y):** Born roughly between the early 1980s and the early 2000s, this group is noted for its optimism. Students tend to view their personal job prospects in a positive light and believe they can use their careers to make a difference. Many students in this group (58%) expect to have multiple job offers to choose from.[4]
- **Generation Z:** Opinions differ as to the year Generation Z first appeared. Names for this group also vary, but they are revealing—they are often referred to as the iGeneration, Gen Tech or Digital Natives. Growing up in the digital age, they tend to value technology. Influenced by an extended recession (and being the children of Gen Xers), they are more realistic than the Millennials about their job prospects.[5]

Technology Trends

These are closely related to industry trends. In addition to affecting industries, such as travel, music, video rentals, newspaper and print media, and bookstores, trends in technology also change the way people engage in their day-to-day work.

> This [rapid technological change] poses an enormous challenge, because humans are creatures of habit. Businesses desperately cling to familiar but no-longer-competitive modes of operation.... Most of us prefer stability to unpredictable change. We fear the unknown; yet the unknown is what technological change portends and is thrusting upon us.[6]

TRENDS

Select and complete **one** of the following journal questions.

Choice A: Generational Trends: Determine which group you or one of your family members belongs in and describe how generation has had an impact.

OR

Choice B: Technology Trends: How do you tend to respond to technology trends? Do you see yourself as a creature of habit? Do you prefer stability or change? How might your natural tendencies affect your ability to adapt?

Consider Other Trends

Think about other trends, such as new advances in biology, the growth of entrepreneurship, increasingly complex international relationships and changes in security measures. Consider how they will impact your future interests and possibilities.

Be a Lifelong Learner and Embrace Challenges

You may have heard the term "lifelong learning." That means continuing to learn and adapt no matter what circumstances you face. Whether you are in the process of seeking opportunity or responding to an unexpected challenge, continual growth and learning are critical.

"Commit yourself to lifelong learning. The most valuable asset you'll ever have is your mind and what you put into it."

– -BRIAN TRACY

SUMMARY

We have learned how common it is for people to have many jobs over their lifetime. Job change is a result of people learning and advancing in their career path and it is a result of trends that affect the job market. Your career path is partly predictable by knowing and developing your talents and by researching trends. However, sometimes you have to respond to situations you can't see coming. You will make mistakes and sometimes things won't go as planned—that is OK. The key is to always be learning and developing your knowledge and skills. Just as it was for Steve Jobs, you never know how or when your talents will come in handy.

CONNECTING THE DOTS

In Steve Jobs' speech, he said that you often can't see how the dots connect until after it has happened. However, by doing what you love and having trust, you can achieve success and satisfaction. "You have to trust the dots will somehow connect in your future. You have to put your trust in something...." Using Steve Jobs' story as an example, consider the following two questions.

Choice A: What talents or abilities do you put your trust in? What do you love to do? How do you hope your dots connect?

OR

Choice B: Is there someone you know who connected their dots (similar to the Steve Jobs story)? How did they do it—how were they prepared for each challenge?

Choose one of the two questions above and write your response below.

CHAPTER 3 QUIZ

Career Awareness

Select the BEST answer for each of the following.

1. A career is:
   a. A job
   b. A job or profession someone does for a long time
   c. A grouping of similar jobs
   d. An estimated amount of money you will earn

2. Which kind of career information does a career profile typically NOT include?
   a. Typical salary range
   b. Job outlook
   c. Names of companies that hire for that position
   d. Skills and education required

3. Which word or phrase does NOT mean or refer to "industry"?
   a. Sector
   b. Group
   c. Certification
   d. Field of related products or services

4. Which if the following is typically NOT a way that careers are grouped or classified for general understanding of career options?
   a. Location
   b. Industry
   c. Education required
   d. Job family

5. If I pick one job family or one industry, I should try to stay in that family or industry my whole working life.
   a. True
   b. False

6. Which is NOT a key factor to consider in determining your career path?
   a. Requirements or qualifications
   b. Popularity or prestige
   c. Job outlook
   d. Activities and skills used

7. Which of the following is NOT an example of a lifestyle factor to consider when pursuing a career?
   a. Work-life balance
   b. Financial goals
   c. Qualifications
   d. Geography/Location

8. Which generation tends to be the most optimistic about finding employment (perhaps even too optimistic)?
   a. Baby Boomers
   b. Generation X
   c. Millennials
   d. Generation Z

9. Steve Jobs is an example of someone who:
   a. Lived out the idea of "do what you love"
   b. Used a variety of experiences and setbacks
   c. Developed interests and seized opportunities
   d. All of the above

10. Which of the following is NOT a major factor influencing industry trends?
    a. Population levels
    b. New technology
    c. Foreign competition
    d. Economic conditions

CHAPTER 3 SURVEY

Career Awareness

This is a quick survey to measure what you know about this chapter topic, both before and after you complete the chapter. Just be honest and rate how much each of the following statements applies to you now. Give yourself a score of:
1 for Not a bit • 2 for A little • 3 for Some • 4 for Mostly • 5 for Definitely

AFTER CHAPTER

	Not a bit 1	A little 2	Some 3	Mostly 4	Definitely 5
1. I can describe how I might express myself through my work.	O	O	O	O	O
2. I know where to find useful career information online.	O	O	O	O	O
3. I have personal contacts who can help me with my career path.	O	O	O	O	O
4. I know services in my school and community that can help me with my career path.	O	O	O	O	O
5. I can describe at least two career clusters that interest me.	O	O	O	O	O
6. I can explain different ways to categorize careers.	O	O	O	O	O
7. I have used career groupings to explore options I hadn't considered before.	O	O	O	O	O
8. I know how to look up the job outlook for my career choices.	O	O	O	O	O
9. I can describe lifestyle factors that are important to me and might be influenced by work.	O	O	O	O	O
10. I can explain why preparing for one career may not be enough.	O	O	O	O	O

11	I can describe why career transitions happen and what to do when I transition.	○	○	○	○	○
12	I understand what can be gained by exploring different career groups.	○	○	○	○	○
13	I know which career information is most important in helping me choose a career.	○	○	○	○	○
14	I can describe how much impact different levels of education have on unemployment and earnings.	○	○	○	○	○
15	I know of several important industry trends and why they might be happening.	○	○	○	○	○
16	I can describe the career expectations of different generations.	○	○	○	○	○

Add up your scores to determine your **After Chapter** total and write it down here:

Write your **Before Chapter** total here:

Compare your Before and After scores to see how your knowledge of this chapter topic has changed.

CHAPTER 3 FEEDBACK

Congratulations, you've completed Chapter 3! To conclude your learning in this chapter, consider and note the following:

What parts of this chapter were most helpful to you?

How would you improve this chapter?

4

GOAL SETTING AND PLANNING

GOAL SETTING AND PLANNING

This is a quick survey to measure what you know about this chapter topic, both before and after you complete the chapter. Just be honest and rate how much each of the following statements applies to you now. Give yourself a score of:

1 for Not a bit • 2 for A little • 3 for Some • 4 for Mostly • 5 for Definitely

BEFORE CHAPTER

		Not a bit 1	A little 2	Some 3	Mostly 4	Definitely 5
1	I can describe how everyday decisions have a big impact on my life.	O	O	O	O	O
2	I have an effective decision-making model that I use when making decisions.	O	O	O	O	O
3	I understand how decision making, goals, and plans all connect.	O	O	O	O	O
4	I understand that failure and discouragement are natural parts of the learning process.	O	O	O	O	O
5	I know the five attributes of SMART goals and why they are important.	O	O	O	O	O
6	I have a long-term plan to achieve my lifelong goals.	O	O	O	O	O
7	I have created short-term plans to achieve goals in the coming days, weeks, or months.	O	O	O	O	O

©arka38/Shutterstock.com

8	I know how to anticipate things that will contribute to and be obstacles for my plans.	○	○	○	○	○
9	I understand the concept of ABZ planning.	○	○	○	○	○
10	I have reflected on what needs are most important to me in regard to decision-making.	○	○	○	○	○
11	I have identified at least one mentor who can help me with my goals and plans.	○	○	○	○	○
12	I can explain why sharing my goals with others may not be in my best interest.	○	○	○	○	○
13	I can explain the benefits of breaking down goals and plans into smaller steps.	○	○	○	○	○
14	I can recognize the signs that it is a good time to change my plans.	○	○	○	○	○
15	I have anticipated potential contributors to, and distractions from, my goals.	○	○	○	○	○
16	I have seen researched information on decision making and what motivates people.	○	○	○	○	○

Add up your scores to determine your **Before Chapter** total and write it down here:

Key Questions

1. Motivation Check: How do I choose my goals?

2. Why are planning and decision making so important?

3. What is my plan to achieve my goals?

4. How do I stick to my plan and modify it when needed?

©Goritza/Shutterstock.com

CHAPTER SUMMARY

In this chapter, we will walk through the process of goal setting, planning, and activating a plan. Each phase of that process requires:

- Knowledge of who you are
- Knowledge about options available
- Effective decision-making skills

Trying to plan without this knowledge usually results in disappointment and frustration. Worse yet, is not setting goals or planning at all. Recently there has been a backlash to setting goals—some believe they are too limiting or place too much pressure on people.[1,2]. However, we believe those negative aspects come from improper goal setting, planning, and modifying of those plans.

Goals are really about providing inspiration and thoughtful direction. They are not about pressure or restricting your choices later. That is why you need to be very mindful in choosing and developing your goals.

The purpose of this first section in the chapter is to set the stage by making sure you continue to reflect on who you are, that you are exposed to decision-making processes and that you see how goals and plans fit together.

> *"People are not lazy. They simply have impotent goals—*
> *that is, goals that do not inspire them."*
>
> – TONY ROBBINS

MOTIVATION CHECK

How Do I Choose My Goals?

Whether you have goals already picked out for your career or not, it is a good idea to think about them with the following exercise. Choosing the right goals is *the* most important step in the planning process. Otherwise, your motivation to carry out your plan may falter. If you already have career goals, review them after completing this activity. If you don't have career goals yet, this activity might be a great way to get you started figuring out what you want.

©Dusit/Shutterstock.com

Choose one of the following videos to spark your interest and start thinking about setting goals and taking action toward pursuing them. The two videos make the same point, but appeal to the viewer in very different ways. Check your *Do What You Are* report for whether you are a *thinker* or a *feeler*. If you are a feeler, the first video is more likely to appeal to you. If you are a thinker, watch the second video. Or, feel free to watch both if you like.

The dimension of thinking or feeling is related to how we prefer to make decisions.

- *Feelers* should watch the video at Link 4-1
- *Thinkers* should watch the video at Link 4-2. This video takes an approach that *appears* to be negative, but is designed to challenge you to be critical of excuses you may make for yourself and motivate you to pursue your passion.

©Alena Hovorkova/Shutterstock.com

PURSUE YOUR PASSION

Write a short response to the video you chose to watch. How did it make you feel? If you watched both, compare the videos in your response.

SECTION 4-1: DECISION MAKING

Decisions, Decisions

It is estimated that the average person makes thousands of decisions per day. How do you know you will make good choices not only in everyday decisions, but especially in major decisions such as education and career paths? Many of your decisions affect others as well.

The history of the world is a result of decisions people have made. A woman once said, "No, I'm not going to get up from my seat." It changed a country. That woman was Rosa Parks. See Link 4-3 for a profile of her.

Read this story by James Clear, copied from jamesclear.com, April 4, 2014[3]:

> In 2010, Dave Brailsford faced a tough job.
>
> No British cyclist had ever won the Tour de France, but as the new general manager and performance director for Team Sky, a British professional cycling team, Brailsford was asked to change that. His approach was simple.
>
> Brailsford believed in a concept that he referred to as the "aggregation of marginal gains." He explained it as "the one percent margin for improvement in everything you do." If every area related to cycling was improved by just one percent, Brailsford believed, then those small gains would add up to remarkable improvement.
>
> The team started optimizing the things you might expect: the nutrition of riders, their weekly training program, the ergonomics of the bike seat, and the weight of the tires.
>
> But Brailsford and his team didn't stop there. They searched for one percent improvements in tiny areas that were overlooked by almost everyone else: discovering the pillow that offered the best sleep and taking it with them to hotels, testing for the most effective type of massage gel, and teaching

riders the best way to wash their hands to avoid infection. They searched for one percent improvements everywhere.

Brailsford believed that if they could successfully execute this strategy, then Team Sky would might win the Tour de France in five years time.

He was wrong. They won it in three years.

In 2012, Team Sky rider Sir Bradley Wiggins became the first British cyclist to win the Tour de France. That same year, Brailsford coached the British cycling team at the 2012 Olympic Games and dominated the competition by winning 70% of the gold medals available.

In 2013, Team Sky repeated their feat by winning the Tour de France again, this time with rider Chris Froome. Many have referred to the British cycling feats in the Olympics and the Tour de France over the past 10 years as the biggest accomplishment in modern cycling history.

SMALL DECISIONS AND BIG EFFECTS

We make many decisions every day. Some feel like big decisions, and some not as big. However, as the story above reveals, small decisions can have a big effect when added together. Can you think of a situation when some small decisions, perhaps even one small decision, had a big impact on your life? Describe the decisions and the impact they had.

We started with the idea of small decisions because they are important in achieving goals and carrying out a plan. In the example of the British cycling team, choosing the goal was the easy part—winning the Tour de France. It was the planning and execution of that plan that were the difficult parts. Those parts are difficult because they involve many smaller decisions compared to the decision of choosing a goal, and people often forget the impact those small decisions have.

Let's think about a student example. Many times during the day, you make a decision about how to spend your time. You may choose to check Facebook, Twitter, and play a few game apps whenever there are a few minutes to spare. Or, you can read over your class notes, skim the textbook, and update a schedule of your assignments and study time. You may choose to take easier classes rather than ones that maximize skill development and chances for a successful transfer program. Think about the impact of those decisions on your grades, knowledge and skills, and on your future career.

> *"Success is a few simple disciplines, practiced every day; while failure is simply a few errors in judgment, repeated every day."*
>
> —JIM ROHN

Why You Make the Choices You Do

We have established that decisions have a huge effect on your life. Now we will try to understand the motivation behind your decisions. To do this, we use a presentation from a motivational speaker.

There are many motivational speakers and "life coaches" (see Link 4-4 for a description of this), each ready to explain his or her "secret" to success. Rather than following the advice of any single one, we advise you to listen to many and pick and choose bits of information from each one. Use critical thinking to judge the advice given—not all of it will be useful. Great athletes will tell you that they learned something from every coach they had. We will use the advice of one speaker here, but remember that there are others as well.

The video presentation at Link 4-5 is the TED Talk *Understand Why You Do What You Do* by Tony Robbins. After you have watched the video, and at various points throughout this lesson, we will ask you to reflect upon some of the ideas presented and apply them to your life.

Warning: the video contains some coarse language.

WHY YOU DO WHAT YOU DO

Emotion is the ultimate resource. Human emotion is huge—if we have the right emotion we can accomplish much. One thing Tony Robbins talked about in the video were six needs that all of us share. In other lessons, you have considered how you would prioritize your interests and values. This time, try prioritizing your needs.

Indicate the importance of each need to you. The range is from least important (1) to most important (5).

		1	2	3	4	5
1	The need for certainty	○	○	○	○	○
2	The need for uncertainty/variety	○	○	○	○	○
3	The need for significance	○	○	○	○	○
4	The need for connection/love	○	○	○	○	○
5	The need for growth	○	○	○	○	○
6	The need to contribute	○	○	○	○	○

WHAT MOTIVATES YOUR CHOICES

As we said before, it is best to take away at least one thing from every "coach" you meet. In the video, Robbins spoke about what causes people to make the choices they make and gets people to think about how they can make better choices that result in happiness and success. In regards to how you can make better choices, what will you take away from that presentation?

Decision Models

Because decision making is a part of every step of the goal-setting and planning process, we wanted to make sure you began to think about it early in the chapter. There are decision-making models that help you make important decisions. At the same time it is important to realize that, since we are making thousands of decisions each day, we won't be able to use a model for every decision.

Remember, the most important part of decision making is that you consider your own strengths, interests, and values as you make decisions. Most often, there is not just one "right" answer. You can choose the decision-making model that works best for you! For now, let's try a model that is summarized by the graphic and explained below. Conveniently, it is summarized with the acronym "D.E.C.I.D.E."

The D.E.C.I.D.E. Model

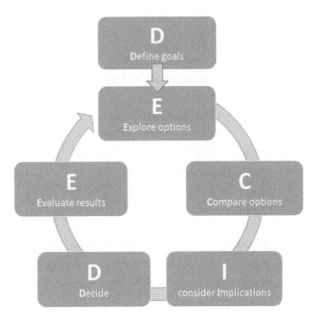

1. **Define goals**. Knowing exactly what you want as a result of your decisions is of paramount importance. This is when you will use your self-knowledge to clarify what you really want, not just what might be convenient or appealing in the moment. Clarifying and remaining aware of your goals helps you make decisions based on long-term outcomes. If you know your goal is to graduate with certain grades, you will likely *decide* to spend a little more time studying than going out every weekend.

2. **Explore options**. This can be considered a brainstorming step. You want to ensure you are not missing possible options. An example would be when you are researching career information and using career groups to consider careers you may not have known about.

3. **Compare options**. Now it is time to look at the details of each option. Does it fit with your goals? Does it fit with your interests, values, and personality? Don't worry too much about what it would take to carry out your decision—you can save that for the planning phase.

4. **Consider implications**. Sometimes an option may fit with your goals, but there are negative implications. For example, plagiarizing might get you a good grade, but it might also get you kicked out of school. Diet pills might cause weight loss, but can seriously damage your health in other ways. Those examples may be fairly obvious. Some negative implications are more subtle. You may need to create a pros and cons list to help you make your decision.

5   **Decide**. While this may seem like an obvious step, many people get caught up in the previous steps for so long that they delay their decision—and this can have negative consequences. Check your *Do What You Are* report again. Are you *judging* or *perceiving*? Perceivers tend to delay making decisions. If you tend to delay making a decision, remind yourself that you will learn more by making the decision. Then, you can use that information in future decisions which are sure to come up quickly.

6   **Evaluate results**. The process does not end with the final decision. You need to evaluate the decision itself and what you did in the process to get to that decision. You may have missed implications, overestimated benefits or even realized that you need to adjust your goals. Everything you learn can be used in your next decision. Sometimes a decision is a one-time affair. For example, deciding to apply for a specific job opening that comes up. The opening may get filled, but perhaps you could find a very similar job later on if you realize that it is something you really want.

Notice that the diagram shows the process as a loop that repeats itself, but that "define goals" is outside that loop. While many decisions are made leading up to a goal, your goals should remain constant most of the time. Occasionally, however, you may need to adjust your goals based on what you learn in the evaluation step. Just be sure that your goals remain aligned with what you really want for yourself. Keeping that in mind, you may need to attempt several options before you are happy with the results.

You can apply this decision-making model to questions such as:

- What should I choose as my major?
- Should I live on or off campus?
- What should I do with my summer?
- Should I buy a car or use public transit?

You can even use this model with some relationship decisions. While it may seem cold and calculated at first, the fact is that you would be putting real thought into your decisions. You might also avoid the bad decisions often made when based purely on emotion.[4] Putting careful thought into decisions about relationships shows *caring*, and not the opposite.

Let's apply the D.E.C.I.D.E. model to the general (and fun!) question "Where would I like to vacation someday?" Follow the pattern of the model except for the evaluation step, which you should eventually do after you go on your dream vacation!

What would be the main goal for your ultimate vacation? What do you want to get out of it?

What vacation options would you consider?

Compare the options. Do a little research here—use some travel sites. Record the main points of your comparison as they relate to you and your goals.

Record your final choice and a brief explanation of why it's your choice.

Describe another real choice that you will make in the near future to which you could apply this decision-making model.

Goals & Plans

The next couple of sections will focus on goals and plans. Think about needs before you think of goals. This sets a context that goals are really only meaningful when viewed from the perspective of these needs. Then think about goals before you think about plans.

Goal: something you are trying to do or achieve.[5]

Plan: a set of actions that have been thought of as a way to do or achieve something.[6]

SECTION 4-2: GOAL SETTING

Learning Objectives

- Learn a goal-setting strategy for short- and long-term goals
- Use knowledge of your abilities and interests while goal setting
- Set challenging academic goals for post-secondary education
- Communicate with mentors who can help with achieving goals

You Decide What Failure Is

We've all heard the stories. Bill Gates didn't finish college. Michael Jordan was cut from the high school basketball team. Aspiring after goals amidst inevitable challenges is really a matter of perspective. For one of Thomas Edison's inventions, for example, it took 10,000 experiments to get it right. When a friend told him not to feel bad about failing, Edison replied, "Why, I've not failed, I've just found 10,000 ways that won't work."[1]

"What would you attempt to do if you knew you would not fail?"

–ROBERT H. SCHULLER

©Sofi photo/Shutterstock.com

NO CONCERN FOR FAILURE

What would your career goal be if you weren't concerned about "failure?"

Remember Who You Are

While the career research you've done so far will be helpful in setting goals, what will hopefully be even MORE helpful is what you have learned about yourself.

Review the section of your *Do What You Are* report called Career Satisfiers. Re-familiarize yourself with the things that bring you satisfaction at work. Those satisfiers should be considered when you set your goals.

"Life can be pulled by goals just as surely as it can be pushed by drives."

– VIKTOR E. FRANKL

How to Set Goals: SMART Goals

You'll do better in school this year—and in life generally—if you have clear goals you're working to achieve. What do you want to accomplish before you finish school?

SMART Goals[2]
- **Specific**
- **Measurable**
- **Achievable**
- **Relevant**
- **Time-oriented**

- **Specific**: A goal that is specific has a much greater chance of being accomplished than one that is vague. A vague goal would be, "I want to do well in school this year." A specific goal would be, "I want to get above a 3.0 GPA."
- **Measurable**: A measurable goal includes concrete criteria for measuring progress. When you measure your progress (through grades, classes taken, clubs joined, attendance or homework completed), you are more likely to stay on track and keep working toward your goals.
- **Achievable**: Goals should challenge you enough to help you grow and achieve something meaningful, but must be realistic and achievable for the time period chosen.
- **Relevant**: Each goal should list something you want to do or want to make happen that is meaningful in your own life. Some would also describe this as rewarding.
- **Time-oriented**: Goals are more likely to be achieved when there is a target date. You will have many opportunities to develop long-term goals in your life. In the following exercise, you will set some goals that are long term (over a year or a lifetime) and some that are short term (something you are able to accomplish by the end of the school year).

It is important to note that goals can be long-term (achievable within a year or further off in the future) or short-term (achievable within days, weeks or months). In this activity, you will develop some of each.

You will probably need to work on this in more than one sitting. In the first sitting, you are required to complete your three career goals and three academic goals. Once you have completed those required responses, you can return later to edit your responses at any time **until you complete this chapter**.

Career Goals

Describe three long-term career goals for yourself:

Career goal 1:

Career goal 2:

Career goal 3:

Choose **ONE** of the three career goals above and answer the following questions related to the SMART goal-setting strategy. Are you being specific enough? Can it be any more specific? Explain.

How will you measure it?

Explain why you think it is challenging but achievable.

Explain how it is relevant or meaningful to you.

What is the time-frame?

Describe three short-term academic goals for yourself:

Academic goal 1:

Academic goal 2:

Academic goal 3:

Choose **ONE** of the three academic goals above and answer the following questions related to the SMART goal-setting strategy. Are you being specific enough? Can it be any more specific? Explain.

How will you measure it?

Explain why you think it is challenging but achievable.

Explain how it is relevant or meaningful to you.

What is the time-frame?

GOALS MENTOR

Talk to someone who might be able to mentor you with your goals. Pick someone who has followed a path that reflects the goals you have chosen. For example, you can choose someone who is working in an area close to your career goals.

If you cannot find a live person to talk to, look for articles, blogs, books, or other media that reveal advice and perspectives from someone whose experiences mirror your career goals. You might even be able to find information by doing a web search for "What is it like becoming a...?" Just be wary that people who complain tend to be more vocal than those who are happy. To keep it balanced, look for articles that look at the good *and* the bad.

Summarize what you learn from your mentor and use the following questions to guide you. Feel free to alter the questions slightly to better fit the situation.

- Why did you choose that goal?
- What challenges did you encounter and how did you deal with them?
- What helped you the most along the way?
- Would you do anything differently? What?
- What advice would you offer to someone in my situation?

SECTION 4-3: BUILDING PLANS

Break It Down

In many ways, creating a plan is similar to breaking longer-term goals into shorter-term goals. Goals and plans are directly related. Here is a story to bring that to life:

In 1984 at the Tokyo International Marathon, a Japanese athlete named Yamada Motochi unexpectedly won the world championship. When reporters asked what made him such a startling success, he said: "I use wisdom to defeat [my] opponent." Many people didn't believe him. Marathon running requires both physical strength and endurance.

Two years later, at the Italian International Marathon, Yamada won the championship again. A reporter said to him, "You have won the championship again. Can you talk about your experience?" Yamada gave the same answer: "I use wisdom to defeat [my] opponent." Everyone was puzzled by his so-called wisdom.

Years later, when Yamada wrote his autobiography, the mystery was solved.

"Before each race," he wrote, "I will travel the whole route and check it carefully. I will mark some important points along the road, such as the first point is a bank, the second point is a tree, the third point is a red house, and the end is the last point. When the race begins, I run as fast as I can towards the first goal, the bank. When I arrive at the bank, I will strive for the second goal, the tree. I break the whole marathon route into many small goals and finish them one-by-one more easily. Before I used this method, I set my goal to be the end of the 40 kilometer marathon. I would get exhausted in the first 10 kilometers because I was frightened by the remote distance."

This story is inspirational. You can learn a lot from it. A great dream can be achieved through many small goals. These small goals are your short-term goals. Sometimes we fail not because the goal is too hard, but because we don't break the long-term goal into several small goals. So we feel that success is too far away.

Many of us will set only short-term goals and ignore the long-term goals. Are you busy working on many small goals and don't even have a long-term goal? This will not lead you to success either, because these small goals grouped together can't give you a good result. They are not relevant and cannot contribute much to your future success.

Now you know the relationship between short-term and long-term goals. The key is to start with a long-term goal and break it into several small goals. Those small goals are your short-term goals.

REVIEW QUESTION

Which words describe the five attributes of SMART goals?

- Smart, Measurable, Achievable, Rewarding, Time-Oriented

- Specific, Mobile, Achievable, Relevant, Time-Oriented

- Steps, Measurable, Achievable, Rewarding, Time-Oriented

- Specific, Measurable, Achievable, Relevant, Time-Oriented

Answer: Specific, Measurable, Achievable, Relevant, Time-Oriented—these are the five attributes of SMART goals.

Remember, making a plan is part of an ongoing process. In the last lesson you identified goals. Now you will work to create a plan, and in the next lesson you will check to see if it is working and what actions to take next.

To Share or Not to Share

A lot of people think the first two things they should do after setting a goal are:

- Tell someone, and
- Create a plan to achieve the goal

This lesson will focus on the latter—creating a plan. Before you do, we want you to think about whether you should share your goals! Conventional wisdom says, "Tell someone your goal so they can hold you accountable." Think about how this message is used in weight loss commercials, for example.

The video in Link 4-6 encourages the opposite approach. There may be exceptions to the negative implications discussed in the video. For example, you may need the direct help of someone else to achieve your goal. If your goal is to complete a marathon, you probably want to tell a coach or trainer so you can receive specific advice on how to train. The video is likely referring to telling others who are not directly involved in completing your goal.

Whether you tell others your goals or not, there are some very practical reasons why *planning* for them is a good idea. It can save you time, money and dashed dreams.

My Plans

Given the exploration you have done to better understand yourself, your potential career interests and your goals, it is time to summarize them in a concise plan.

TURNING GOALS INTO PLANS

Complete all of the following as an outline of a career plan. You will probably need to work on this in more than one sitting. Only the first two questions are required for now. Once you have completed the required questions, you can return to add information and edit the page at any point **until you complete this chapter**.

Goals Summary

Post-secondary Goals (required). Check all that apply.

_____ Complete a two-year degree

_____ Complete a four-year degree

_____ Go to graduate school

_____ Get a job first

_____ Join the military

_____ Apprenticeship or other certification program

Other post-secondary goals:

Completed Planning Steps (required). Check all that apply.

_____ Completion of a plan (such as this one)

_____ Course registration

_____ Informational interviews in target career areas

_____ Career planning: resume, career fairs, etc.

_____ Researched next school or first job options

_____ Completed job or grad school applications

_____ Budget planning: bills, spending, and savings

Other planning steps that you have completed but are not listed above:

Education

Current school:

Future schools (if planned):

Current or planned majors:

Total credits required for graduation:

Credits required within major:

Credits required within minor:

Other course or grade requirements:

Work-related Experience (identify what you have done for each)

Volunteering:

School projects:

Extracurricular activities:

Internships:

Other:

Exams (identify all exams required for graduation, certification or admission to your next program)
Examples include GRE, ASVAB, and UCPAE:

The previous activity is just one way of thinking about a long-term plan—there are lots of others. Some people like to build pyramids or use spreadsheets, write a narrative or use other formats.

TIP: Here's a really simple framework that you can use for any planning. Notice how it works backward from the end-goal:
- What do I need to do within five years?
- What do I need to do within two to three years?
- What do I need to do within the next year?
- What could I do in the next month?
- What can I do in the next week?
- What could I do today?

Short-Term Goals and Plans

Hopefully you found the process of developing a longer-term plan to be fun and helpful. It can also sometimes feel overwhelming. It's OK if you don't know exactly what you will do or precisely how to do it. Keep at it! Remember, long-term goals are really just a collection of short-term goals.

©Alex Valenj/Shutterstock.com

"Faith is taking the first step even when you don't see the whole staircase."

–MARTIN LUTHER KING, JR.

SHORT TERM PLAN

Here is a simplified activity that can give you additional practice building a plan for a short-term goal such as completing a race, getting an A in a class, learning a new skill or finishing your resume.

In the activity, you will identify a short-term goal, describe three steps to achieve that goal, and describe when you will complete those three steps.

EXAMPLE: My short-term goal is "choose my major." Three things that will help me accomplish that goal are:

- Narrowing my choices to two options based on results from the assessments in this program. I will set aside two hours this weekend to do this.
- Researching my two choices by using O*NET Online at Link 4-7 and talking to people who have completed those majors or are well into the programs. I will do this over the next week and complete it by next Sunday.
- I will compare the two choices using the research I did in the previous step and make my decision one week after I finish my research.

Describe a short-term goal you would actually like to complete within the next few months.

Below, describe the three steps and when you will do each step.

First, I will...

The time I will do this is...

Second, I will...

The time I will do this is...

Third, I will...

The time I will do this is...

SECTION 4-4: MODIFYING PLANS AND BACKUP PLANS

"Failed plans should not be interpreted as a failed vision. Visions don't change, they are only refined. Plans rarely stay the same, and are scrapped or adjusted as needed. Be stubborn about the vision, but flexible with your plan."

– JOHN C. MAXWELL

Learning Objectives

- Understand the importance of flexibility in carrying out plans
- Recognize important contributors and obstacles to career and academic plans
- Know how to create backup plans and know when to use them

You Can Change Plans

In Greek mythology, Sisyphus was a king of Ephyra (now known as Corinth) punished by the gods for chronic deceitfulness. For all eternity, Sisyphus was condemned to roll an immense boulder up a mountain, only to have the stone roll down again as soon as it reached the top. The gods thought, with some reason, that there could be no more dreadful punishment than futile and hopeless labor.[1]

If you start feeling like Sisyphus and find yourself engaged in "futile and hopeless labor," it may be time to modify your plans. Sometimes goals and plans feel like work. They should—that's normal. But if it feels like drudgery, or there are changes or opportunities to take advantage of—be ready to adapt!

©PHOTOCREO Michael Bednarek/Shutterstock.com

Remember, making a plan is part of an ongoing process. In the last couple of sections, you have identified goals and created a plan. Now it is time to develop skills that help you assess if the plan is working and consider what actions can be taken when it is ... and when it isn't.

WHAT HELPS KEEP YOU GOING?

What helps keep you going? Have you ever felt like you are enduring futile and hopeless labor? When have you been part of something that has felt fulfilling?

REVIEW QUESTION

How are plans connected to goals?

- plans move you into action toward your goal

- good plans are smaller, less intimidating steps toward your goal

- plans provide guidance and direction toward your goals

- All of the above

Answer: All of the above are true for plans.

What is Helping Your Plans?

There is power in having a plan. That doesn't mean you can't change it or that circumstances won't change it for you. Plans are intended to serve you and provide clear direction, not to make you a slave to what you once said you would do. There are times to buckle down and "work the plan." But if you begin to feel like Sisyphus, it may be time to think of other options.

There will be things that contribute or help you to pursue your plan and other things that are obstacles or distractions. Because of that you will need to make important decisions about how you spend your time and effort. Remember the decision-making strategy D.E.C.I.D.E. you learned earlier in the chapter. In the next activity, you can use that strategy to identify the key contributors and obstacles to your goals.

"I think when things linger, that's when they become a distraction. I don't want any distractions."

– DEREK JETER

CONTRIBUTORS AND DISTRACTIONS

List two of your top goals. For each, identify key contributors that could help you achieve these goals. Also predict obstacles or distractions that could prevent achievement of your goals.

Identify one of your short- or long-term goals.

Describe at least two **key contributors** to that goal.

Describe at least two **key obstacles or distractions** to that goal.

Identify a second short- or long-term goal.

Describe at least two **key contributors** to that goal.

Describe at least two **key obstacles or distractions** to that goal.

You've been asked to record a lot of information about your goals and plans. Now we want you to sit back, relax, and watch one more video. The goal of watching this next video is for you to think deeply about your motivations and decisions as they relate to your goals and plans. You have three options. You only need to choose one, but you are welcome to watch two or even all three.

Video Choices:
- **Option A**: Use Link 4-8 for a video on feeling good about your work
- **Option B**: Use Link 4-9 for a video on making it easier to choose
- **Option C**: Use Link 4-10 for a video about decision making

GOALS AND PLANS: YOUR MOTIVATION

What information from the videos did you find useful or interesting?

ABZ Planning

You will often get contradictory advice on career development. Some people will tell you to think about where you want to be in 10 years, work backwards, and construct a long-term career plan for realizing your ambitions. Others say that firm plans are like a straitjacket; they will blind you to unexpected breakout opportunities. It's better, they say, to remain nimble and opportunistic.

Who's right? Both are not only right, but critical. We can learn from entrepreneurs who are *flexibly persistent.* LinkedIn's Reid Hoffman says the best entrepreneurs he has worked with engage in serious *planning and strategy,* but they do not set *fixed plans.* In his book, co-written with Ben Casnocha, *The Start-Up of You: Adapt to the Future, Invest in Yourself, and Transform Your Career,* the authors set out to show how any professional can apply entrepreneurial techniques to their career, even if they never plan to start a company. The following is an excerpt from the book.

Plan A

What you are doing or pursuing right now

This should be what you currently think is your ideal career

More Info/Example:
For Flickr co-founders Caterina Fake and Stewart Butterfield, the original Plan A was *Game Neverending,* a multi-player online game. Unlike most games of the time, which enabled play between a few opponents through a fixed experience, Fake and Butterfield wanted their game to have hundreds of users playing concurrently and creating new things in the game forever. To engage users, they built social features like groups, instant messaging, and—crucially—a feature that allowed players to share photographs with one another.

Plan B

What you pivot to when you need to change the goal or route

This is really a modified Plan A based on what you have learned in working toward your original goal

More Info/Example:
At Flickr, unexpectedly, the photo-sharing feature eclipsed the game itself in popularity. Fake and Butterfield were faced with a choice: Should they stick with their Plan A or put the game (and its 20,000 avid users) on hold to focus exclusively on the photo-sharing feature? They shifted to Plan B. They were still following their original idea to build an online social space—they just saw greater potential in photo sharing than gaming.

Fallback position: A reliable and stable plan if none of your career plans work

A plan Z helps you know when you're heading toward a worst-case scenario and what to do should that happen

More Info/Example:
Maybe when your credit card debt climbs to a certain amount you cash out your retirement savings or get a job at a coffee shop. The certainty of a Plan Z is what allows you to take on uncertainty and risk in your career. When Hoffman started his first company, Socialnet, his parents offered him a room in their house in the event things didn't work out. Living there and finding another job was his Plan Z. It gave him the confidence to throw himself into the business knowing that if it all went to hell, he wouldn't end up on the street. You want to be able to survive failure in order to play again.

You likely noticed that the order of the letters skips from B to Z. If you guessed that you might need to go to Plan C, D, or further, you are right. Your original plan may need several modifications before you find real success. Remember the story of Thomas Edison and the many attempts he made before getting the light bulb right. Right now, you can't know that many steps ahead. However, you probably have a good idea of one change you can make to your current plan if things don't work out the way you intended—hence the letters A, B, and Z. You can't know how many plans you will go through before you have to use your Z plan, but going through the whole alphabet is unlikely. Remember that you need to think about the difference between when your plan feels like it is just work and when it feels completely hopeless. You also need to consider the resources you can gather to make each plan happen.

If you haven't thought of a plan B yet, now is a good time to start. You were recently asked to think of possible obstacles to your goals. Choose one or more of those obstacles and imagine how you might change your plan A to a plan B that would eliminate those obstacles. Even if you end up using a different plan B because the situation turns out differently from what you expected, it is good to know you can create a plan B at all.

"Plans are only good intentions unless they immediately degenerate into hard work."

– PETER DRUCKER

YOUR A, B, AND Z PLANS

Take inspiration from the previous examples and briefly describe your A, B, and Z plans.

CHAPTER 4 QUIZ

Goal Setting and Planning

Select the best answer for each of the following questions.

1. Which of the following is **NOT** a key part of goal setting and planning?
   a. Self-knowledge
   b. Knowledge of trends
   c. Knowledge of available options
   d. Decision-making skills

2. Which of the following is **TRUE** regarding decisions we make every day?
   a. Small decisions can have a very large impact on our lives
   b. Goals only need to be considered for large decisions
   c. Once you make a decision, move on and do not think about that decision anymore
   d. Decisions are best made by instinct rather than using a model or strategy

3. In the Tony Robbins video, which of the following was **NOT** described as a human need to be considered when making decisions?
   a. Need for certainty
   b. Need for significance
   c. Need for travel
   d. Need for connection/love
   e. Need for growth

4. Which of the following is **NOT** part of the D.E.C.I.D.E. decision-making model?
   a. Explore options
   b. Consider implications
   c. Ignore distractions
   d. Decide

5. Which words fit the SMART goals process?
   a. Smart, Measurable, Achievable, Rewarding, Time-Oriented
   b. Specific, Mobile, Achievable, Relevant, Time-Oriented
   c. Specific, Measurable, Achievable, Relaxing, Time-Oriented
   d. Specific, Measurable, Achievable, Relevant, Time-Oriented

6. Which of the following is **NOT** recommended when setting goals and making plans?
   a. Break long-term goals down into smaller steps
   b. Share your goals with as many people as you can
   c. Have a target date in mind
   d. Find a mentor who has achieved similar goals

7. Which of the following should be considered when working toward your goals?
   a. Contributors or helpers
   b. Obstacles or distractions
   c. Both of the above
   d. Neither of the above

8. What is a good sign that you should change your plans?
   a. When it starts to feel like hard work
   b. When it starts to feel hopeless and futile
   c. Both of the above
   d. Neither of the above

9. Which of the following best summarizes ABZ Planning?
   a. Have one plan for each letter of the alphabet
   b. Choose your two favorite things and your least favorite
   c. Have a primary plan, be willing to adapt it, and have a backup plan
   d. Have one plan for each phase of your life

10. In ABZ planning, which of the following is **NOT** true?
    a. Plan B is a completely new plan compared to A
    b. Plan Z is the most stable or safe plan
    c. You may end up using plan C or D as well
    d. All of the above are true

GOAL SETTING AND PLANNING

This is a quick survey to measure what you know about this chapter topic, both before and after you complete the chapter. Just be honest and rate how much each of the following statements applies to you now. Give yourself a score of:
1 for Not a bit • 2 for A little • 3 for Some • 4 for Mostly • 5 for Definitely

AFTER CHAPTER

		Not a bit 1	A little 2	Some 3	Mostly 4	Definitely 5
1	I can describe how everyday decisions have a big impact on my life.	○	○	○	○	○
2	I have an effective decision-making model that I use when making decisions.	○	○	○	○	○
3	I understand how decision making, goals, and plans all connect.	○	○	○	○	○
4	I understand that failure and discouragement are natural parts of the learning process.	○	○	○	○	○
5	I know the five attributes of SMART goals and why they are important.	○	○	○	○	○

6	I have a long-term plan to achieve my lifelong goals.	○	○	○	○	○
7	I have created short-term plans to achieve goals in the coming days, weeks, or months.	○	○	○	○	○
8	I know how to anticipate things that will contribute to and be obstacles for my plans.	○	○	○	○	○
9	I understand the concept of ABZ planning.	○	○	○	○	○
10	I have reflected on what needs are most important to me in regard to decision-making.	○	○	○	○	○
11	I have identified at least one mentor who can help me with my goals and plans.	○	○	○	○	○
12	I can explain why sharing my goals with others may not be in my best interest.	○	○	○	○	○
13	I can explain the benefits of breaking down goals and plans into smaller steps.	○	○	○	○	○
14	I can recognize the signs that it is a good time to change my plans.	○	○	○	○	○
15	I have anticipated potential contributors to, and distractions from, my goals.	○	○	○	○	○
16	I have seen researched information on decision making and what motivates people.	○	○	○	○	○

Add up your scores to determine your **After Chapter** total and write it down here:

Write your **Before Chapter** total here:

Compare your Before and After scores to see how your knowledge of this chapter topic has changed.

You are at the end of the chapter on goal setting and planning. Before you continue, **make sure you have completed all the chapter activities**.

CHAPTER 4 FEEDBACK

Congratulations, you've completed Chapter 4! To conclude your learning in this chapter, consider and note the following:

What parts of this chapter were most helpful to you?

How would you improve this chapter?

CHAPTER 5

LEARNING AND PRODUCTIVITY

©arka38/Shutterstock.com

LEARNING AND PRODUCTIVITY

This is a quick survey to measure what you know about this chapter topic, both before and after you complete the chapter. Just be honest and rate how much each of the following statements applies to you. Give yourself a score of:

1 for Not a bit • 2 for A little • 3 for Some • 4 for Mostly • 5 for Definitely

BEFORE CHAPTER

		Not a bit 1	A little 2	Some 3	Mostly 4	Definitely 5
1	I can describe mindset, grit, self-control, motivation and how they affect achievement in school and work.	○	○	○	○	○
2	I understand the difference between extrinsic and intrinsic motivation.	○	○	○	○	○
3	I know several proven strategies to improve motivation.	○	○	○	○	○
4	I know the most common ways motivation can be decreased and how to avoid them.	○	○	○	○	○
5	I know what critical thinking is and how to develop my ability with it.	○	○	○	○	○
6	I can describe my preferred learning styles and strategies to accommodate them.	○	○	○	○	○

7	I know what metacognition is and how to develop my ability to use it.	○	○	○	○	○
8	I know the pitfalls of technology and how to ensure it benefits my education.	○	○	○	○	○
9	I know where to go for help with technology if I need it.	○	○	○	○	○
10	I know several good listening techniques.	○	○	○	○	○
11	I know several note-taking strategies and when to use them.	○	○	○	○	○
12	I know good research-supported reading techniques.	○	○	○	○	○
13	I know the steps and where to go to perform good research and information analysis.	○	○	○	○	○
14	I can describe several effective memory techniques and why they work.	○	○	○	○	○
15	I know the expectations for good writing in college and how to meet those expectations.	○	○	○	○	○
16	I can describe several effective studying and test-taking strategies.	○	○	○	○	○

Add up your scores to determine your **Before Chapter** total and write it down here:

LEARNING AND PRODUCTIVITY

Key Questions

1 Motivation Check: How do I work hard, perform well, and enjoy myself while doing so?

2 What are some tips for increasing motivation?

3 What is critical thinking, and how can it help me?

4 What are the best ways for me to learn and work?

5 What study skills will help me most?

    A. Using Technology
    B. Listening and Taking Notes
    C. Reading
    D. Research and Information Analysis
    E. Memory Tricks
    F. Writing
    G. Studying and Test Taking

©g-stockstudio/Shutterstock.com

MOTIVATION CHECK

How do I work hard, perform well, and enjoy myself while doing so?

That may seem like a lot rolled into one question, let alone actually doing it. However, it is possible. In fact, all three parts of that question—hard work, performance and enjoyment—are related to one another. Working hard develops your skills to perform well. Performing well leads to enjoyment. Seems logical, right? But perhaps it works in a different order. Enjoying yourself leads to motivation, which causes you to perform well.

Reflect on the quote below and then use Link 5-1 to watch a related video. The video takes the stance that happiness leads to success, as opposed to the more traditional viewpoint that success leads to happiness.

> *"Ability is what you're capable of doing. Motivation determines what you do. Attitude determines how well you do it."*
>
> – LOU HOLTZ

WHICH COMES FIRST, SUCCESS OR HAPPINESS?

Which do you think comes first? Do you need success to have happiness? Or is it the other way around? Explain.

Generating Happiness

If positivity and happiness are needed for productivity and success, how do you generate positivity and happiness? Good question. The answer has to do with mindset and gratitude. In the video, **expressing gratitude on a daily basis is a key way to increase happiness**. In the next section we will discuss gratitude further, ways to improve mindset, and other concepts proven to increase your productivity.

SECTION 5-1: EFFORT AND MOTIVATION

Now that you know what careers are out there and you have begun to set some goals, it is time to focus on some things that will help you achieve success on a day-to-day basis.

We can break the elements of success into two simple factors:
- Effort
- Ability

We will focus on effort in this section, and then look at how to maximize your ability in the later sections.

Effort

Effort is a combination of many things. We have already covered some of those things in other chapters, and learned early in this chapter that happiness is a big factor in how much effort one puts in. Take a look at the graphic with the words that associate with "effort." Think about what the words mean to you and what other words you might add.

What Creates Effort

The previous page introduced the idea that effort is a combination of things. Here we will look at some of those things so that you can understand how to maximize your effort in school and in your career. While we can separate effort into different words and ideas, you will quickly see how these different ideas overlap with each other. Don't worry about the exact differences between the following concepts. We separated them out to give you more choice in the strategies you can use to maximize your effort.

Mindset

Very generally, "mindset" refers to how you think or to your beliefs. In earlier chapters we talked about the importance of a growth mindset. In essence, it is the belief that abilities can be developed through dedication and hard work.[1] If you believe you can improve and grow, you are more willing to put the effort into school and work.

Refer back to the start of the chapter College Awareness for some strategies on how to foster a growth mindset.

Grit

Another important set of research came out of the University of Pennsylvania from Professor Angela Lee Duckworth. She asserts that something called "grit" is the most important predictor of success.[2] Check out the video at Link 5-2 to learn more about grit.

You can also get your grit score from a research survey being conducted by the University of Pennsylvania. Check out the site at Link 5-3 for information. Note, however, that this assessment is not part of CollegeScope.

So, how can you improve your grit? At this point even Dr. Duckworth is unsure, but she indicates that developing a growth mindset may be one way. Be sure to review the strategies for developing a growth mindset from the earlier chapter.

Self-control

The ability to control your emotions, behavior and even desires in the face of outside influence is self-control. A simple example is when you are offered a delicious-looking chocolate doughnut right after you have promised yourself you'll cut back on treats. Good self-control would help you say, "No, thank you." Less self-control would likely result in you enjoying a delicious chocolate doughnut—but also the failure, or at least delay, of achieving your goal. Self-control also helps you study and focus in class when distractions like Facebook, video games and partying can be very tempting.

Taking responsibility for your actions and exercising self-control are very important. These are among the traits that will be expected of you in school and work. Sometimes exercising self-control includes delayed gratification, which means that you can wait to receive a reward. This ability has been shown to be a major predictor of success, adjustment, and happiness.

Psychology professors at Stanford University originally conducted what has come to be known as The Marshmallow Experiment. This experiment about delayed gratification was reproduced and captured in a video that you can view at Link 5-4.

The experiment has been reproduced many times and one of the important things we have learned from the research is that self-control can be learned.

Check out the article at Link 5-5 for some tips on how to develop more self-control.

Motivation

Motivation is a fairly general term for how much you are willing to do something. We are choosing words carefully and not saying it is how much you "want" something. Many people want many things but are not willing to do what it takes to get those things.

In this lesson, the terms "desire" and "drive" are considered part of motivation. Because motivation is difficult to define and is affected by so many factors, learning about it can be confusing or overwhelming. We will attempt to keep things simple here, but you are encouraged to use other sources and your critical thinking skills to expand your knowledge of motivation. As your knowledge grows, you will improve your ability to **be** motivated to achieve your goals.

"Some people want it to happen, some wish it would happen, others make it happen."

– MICHAEL JORDAN

Motivation

There are two main types of motivation.

Extrinsic Motivation

Extrinsic motivation occurs when we are motivated to perform a behavior or engage in an activity in order to earn a reward, avoid a punishment or for something other than the activity itself.

Examples of behaviors that are the result of extrinsic motivation include:

- Studying because you want to get a good grade
- Cleaning your room to avoid being nagged by your parents (or roommates)
- Competing in a sports event in order to win

In each of those examples, the behavior is motivated by a desire to gain a reward or avoid a negative outcome.

Intrinsic Motivation

Intrinsic motivation involves engaging in a behavior because it is personally rewarding. You perform the activity for its own sake rather than the desire for some external reward.

Examples of behaviors that are the result of intrinsic motivation include:

- Studying because you find ways to keep the topic interesting
- Cleaning your room because you enjoy making things tidy
- Competing in a sports event because you love the sport and the challenge of competition

In each of these instances, the person's behavior is motivated by an internal desire to participate in an activity for its own sake.[3]

EXTRINSIC VS. INTRINSIC

Look at the statements below describing why a person would perform an activity. Identify each statement as being related to extrinsic or intrinsic motivation.

		Extrinsic	Intrinsic
1	Work hard to get a promotion	◯	◯
2	Stay under the speed limit to avoid getting a ticket	◯	◯
3	Dress nicely because it makes you feel good	◯	◯
4	Study hard to get a good grade on a test	◯	◯
5	Go to a party because you don't want to disappoint your friends	◯	◯
6	Volunteer because it will look good on your resumé	◯	◯
7	Donate to a charity because you believe it is the right thing to do	◯	◯
8	Participate in intramural sports so you can see your friends and meet other people	◯	◯
9	Play guitar because you enjoy the challenge and want to get better	◯	◯

Answer: The extrinsic statements are numbers 1, 2, 4, 5, 6 and 8. All the others are intrinsic.

Extrinsic versus Intrinsic

Intrinsic motivation tends to result in someone persisting in an activity for longer and with greater effort. It also leads to greater happiness, since the activity itself brings satisfaction rather than just the reward (that can make the activity feel like a chore to get over with in order to receive the reward).

Think about the following scenarios that contrast students who are only extrinsically motivated with students who are strongly intrinsically motivated.

Extrinsic: These students strive solely for good grades and have to force themselves to learn the material, no matter how tiresome it feels to them. All the while they think about a reward some day in the future. Most of their school experience involves doing things they don't enjoy, in order to reach an endpoint. Their studying is less effective because they view it as a chore. When they finally graduate with a decent grade point average, they quickly realize the reward is over and now they will be starting jobs that require them to do something very similar to what they were doing in school.

Intrinsic: These students find interest in what they study. They are curious to learn more about the topics covered in class. This helps them learn the material at a deep level and perform well on assignments and tests naturally. They get enjoyment from their studies and are generally happy individuals as a result. Graduation brings them as much excitement as it does the extrinsically motivated students. But the intrinsically motivated students are also excited to start a new job, where they get to continue doing what they enjoyed doing in school.

You may get a sense that intrinsic motivation is better than extrinsic. That is **not** always true. In some cases, starting an activity for an extrinsic reward can, over time, allow a person to develop an intrinsic motivation for the activity.[4] This is especially true with young children, who may not be able to perceive the intrinsic benefits of the activity. Also, extrinsic rewards can reinforce healthy behaviors such as in losing weight or exercising. In other cases, extrinsic rewards can cause a reduction in intrinsic motivation for a behavior.[5]

It comes down to using extrinsic reward properly. Extrinsic reward can help you get started in a healthy or productive behavior, especially if you don't initially enjoy the activity. Then, to develop intrinsic motivation for the behavior, use the following strategies:[6]

How to Develop Intrinsic Motivation for an Activity

- **Have a growth mindset** – remind yourself that you can do well if you work at it. You may not have all the skills to perform well at first, but you can learn them.
- **Take ownership** – when there are any results or improvements from good performance, make sure you take ownership of the good performance. Remember that you did it: you worked hard and earned that result.
- **Seek mastery** – make it a goal to learn more than you *need* to learn. Don't stop at the minimum required for the course. When there is a chance to learn more, take it.
- **Make it personal** – look for connections in what you learn to other areas of your life. Think of how you might apply the knowledge you gain.

Here is an example of the above strategies at play in your own role as a student.

You motivate yourself to study more with the extrinsic reward of a fun social activity at the end of the week—if you have completed four two-hour study sessions in that week. During those study sessions you do the following to develop your intrinsic motivation for studying:

- *You remind yourself of how you are improving your knowledge and skills, and how your brain is developing during those times.*
- *After each study session, you give yourself small quizzes to measure what you have learned. You take pride in doing well on those quizzes.*
- *When you get a chance, you go online to learn more about the topic than what is required in the course. You even find some websites that allow you to discuss the course topics with other students.*
- *If you are learning about psychology, for example, you think about how the theories discussed apply to your own behavior and the behavior of the people you know.*

DEVELOPING INTRINSIC MOTIVATION

Let's make learning about motivation *personal*. Out of the four strategies for developing your intrinsic motivation, which one do you feel you could work on to help your motivation? Explain how you could apply that strategy to your situation.

Let's take your learning of motivation and effort to a mastery level—or at least closer to it. Watch the video at Link 5-6, which examines the puzzle of motivation, starting with a fact that social scientists know but most managers don't—traditional rewards aren't always as effective as we think.

Avoiding Motivation Busters

In addition to knowing how to improve motivation, it is important to know how to avoid losing motivation. There are challenges out there that can spoil your motivation if you are not ready to deal with them properly. It is easy to get distracted by negative thoughts or fears about the future. It is normal to face doubt and worry. What separates the successful from the not-so-successful is the ability to keep moving forward with strategies to deal with those challenges.

Motivation Busters
- Lack of gratitude
- Lack of focus
- Lack of direction

There are three main reasons we lose motivation. We will take a look at each of these "motivation busters."

1st Motivation Buster: Lack of Gratitude

If you don't appreciate what you have or what you have done, why try to do more? This can often happen when we focus on what we *want* while neglecting what we already *have*. When you only think about what you want, your mind creates explanations for why you aren't getting it. This creates negative thoughts. Past failures and bad memories might dominate your mind. It's easy to compare yourself to others and lose confidence as a result.

How to beat it: regularly record what you are thankful for. Set aside time to focus on everything positive in your life. Make a mental list of your strengths, past successes, and current advantages. By making an effort to feel grateful, you'll realize how competent and successful you already are. This will rejuvenate your confidence and motivate you to build on your existing successes.

©Alena Hovorkova/Shutterstock.com

GRATITUDE

List five things you are grateful for right now. Be specific. Don't just use clichés like "my family" and leave it at that. Say exactly why you are grateful for your family.

1

2

3

4

5

Check out the website at Link 5-7 for advice on how to develop gratitude and other positive behaviors.

2nd Motivation Buster: Lack of Focus

If you don't know what you want, do you really want anything? How often do you focus on what you don't want, rather than on a concrete goal? We normally think in terms of fear—fear of being alone, of not being respected, or of not being able to support a family. The problem with this type of thinking is that fear alone isn't actionable. Instead of doing something about our fear, we allow it to feed on itself and drain our motivation.

How to beat it: take action toward goals. If you're caught up in fear-based thinking, the first step is focusing that energy on a well-defined goal. By defining a goal, you automatically define a set of actions. Instead of worrying about the future, you will start to do something about it. This is the first step in motivating yourself to take action. When you know what you want, you become motivated to take action. If you find you get distracted from your goal, remember the earlier section on *self-control* and *grit*. Those sections offer strategies to help keep you on track to your goals.

FOCUS

What is one thing you can do TODAY to move toward one of your goals?

The final piece in the motivational puzzle is direction. If focus means having an ultimate goal, direction is having a day-to-day strategy to achieve it. A lack of direction kills motivation, because without an obvious next action we procrastinate. An example of this is a person who wants to have a popular blog, but who spends more time reading posts about blogging than actually writing articles.

How to beat it: find and prioritize direction. The key to finding direction is identifying the activities that lead to success. For every goal, there are activities that pay off and those that don't. Make a list of all your activities and prioritize them based on results. Then make an action plan that focuses on the activities that lead to big returns.

Scan the items below. If you wanted to publish a blog, what do you think the three most important things to accomplish your goal would be?

- Read other blogs
- Write content
- Research relevant topics
- Network with other bloggers
- Optimize design and ad placements
- Answer comments and email

Answer: We hope you identified *write content* as one of your top three! Keeping track of your most important tasks will direct your energy toward success. Without a constant reminder, it's easy to waste entire days on filler activities like social media, email, and random web surfing.

SECTION 5-2: CRITICAL THINKING

Learning Objectives

- Understand critical thinking skills and their importance
- Learn strategies to develop critical thinking skills
- Identify resources to continue developing critical thinking skills

The previous section covered the kind of effort necessary to maximize learning and productivity. Now we will discuss some of the skills needed to do the same. One particular set of extremely important skills is that of critical thinking.

What is Critical Thinking?

There are many definitions, but here is one of our favorites:

> **Disciplined thinking that is clear, rational, open-minded, and informed by evidence.**[1]

Critical thinking is about being *critical* of information you receive. Critical, in this case, means being skeptical or careful, not necessarily negative. For example, imagine someone is telling you about a party she attended. A critical thinker would be thinking...

* She has her own viewpoint, which will affect what she tells me.
* From what I am being told, what was directly observed and what is being assumed or re-told from another person with another viewpoint?
* From what I am being told, what are statements of fact and what are statements of opinion?
* What is my current mood and could it affect how I interpret what is being said?
* What beliefs or opinions do I have that might affect how I interpret the information I am hearing?

Critical thinkers do not believe everything they hear. They ask questions, get information from multiple sources, evaluate those sources, and avoid jumping to conclusions. They also interpret meaning carefully and are usually able to learn much from what they observe. Critical thinking isn't easy, however. It takes persistence and practice, but the benefits are huge. Significant historical advancements in civilization can be attributed to philosophers using critical thinking, from Early Islamic philosophy (see Link 5-8) to Hundred Schools of Thought (see Link 5-9) to Classical Greece (see Link 5-10) to the Age of Enlightenment (see Link 5-11) in Europe. These periods were noted for advancements in science, justice, equality, economics, medicine, human rights, and government—most of them thanks to critical thinking.[2]

> *"Thinking is the hardest work there is, which is probably the reason why so few engage in it."*
>
> – HENRY FORD

©graphixmania/Shutterstock.com

Critical thinking skills are also extremely important for success in school and your career. Maybe you've already heard that many times, but haven't been taught how to think critically. College students and young professionals are told why they need to develop these skills, but often without an explanation of what critical thinking skills are and how to develop them.

To help you understand critical thinking better and how to develop it, start with the video at Link 5-12, which looks at what employers think about critical thinking skills. On the next page we will go one step further and discuss six key critical thinking skills, conveniently abbreviated by the acronym C.R.I.T.I.C.

C.R.I.T.I.C.al Thinking Skills

CRITICal Skills
- **Catch**
- **Reveal**
- **Investigate**
- **Traps**
- **Infer**
- **Communicate**

If you were to Google "critical thinking skills" you would see more than 21 million results. We have filtered it all down to six key critical thinking skills. We will explain them and let you practice so that you can apply them in your classes and in your life.

1   Catch the Right Information

How to do it: Take in the information presented to you and "catch" the connections between that information and what you already know or other information presented to you. This is also about "catching" the important information for the issue at hand, as opposed to focusing on irrelevant information.

Practice: On a piece of paper, write down eight emotions that you think have specific facial expressions. For example, smiling relates to happiness. Just write the name of the emotion, don't describe the facial expression. Give your list to someone you know who will perform a facial expression for each emotion in random order. You have to "catch" each facial expression and guess the correct emotion. Record whether you guess correctly each time.

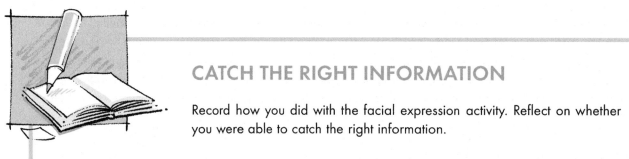

CATCH THE RIGHT INFORMATION

Record how you did with the facial expression activity. Reflect on whether you were able to catch the right information.

©Alena Hovorkova/Shutterstock.com

How to do it: Analyze the information carefully in order to reveal what the intended meaning. Sometimes communication can be explicit and straightforward. Other times, you have to consider if there is more meaning than what is plainly obvious. Having this skill will better provide you with the ability to "read between the lines" and get more meaning out of the information you receive. Be careful not to confuse this with jumping to conclusions, which is assuming certain meaning that does not exist.

Practice:

"You've got to go out on a limb sometimes because that's where the fruit is."

– WILL ROGERS

What do you think the quote means? Think of your response before you read the paragraph below.

Answer: There is a double meaning in the quote. There is literal meaning in that fruit is on the limbs of a tree. But going out on a limb also has the metaphorical meaning of taking risks. The fruit also has the metaphorical meaning of a reward. Therefore, the quote is really trying to say that sometimes you need to take risks in order to gain rewards.

3   Investigate Sources

How to do it: Investigate the credibility of your information sources to place a value on the information itself. Remember that people have their own viewpoints that affect how they interpret and communicate information. Also remember that people are behind every bit of information you see, whether that information is spoken to you, posted online, or printed in a book or magazine. Some sources have rules about how they communicate information, and those rules can make the information more reliable. Examples of sources with good rules are reputable journals such as *Reuters, Huffington Post,* and the *Wall Street Journal.* Scientific journals and Wikipedia (depending on its sources) can also be good sources. This may sound like a conflict of interest, but Wikipedia does have a good article on identifying reliable sources, which you can read at Link 5-13.

Practice: Do an online search on how to be a leader at school or work. Identify two excellent sources and two less-than- excellent sources. Record what you find and complete the journal below.

INVESTIGATE SOURCES

Record the results of your search on how to be a leader. List all four sources, identify which were excellent, and explain why you gave them the rating you did.

4 Avoid Traps

How to do it: Whether we realize it or not, we all have certain biases and viewpoints based on our past experience that can "trap" us into certain ways of thinking. In order to avoid these traps, we need to avoid making assumptions based on our previous experience. This can be a tricky balancing act because we also need to use previous knowledge to help fill in any gaps in the information. Avoid bad assumptions by gaining awareness of your biases.

Practice: Try the mind puzzle below—it is an old one and you may know it, but it is a good example of assumptions getting in the way of clear thinking.

> *A father and his son, his only child, got into a car accident. The father died but the son survived and was taken to the hospital for surgery. The surgeon came in and said, "I can't do surgery on this boy, he is my son!"*

What is going on? Think of your response before reading the answer.

Answer: The surgeon is the boy's mother. Some people might assume the doctor is a man because the profession used to be male-dominated. If you grew up seeing all or mostly male doctors, you may assume the doctor in the puzzle was male and had to be the boy's father, which doesn't make sense.

How to do it: Examine all the information you have available and reach the best conclusion or hypothesis despite missing some pieces of information. It is like making an educated guess based on clues. This skill also involves knowing what additional information may be needed to make the hypothesis stronger. Scientists and detectives would use this skill a lot.

Practice: Try this mini-mystery puzzle:

An old man lives alone in a house. His mobility is reduced so most things are delivered directly to his house. A neighbor, who helps the old man by cutting his lawn on Thursdays, notices that there are many items sitting outside the old man's door—much more than usual. Suspicious, the neighbor peeks in the window and sees that the old man has been murdered in his kitchen. When the detective arrives, she takes note of the items left outside the door. There are stale groceries delivered by the grocer, wilted flowers from a family member, Monday's newspaper, some unopened mail, and some boxes from an online retailer. The detective then says, "I think I know who did it."

How did she know? Think of your response before reading the answer.

Answer: The fact that only Monday's newspaper was there implicates the paperboy because only he would know not to deliver the paper the rest of the week after the old man was murdered.

INFER A HYPOTHESIS

If you solved the mystery, what important clues caught your attention? If you didn't solve it, do you now see why the Monday paper was a clue that stood out from the others? What other information could the detective seek if she wanted to strengthen her case against the newspaper carrier?

How to do it: Just repeating information or blurting out a series of facts is not helpful. You need to add organization, clarity and perspective to the information, so it can be fully understood by each particular audience. It's important to remember not everyone has the same background, goals or preferences that you have.

Practice: Explain to two different types of people something complex that you have knowledge about. One person should be well-versed in the subject and the other should be new to the subject. For example, discuss the strategy of a play in football with someone who knows football and then explain it to someone who doesn't.

COMMUNICATE CLEARLY

Choose an idea or action that you know well and think about how you would explain it to someone who is familiar with the topic and how you would explain it to someone who is not familiar with the topic. You can either write a summary of your two different explanations (if you can't easily find two people) or how the two people you chose responded to your different explanations.

Critical Thinking Resources

There are many good websites that can help you learn more about critical thinking and provide you with additional practice. See Link 5-14 and Link 5-15 for a couple of good places to start.

Some colleges support their own critical thinking resources for students. Check with your student services department. In the meantime, check out the critical thinking website at Link 5-16 specifically for college students.

SECTION 5-3 LEARNING STYLES AND METACOGNITION

REVIEW QUESTION

Which of the following is **NOT** a critical thinking skill?

- getting the relevant information
- being aware of bias
- using every source available
- communicating clearly

Answer: Using every source available. While using sources is good, critical thinkers evaluate their sources and only use credible sources of information.

Learning Objectives

- Discover personal learning preferences and strategies to take advantage of them
- Understand metacognition and how it helps with learning
- Know how to use and develop metacognitive skills

We have looked at critical thinking, which is a method that everyone can use to maximize their success in school and at work. In this section, we will look at your personal learning style and metacognition, which is how you think about learning.

Learning Style

"The only person who is educated is the one who has learned how to learn and change."

– CARL ROGERS

Have you ever noticed how different people tend to remember things in different ways? For example, some people may recall what they hear very well, while others are better at remembering what they see. Still others may best remember what they do when they are working with their hands. These differences are called learning styles. You have a unique set of learning styles, which we will uncover using an assessment called the *PEPS Learning Style Inventory*. PEPS stands for Productivity Environmental Preference Survey. This is just a fancy name for a survey that finds out which environment allows you to be most productive. Learning and productivity are closely related.

Once you complete the survey questions in the *PEPS Learning Style Inventory*, you will get a report that will show you your preferences in 16 different areas and strategies designed for your specific preference in each area. Those strategies should help improve your learning and productivity in school and at work.

To get started, open a browser and go to www.humanesources.com. Click the Login link at the top of the page. If you have not already registered, follow the instructions to register with your Access Key. In your portfolio, select the link for the *PEPS Learning Style Inventory* to begin the assessment.

Your *PEPS* report displays 16 learning and productivity styles. The chart shows which side of the preference spectrum you are on and to what degree. The ones furthest to the left or right are your strongest preferences, while those in the middle are ones for which you show little or no preference. Below the chart are suggested tips for you to adapt your study habits or learning environment to maximize your success. The strategies are specific to *your* preferences.

Review your results from the *PEPS* assessment online. Scan the chart and one or two of the preferences, then complete the Tips for Better Learning activity below. It will help you get the most out of your report information without having to read the whole report at once.

Focus on Strongest Preferences

Trying to use tips for all 16 learning and productivity preferences at the same time would get confusing. The following activity will help you to focus on your strongest preferences so you avoid confusion and get maximum benefit from the tips in the report.

TIPS FOR BETTER LEARNING

Examine the chart in your *PEPS* report. Identify the three strongest preferences (furthest from the middle) and write them down. From each of those three preferences, identify two tips that you could actually try in the next few weeks and record those. You can also modify a tip or create your own to better fit your circumstances. Record the three learning preferences and six tips in the spaces below.

Learning preference 1

Tip A:

Tip B:

Learning preference 2

Tip A:

Tip B:

Learning preference 3

Tip A:

Tip B:

Learning and Personality

The *PEPS Learning Style Inventory* takes one view of how you learn. It tends to focus on how you best receive information. You may remember that the *Do What You Are* assessment also examined how you learn based on your personality type. It tends to focus on how you process, or think about, information. The journal activity below will help you combine information from both assessments to gain greater perspective on how you learn and work best. Get your paper and pencil out again—you may need to take some notes as you navigate back and forth between your assessment reports.

Two Perspectives on Learning

Look again at your *PEPS* report online. Read the sections below the chart labeled "structure", "persistence", "alone/peer" and "authority figures present." Next look at your *Do What You Are* report and read the statements under the section labeled "Your Preferred Learning Style." Reflect on the information from both reports and think about how you usually approach learning and studying.

©Sofi photo/Shutterstock.com

MY APPROACH TO LEARNING

Based on what your *PEPS* and *Do What You Are* reports suggest, do you think you have been taking an approach to learning that is best suited to you? Explain.

Metacognition

The best way to describe metacognition is that it is thinking about and controlling how you learn and problem solve. People who use metacognition would not stop at just memorizing that definition. They would think to themselves, "I should find an example of metacognition so I can truly understand it." Here are two examples for you:

People who **do not** use metacognition would... read the definition of metacognition over and over until they memorized it. They would complete assigned readings and probably even take notes in class, but their notes would more likely be copied than written in their own words. While they read, they would **not** ask questions such as, "Why is this important?" or "How can I think about this in a way that makes more sense to me?" People who don't use metacognitive skills don't use strategies to help them understand information. They simply follow instructions and take things at face value.

People who **do** use metacognition would... think of different ways to understand the word "metacognition". First they might seek the definition from other sources that have helped them before. Check out Link 5-17 for a well-defined explanation on Wikipedia. Next they might determine what metacognition *is* and what it is *not*—as we have done with the two examples here. They might also try to make connections to similar concepts they already know about. They might think of an analogy that compares information to food and learning strategies to cooking.

I remember when I used to just follow recipes to cook. Sometimes the final product turned out well and sometimes it didn't. I was dependent on the recipe and never really thought about what was happening to the food when I cooked it. Then I decided to find out how the different ingredients and cooking methods affected the final product. I learned different strategies to prepare and cook certain types of food and why some strategies worked better in certain situations.

Now I pay close attention to my ingredients and how I prepare them. From start to finish, I am aware of what I am doing in the kitchen and realize that everything I do affects the final product. I get a better final product and enjoy cooking a lot more.

One might say that students who use metacognition regularly are "master chefs" of their own learning, while students who don't are just "line cooks."

Don't get discouraged if you realize that much of your learning up to now has been done in line cook style. Every master chef has had to start somewhere. The next page will help you begin to develop your metacognitive skills so you can master your own learning.

HOW METACOGNITIVE ARE YOU?

How often do you think about *how* you are learning? Do you think about how your brain is recording and storing the information? Do you try different learning strategies and pay close attention to how you learn best? Be honest and describe how much of a master chef you are when it comes to learning.

Developing Your Metacognitive Skills

Before we go any further, we should recognize that there is one major difference between a master chef and a metacognitive learner. Not everyone can be a master chef, but everyone can become a metacognitive learner. After all, your metacognitive "kitchen" is your mind, and you know it best.

You have already completed the first steps in developing your metacognitive skills—learning what metacognition is and that you can develop your ability in it.[1]

The next steps include:
- Remaining self-aware during learning so that you can stop yourself when you are just receiving information without truly thinking about it.
- Being able to "switch" your focus to really trying to understand the information.
- Developing a wide variety of "kitchen tools" to use when trying to understand information, especially new and complex information. Examples of kitchen tools are techniques for listening, note taking, reading, research, memory, and self-quizzing.
- Using the best tool for the job. Some topics are better suited to one technique than another. For example, reading and taking a lot of notes on how to solve algebra problems may not be a good idea. It is likely better to do a lot of practice problems and reflect on any patterns in how you solved them. Look for what you did well, where you made mistakes, and adjust how you solve the algebra problems.

Thinking Aloud

A good habit that metacognitive learners use in group situations is thinking aloud. They talk to others about how they understand information, how they might approach questions, and the steps they take to solve problems. It may sound like they are narrating what is going on in their head, and that is exactly what they are doing! Describing your thought process forces you to slow down a little and reflect on how effective your strategy is. It also invites others to examine your strategy and provide feedback or suggestions, which can give you more tools to work with.

©Antoniu/Shutterstock.com

Getting More Tools

Hopefully, when you read the steps for developing your metacognitive skills, you started thinking about the "kitchen tools" you have for studying—stopping to think like that is an example of metacognition. You already have some potential tools in your *PEPS* and *Do What You Are* reports. In addition, the next sections are all about different learning tips and tricks you can use at school and at work. In other words, you will be able to really stock up your "kitchen" in the next sections.

SECTION 5-4: STUDY SKILLS

This is a special section of CollegeScope. It is divided up into seven subsections dealing with different study skills. The sequence is...

- 5-4A Using technology
- 5-4B Listening and taking notes
- 5-4C Reading
- 5-4D Research and information analysis
- 5-4E Learning and memory
- 5-4F Writing
- 5-4G Studying and test taking

We hope you find lots of useful tips and strategies to help you maximize your success in school.

SECTION 4A: USING TECHNOLOGY

Learning Objectives

- Learn what technology is and some of its forms
- Describe what is needed for technology to benefit learners
- Identify technology skills needed by students and people entering the workforce
- Identify some general dos and don'ts regarding technology in college

What is Technology?

In our age, technology seems to be ever-present and ever-changing and developing. But what do we mean by phrases like "high tech" and "technological advancement"? Technological advancement is actually dependent on scientific knowledge. Technology is organizing or applying scientific knowledge for practical purposes.

"Technology is anything that wasn't around when you were born."

– ALAN KAY

Nowadays, being a successful student and productive member of the working world absolutely requires a certain level of technological know-how and sophistication. Watch the video in Link 5-18. It may still look a little like science fiction, but virtually all the technology shown in the future classroom is already possible.

The video demonstrates a form of technology that most of us imagine when we hear the word "technology": computers and electronics. Remember, however, that the definition of technology does not require the presence of computers or electronics.

Watch one more video, at Link 5-19, to remind yourself of the other forms technology can take.

©everything possible/Shutterstock.com

Technology in Education

You have probably already experienced many forms of technology in your education. From the following list, identify the technologies you have used as part of your education.

- SMART Board
- An online course
- Online portfolios or learning management system
- Edmodo
- Khan Academy

- Mobile classroom quiz/poll app (such as, eClicker)
- TED-Ed videos and lessons
- Teacher/instructor-made website
- Wikipedia
- Evernote

EDUCATION TECHNOLOGIES

Copy any technologies from the list above that you have used and add any others you can think of.

Is Technology Always Better?

Many people assume that technology automatically helps make education better. And, in many cases, it does. A review of over 700 research studies showed gains in standardized tests and other national test scores when students had access to certain types of learning technology.[1] However, in some cases, technology is of no help and can even be harmful to education.

Watch the short video in Link 5-20 for a funny look at some of the pitfalls of technology.

With the potential for pitfalls, it is important to use technology properly so that actual gains in academic achievement happen. Gains in achievement occur when the following criteria are met:[2]

* The technology is focused on the learning objectives
* The technology aims for deeper understanding of the objectives rather than just making learning easier or more convenient
* The learners and educators feel comfortable using the technology
* The technology can accommodate differences between individual learners
* The technology promotes a high degree of interaction with the learner
* The technology allows for the learner to contribute content

While many students in college are comfortable using most technologies, not everyone has grown up with the same opportunities or had the same exposure to technology. Luckily, most schools have a help desk or similar department under the auspices of student services or academic support.

You may be able to find information about your school's help or IT desk on your school's website. The help desk can provide assistance with using your college's learning system (such as, Blackboard, Moodle, etc.), your school email account, or access to a computer lab.

"The human spirit must prevail over technology."

– ALBERT EINSTEIN

Developing Technology Skills

Because technology is everywhere, a major factor for success in college and the workplace is using technology effectively. There are many technology skills to learn, but for some basic skills to get you started, check out the article in Link 5-21.

The skills mentioned in the article are just a starting point.

The following list reveals some of the most sought-after technology skills by employers and colleges now and into the future.[3]

©dizain/Shutterstock.com

- **Mobile technology**. Use smart phones and tablets for productivity and collaboration.
- **Cloud technology**. Manage shared storage areas, perform project updates and tracking, and create collaborative work projects. Examples include Amazon Web Services, Google, HP Cloud, IBM and Microsoft.
- **Social media**. Yes, this can be used for more than just keeping up with what your friends are doing. Businesses want to be able to run marketing campaigns, collect feedback, extract market research, and even run customer service out of multiple social media platforms. Examples include Facebook, Pinterest, LinkedIn, Twitter, Tumblr, and Instagram.
- **Big data**. We now communicate in many different ways, and much of that communication is tracked and analyzed. A lot of companies want to use that information. You have likely seen ads on Facebook or Google that seem to know your interests. Even the predictive text feature on your phone knows what words and phrases you tend to use most. This is all done by analyzing "big data." Mathematical ability, mostly statistics, and knowledge of applications to crunch the numbers is something employers like to see. Ability with big data can occur on a small scale with a simple spreadsheet and a few formulas, or on a much larger scale with sophisticated databases and complex algorithms.
- **Enterprise resource planning (ERP) tools**. These are software applications that store and track information on everything from customers to employees to the financial and physical assets of a company. For many businesses, they are the core application for the company. They are used by sales, marketing, customer support, accounting, development and management departments. Examples include Oracle, SAP, Salesforce, NetSuite, Intacct, Sage and Microsoft Dynamics. Becoming familiar with one of these applications can get you started and help you adapt to one of the others if your work requires it.
- **Programming**. While this skill is an obvious must for many IT positions, it is also useful for non-IT positions. A basic understanding of HTML and other programming languages can help you reap benefits in other areas. For more information, check out the article in Link 5-22.

We still have only scratched the surface of what you will likely need to know. If many of the skills in the list seem unfamiliar, now is a good time to start learning more about them. A lot of them can be developed as you prepare for and even enter the workforce. For now, you can probably get away with some basic skills, which we have listed below.

Word processors: Just about everybody uses a word processor to help write papers and other assignments. However, we have all seen the problems that can occur when we trust technology to correct what we write. Just search the web for "autocorrect fail" and you will see the results.

Do:

* Use them to help with formatting and *finding* some of your errors, but don't trust them to *correct* all of your errors.
* Save and back up your information often. Most applications have an autosave or auto-backup function, which you should enable. It is also a good idea to have your work backed up online, so if your device fails, your work can be recovered.

Don't:

* Rely on them to correct errors for you unless you check the "correction" and know it is the right correction.

Online forums and discussions: Many schools and instructors host their own online discussion boards. These are usually the best to use, since they tend to be focused on the right topics. Even if you never contribute to the discussion (you should try), you can gain a lot from reading.

Do:

* Use them to discuss your school-related ideas and work, and to learn from others' ideas.

Don't:

* Spend a lot of your time off-topic.
* Be disrespectful or argumentative.

Devices in the classroom: Whether you like it or not, people will bring and use their devices in the classroom. Smartphones, tablets and laptops can be of some help with taking notes or quickly referencing information when needed. However, they can just as easily become a distraction for the user and for others around the user.

Do:

* Use them when they provide a real advantage over traditional items such as paper and pencil.
* Use them when the instructor encourages it for a specific purpose.

Don't:

* Disturb others with keystrokes, tapping or any other sounds from your device.
* Let the device distract you from your main focus, which is the concepts being discussed. If you have to think about how to use the device, it is distracting you.

Cell phones and plans: This technology has become one of the most ubiquitous technologies in the world. In the third quarter of 2014, 455 million cell phones were shipped by vendors.[5] Over a year that would be almost two billion phones! At the end of 2014, it is estimated that there were about 4.2 billion cell phone users.[6] That is half of the planet's population! That huge market has pushed companies to create all kinds of educational and productivity apps for mobile phones. Many of these apps can be helpful, but there is a negative side, too.

The expense related to owning a mobile phone has quickly become one of the biggest monthly expenses for many students. Recent surveys have revealed that the average monthly bill for mobile phone service is over $100. One carrier had an average of $148.[7] These numbers go up when you add in expenses like paid-for apps, device costs, and accessories. You could end up spending over $2,000 per year!

Another issue with cell phones is their ability to take pictures and video. While the law generally allows you to take pictures and video in public spaces, there is an exception when people have an expectation of privacy, such as in a restroom. The law is even stricter when it comes to posting photos and video online. If the picture in question communicates something that can be considered as private facts, or if the subject of the photo would consider the photo highly offensive, you should **not** post it.[8]

Do:

- Before you buy a new phone, ask yourself what you *need* your phone to do, not what you *want* it to do.
- Research your options. Getting the latest device usually means you pay a premium—maybe not upfront, but add up the monthly plan cost and you will see. Sometimes an older, less sophisticated phone can do all the things you need it to do, but cost a fraction of what the latest device would cost.
- Look into ways of using fewer minutes and less data. Many schools and businesses offer free or low-cost WiFi, which can be used instead of minutes or data from your service provider.
- Use an app to track your data usage. There are many free options available and they can help you be aware of your actual use in real time, instead of when that large bill comes in and it's too late.

Don't:

- Try to keep up with the latest technology just for the sake of having the latest device.
- Use your phone (or any camera) to take pictures that might offend people or invade their privacy.

The Bottom Line

As with most tools, it is best to use your *critical thinking* skills to evaluate whether something is the right tool for the job and what the basic dos and don'ts are for each tool. You should consider this short list of factors for every form of technology you use:

- Does it actually save you time and effort compared to not using the technology? Or does it take more time and effort to maintain and use the technology itself?
- Does your use of the technology interfere with or disturb others?
- How does the cost of the technology affect your overall finances?
- Does the technology compromise your privacy or security? Are there procedures you can use to safeguard yourself and others?

"Once a new technology rolls over you, if you're not part of the steamroller, you're part of the road."

– STEWART BRAND

YOUR TECHNOLOGY ADVICE

We have given you much advice regarding technology. Now it's time to think about what technology advice you would give your peers.

If you had to list one "do" **and** one "don't" for any technology, what would they be?

If you had to recommend one technology skill that you think is crucial for students to know, what would you recommend?

SECTION 4B: LISTENING AND TAKING NOTES

Taking Notes

"He listens well who takes notes."

– DANTE ALIGHIERI

Many students assume the purpose of taking notes is simply to be able to review the information later. While this is true, it is not the only purpose. Taking notes while listening to a lecture, watching a presentation, or even reading a book can make you more engaged as well. We say "can" because taking notes the wrong way can actually do the opposite.

The Wrong Way to Take Notes

Copying down everything you see or hear makes you focus on getting everything down and not on understanding what you are copying. You are not using critical thinking or metacognition. Students who just copy down material tend to do worse on exams when compared to students who paraphrase the information in their own words.[1] Paraphrasing information forces you to think about and understand the information, rather than just hear it.

It has also been shown that students who take notes via a laptop, tablet or other electronic device do more poorly on tests when compared to students who actually write their notes down on paper.[2]

The Right Way to Take Notes

There are many different methods for good note taking, but they all rely on your ability to listen and recognize key concepts. It is important that you understand what you are writing down before you write it down. You need to use critical thinking and metacognition. If you don't understand what you are writing when you record it, chances are you will not understand it when you are reviewing your notes for the test.

If you find it difficult to keep up with lectures or presentations, you may be trying to record too much detail. Instead, focus on what the information means and how it should be organized. What is the main topic? What are the sub-topics? Is there a sequence? What exam questions are likely to come out of this information and what are the answers?

The video in Link 5-23 provides another way to think about taking notes.

TAKING NOTES

Based on what you've learned from the video and the text above, what are the most important things you should and should not do in regard to taking notes?

©Alena Hovorkova/Shutterstock.com

Note-Taking Systems

Now that we have covered the basics of note taking, let's cover some of the details by describing some note-taking systems. There are many systems that can be used in different situations. Various systems may be better suited to a lecture, a textbook or an online presentation. Different subjects, such as math and literature, often merit their own note- taking systems. Finally, you, as an individual learner, may be better suited to different systems.

Scan the Wikipedia page in Link 5-24 to learn about some of the recognized note-taking systems.

What follows are two examples of note-taking systems. Within each example, three different note-taking systems are described. You might say it is meta-note-taking.

Chart Notes on 3 Note-taking Systems

	DESCRIPTION	ADVANTAGES	DISADVANTAGES
Outline notes	Uses hierarchy of topics, subtopics, and details in bullet points. Roman numerals and letters to organize info	• can follow sequence of lecture • highly organized • flexible with type of info	• can be hard to edit once complete
Cornell notes	Three sections: • main area = main ideas • left margin = key points questions • bottom = notes summary	• forces deep processing of information • encourages review of notes • flexible with type of info	• can be hard to keep up with a lecture • may miss some smaller details
Chart notes	Bits of information in a grid or pattern to show relationships or series of concepts	• highly organized • shows patterns in the information	• does not fit all types of information

	Cornell Notes on 3 Note-taking Systems	
Key Points and Questions	**Outline:**
	• hierarchy of topics, subtopics, and details in bullets
	• Roman numerals and letters to organize
Different methods fit different topics	• flexible for content, but hard to change after
	Cornell:
Which method is best for math?	• paper in three sections
	• left margin – key points/questions
	• main area – notes
	• lower area – review/summary
All good note taking uses own words, no copying	• deep processing of info but slower
	Chart:
	• grid with lines
	• organized but only works with certain topics
Review and Summary	
Use a note-taking strategy that fits the learner best AND fits the topic best. Always review notes and never copy what is said or shown—use own words.	

Visual Note-taking Systems

The above systems work well for people comfortable with words and language. Other note-taking systems may work particularly well for you if you are a visual learner. Review your online results from the *PEPS Learning Style Inventory* and *MI Advantage* assessments to identify your learning preferences. Examples of visual note taking are mind mapping and pictorial note taking. These systems appeal to the visual centers in our brain. Pictorial note taking, sometimes referred to as just visual note taking, requires the note taker to draw images rather than words to represent the ideas being learned.

If you enjoy drawing or doodling (no matter the quality of your art), you may want to try your hand at pictorial note taking. Research has now proved that doodling, once considered a mindless activity, can actually be a mindful activity. It seems that doodling actually helps some of us focus better on what we are hearing. If you feel you learn more while drawing or doodling, you may be interested in pictorial note taking.

The following videos explain what visual note taking is and why it works so well for some of us, and provide helpful hints on how to become effective with this type of note taking.

Watch the video at Link 5-25 to help you decide whether pictorial note taking is for you.

If you think visual note taking is for you, take time to watch the video at Link 5-26.

"I remind myself every morning: Nothing I say this day will teach me anything. So if I'm going to learn, I must do it by listening."

– LARRY KING

If you already feel comfortable with a system or two, and they work for you, then that is fine. But if not, try a few of the systems from this section that seem to suit you, and practice until you become comfortable and confident in your ability to listen and take good notes. No matter which system you use, it is a good idea to get together with a few others from your class to compare notes well before each exam. That way you can see if you missed any of the key concepts that might appear on the test.

©Alena Hovorkova/Shutterstock.com

NOTE-TAKING SYSTEMS FOR ME

Name two note-taking systems that you think will work best for you. Describe why you think those systems will work best.

SECTION 4C: READING

The Need to Read

There's no escaping it. Success in college requires a great deal of reading. Many students are overwhelmed by the amount and difficulty of what they are required to read in an average college semester.

If you already like to read, then you are at somewhat of an advantage. However, if you are not much of a reader right now, that's OK.

You can learn to read and better understand college-level texts, and you can become a more skilled reader. Just as exercise improves your body strength, cardiovascular endurance and agility, reading can improve your mental stamina and capabilities.

"Reading is to the mind what exercise is to the body."

– RICHARD STEELE

Two Key Factors to Reading

Speed – usually measured in words per minute.

Comprehension – how well you understand what you read.

Both speed and comprehension are important to your success as a student. Your reading speed develops with practice, just like training for a race. The more you read, the faster you will be able to read. Comprehension can improve by using certain techniques. Think of it as like having a coach who gives you tips for your running technique.

One of the most popular and established techniques is the *SQ3R method*. Watch the video at Link 5-27, which provides a great summary of the SQ3R method. Then answer the questions below. You can review the video as many times as you like to help you answer the questions.

SQ3R PRACTICE QUIZ

We hope you paid attention to that video! This practice quiz will test you on what you remember about the SQ3R reading method.

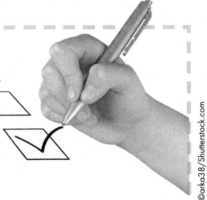

1. Which of the following is the correct order for SQ3R?
   a. Skim, Question, Recite, Read, and Review
   b. Skim, Question, Review, Recite, and Read
   c. Skim, Question, Read, Recite, and Review
   d. Skim, Question, Read, Review, and Recite

2. Which of the following is NOT part of "skim"?
   a. headlines
   b. paragraphs
   c. bold words
   d. diagrams

3. Which of the following is NOT part of "question"?
   a. it makes your reading purposeful
   b. questions are generated when you skim
   c. you find answers to your questions when you read
   d. questions are an optional part of SQ3R

4. Which of the following is NOT part of "recite"?
   a. you should answer your questions in this step
   b. you should talk out loud to yourself
   c. you should take notes in this step
   d. you should copy out some of the text

5. Which of the following is NOT part of "review"?
   a. reviewing your notes
   b. taking additional notes
   c. reviewing at a much later time
   d. talking to someone else about the topic

> *"Words mean more than what is set down on paper. It takes the human voice to infuse them with deeper meaning."*
>
> – MAYA ANGELOU

Try this bonus question: What key feature is the same between the SQ3R reading method and the listening and note-taking method in the previous section? Think of your response before you read the paragraph below.

Answer: There are several similarities, but if you said *putting things in your own words*, you are focusing in on a key point. The point is, it's important to do more than just listen to a lecture or look at the words on the page. You should find meaning and seek to understand. In fact, every step of the SQ3R method is meant to help you understand what you read. Putting things in your own words forces you to understand the information rather than just copy it. If you are thinking this sounds like critical thinking, then you are on the right track again. We keep circling back to that concept, which just goes to show how important critical thinking is.

SQ3R Tips

Now that you have a main strategy for reading, here are some handy tips that can help with the different steps of SQ3R.

SQ3R
- **Skim**
- **Question**
- **Read**
- **Recite**
- **Review**

Skim

- read the inside front and back cover or jacket of books
- read titles, headings and sub-headings first

Question

- have in your mind a purpose for reading (either your purpose or your instructor's purpose)
- bring to your mind any background knowledge you have about the subject
- make predictions about what you might expect to read
- write questions in margins

Read

- mark your texts with pen, pencil, or electronically
- take notes
- highlight or underline key points
- find answers to the questions you recorded in the previous step

Recite

- answer your questions and describe key points out loud to yourself
- discuss questions and concepts with others
- make sure to use your own words when answering questions and discussing topics

Review

- talk with others about what you are reading
- complete exercises, discussions, quizzes, and other activities that the text may have at the end of each section or chapter

When to Use SQ3R

The SQ3R method can be used when:
- reading a textbook section in preparation for class reading
- assigned content for class
- studying for tests
- doing research for writing a paper
- reading a book as part of novel study

"Once you learn to read, you will be forever free."

– FREDERICK DOUGLASS

USING SQ3R

Identify your next opportunity to use the SQ3R method. To help you commit to actually doing it, briefly describe your plan of when, where and on what you will be using the SQ3R method.

SECTION 4D RESEARCH AND INFORMATION ANALYSIS

What is Research?

In basic terms, research is a certain way to answer a question or solve a problem. Good research uses methods that arrive at the best answer. It avoids making assumptions or other factors that can lead to mistakes. Good research allowed us to realize that the Earth orbited around the sun and not the other way around. Research also taught us that infections were caused by unclean hospitals and not by evil spirits or bad luck.

Many people assume research is only used in science and people who assume that have not done their research! One thing that is crucial for doing good research is critical thinking. You should notice a lot of similarity between this section and what you learned in the section on critical thinking.

Just as with critical thinking, all kinds of jobs benefit from having good research skills. Doctors, teachers, accountants, artists, marketers, small business owners, tradespeople, lawyers, reporters, government officials and actors all need to do good research in order to do their jobs effectively. Good research skills are also needed in all subject areas in school. You can even use research skills in your personal life when making major decisions such as buying a house or car, or deciding where to move and which career to seek out.

> *"Research is formalized curiosity. It is poking and prying with a purpose."*
>
> – ZORA NEALE HURSTON

In a sense, you perform research every time you are curious about a topic and seek any kind of information. However, academic or college-level research is a particular type of research with specific expectations, especially for the sources of information you use.

General Rules for Good Research

1. **Start with a question.** Turn your topic into a question. This will guide your research so you don't stray from your topic. If you have the option, choose a question that you are truly curious about, to keep you motivated. Many search engines will let you use a full question in your search. Otherwise, choose keywords.

Try to include as many keywords in a single search as you can. You may have fewer results, but you will have more specific results. You can always use fewer terms or switch your terms if you need more results.

2. **Be objective.** Don't ignore information that goes against your beliefs. Only ignore information if there is no evidence to support it. Research is NOT looking to prove your beliefs on a topic. Your conclusion should be based on the information you find. If you have any beliefs or assumptions about a topic, be ready to discard them if the research leads you there. Your initial beliefs may turn out to be right, but let the evidence prove it.

3. **Use multiple sources.** If you can support your conclusion with a variety of sources, it makes your conclusion strong. Try using at least one book or extended article that provides a more general overview and will be an aggregation of other sources. Also use journal articles that tend to be more specific. Additionally, you can use subject experts, who are likely to be available at your school, for personal interviews. And finally, try to use the most recent sources available. In total, you should have a minimum of three sources, but five or more would be better.

Information Sources

Credibility

Clues for credibility:

- **Internet Domains**: URLs ending with .gov and .edu tend to be most reliable. Sites ending with .com, .org, and .net may or may not be credible.
- **Author**: Websites that list an author are better than sites that do not.
- **References and Citations**: Websites that cite or reference other credible sources for some of the information they present tend to be more credible themselves.
- **Date**: A clearly displayed date is not only a clue to credibility, it also allows you to determine if the information is recent enough to use in your research.
- **Reputation**: Publications like *The New York Times, The Economist,* and *Newsweek* are established periodicals that have a reputation to uphold and are subject to journalistic ethics and standards. The websites of organizations like these are more likely to be credible.

When in doubt about any particular source, ask your instructor or a librarian. Many students forget that librarians are not just "book organizers," they are usually expert researchers!

While there are many sources of information available for doing research, let's narrow the list to the most commonly used ones, and discuss each.

Search Engine Results

When you are just getting started researching a topic, search engines like Google and Bing can be very helpful. They provide a lot of starting points for further research. But keep in mind that websites are created for many different reasons. Some are trying to sell a product or express an opinion. Those sites may offer some facts, but have a great potential for bias and should not be used for academic research—unless the research is specifically about the bias of certain websites! Some websites genuinely present evidence-based information. The problem is that sites often present themselves as "fact-based" or "informational" regardless of whether they are biased or not.

It is your responsibility to identify which sites are truly evidence-based and meet the rigorous standards of academic research. You must be sure your sources of information are scholarly, unbiased (showing no prejudice for or against), and credible (convincing and trustworthy).

Another thing to remember is that websites change and links are removed all the time. What is there today may not be there in three weeks, for example. If a website looks like it uses URLs that are more permanent—for example, if the title or date of the article is in the URL—that is a good sign.

Wikipedia

While we covered websites already, we are going to address Wikipedia separately due to the extent that it is used for research and its somewhat unique format. While it remains controversial in some cases, the use of Wikipedia can be handled in a way that will satisfy even the most discerning college professor.

> *"Facts are stubborn things; and whatever may be our wishes, our inclinations, or the dictates of our passions, they cannot alter the state of facts and evidence."*
>
> – JOHN ADAMS

Watch the video at Link 5-28 to learn how to use Wikipedia for research.

Here is a summary of the key points in the video:

- A Wikipedia article is a great way to become familiar with a topic and its related ideas, and to learn some terms you can use when searching other credible sources in your campus library.
- Generally, you should not cite a Wikipedia article directly as a source.
- You may be able to find a credible source through a Wikipedia article's references.

The Library

This should be your number one source for academic research. You can use either a public library or a campus library. A campus library is more likely to have information specific to your needs as a student and probably has free access to academic journals for which you would normally have to pay.

Academic journals are subject to peer review and follow a specific format, so they are often the most credible sources you can use for academic research. Also, there are thousands of journals that cover just about every subject you can imagine. Just check out the list of academic journals at Link 5-29.

Some students use Google Scholar, ERIC, Mendeley, or other academic search tools that only look up information in academic books and journal articles. Often, however, the entire reference cannot be viewed, so you will also need to use your campus library, which may have access to the full version of the particular reference you need. If you are starting your research online, make sure you find at least several references so that your campus library is likely to have access to at least one. Using your campus library's search tools instead of Google Scholar ensures the full reference will be available.

Using Academic Journal Articles

While academic journal articles are not the only source of information you can use, they are usually the most credible and the most specific to a topic. However, they also tend to be the most difficult to understand, because they are written for the academic peers of the author and often contain language and references particular to that audience. So, we think it is worth spending a little time understanding how best to use an academic journal.

The first step in using academic journal articles is to find the right ones. Most search tools allow you to look for keywords in the title and the abstract. Try using different search terms, including new ones you learn as you are doing your search.

You should be able to identify whether an article will be useful by reading just the abstract, which is a summary of the article. Just about all academic articles are simply trying to answer a question or solve a problem. The key is to find some that are attempting to answer questions similar to the ones you are asking in your own research. You should be able to find at least several articles that you can use.

From your selected set of articles, approach each article one at a time. Some articles may seem intimidating at first, but they all usually follow a similar format of five main sections. If you are familiar with the sections, and focus on one section at a time in the order suggested below, you should find things easier.

Academic Journal Article Structure

SECTION	WHAT IT COVERS	HOW YOU CAN USE IT	SUGGESTED READING ORDER
Abstract	basic summary of the article, usually includes the question or problem and what was discovered	useful when you are scanning articles and looking for the right one	1
Introduction	summarizes previous research and identifies the question or problem the new research is attempting to answer	good to understand the background	2
Method or Procedure	details exactly how the research was done	you might want to scan this section for certain details you need, but focus more on the other sections for research	5

Results	details the exact results from the research as they were observed	good information to have, but the discussion is likely to have a nice summary of the same information	4
Discussion or Conclusion	discusses the meaning of the results, how well the question or problem was answered, and what further research could be done	probably the most important part of the research article. You will likely quote or paraphrase from this section	3

USING AN ACADEMIC JOURNAL ARTICLE

Let's try out a strategy for reading and interpreting an academic journal article. We will use a real article on study strategies. For the article, read only the abstract and the discussion. You can skip the introduction, method and results in this activity to save time. You can skim the other sections if you like, but they are optional.

Read the article at Link 5-30 about study strategies of college students. Then answer the questions below.

Name three strategies that were shown to improve student achievement.

Name two strategies that did not improve student achievement in this study.

Name two factors, described in the discussion, that might have affected the results of the study.

Documenting Your Sources

You must give proper credit to any source you use in your research and in the work you submit to your instructors. Here are just some of the reasons you need to document your sources:

- It gives proper credit to the authors who came up with the original idea or observation, so that you avoid plagiarism.
- It allows the reader to know where to look if he or she needs more information.
- It gives your work more credibility.

How you give credit to your sources depends on your instructor. You may have to list your sources differently for different classes. Your course syllabus usually identifies how. If not, ask your instructor to be sure.

Usually, there are two parts to naming each of your sources:

- **In-Text Citation** – this is a short mention of the source in the body of your text, right next to where the information is discussed.
- **Reference** – this is a full description of the source at the end of your document, usually grouped with all of your other sources.

There are several different formats for citations and references. Again, ask your instructor to find out which one should be used for any particular course. The most popular formats are American Psychological Association (APA), which is used in social and behavioral sciences, and Modern Language Association (MLA), which is used in the liberal arts and humanities. Check Link 5-31 for details on how to format your citations and references.

APA FORMAT

Let's practice documenting a resource using APA format. Models and examples of APA format are shown.

APA Format

citation model: (author's last name, year)

citation example: (Jones, 2014)

reference model: Last name, initials (year). Article Title. *Journal Title*, issue number, page numbers.

reference example: Jones, A. (2014). Sample Title. *Sample Journal,* 1, 5-10.

For the article on study strategies that you were asked to read earlier, complete a citation and a reference in the spaces provided.

Citation:

Reference:

SECTION 4E: LEARNING AND MEMORY

To put it simply, learning is remembering. Therefore, improving your memory will improve your ability to learn. You may have heard of short-term (see Link 5-32) and long-term memory (see Link 5-33). You may even have heard of different types of long-term memory: declarative (see Link 5-34) and procedural memory (see Link 5-35). Feel free to research those topics more on your own. This section will focus on general long-term memory, which we will refer to as just "memory," because it is most closely related to learning.

"Memory is the mother of all wisdom."

– AESCHYLUS

Memory is a Skill

Contrary to what some think, memory experts tell us that having a "good" or "bad" memory is much more a matter of skill than it is inborn talent. And that is a good thing because it means every one of us can improve our memory.

©Nenov Brothers Images,/Shutterstock.com

Memory works by building upon itself. Think of memory as a Lego® structure. The neurons in your brain are the building blocks. Your neurons fit together in different ways to form what you know and remember. As you learn new things, or forget them, you are changing the structure in your brain.

Quick note: Your brain does not add, put together, nor take apart neurons like a Lego structure! It is more accurate to say that your brain strengthens or weakens the connections between the neurons that are already there. However, because it is much easier for most people to imagine a Lego structure than the inside of a human brain, we will use the Lego example.

There are three mechanisms that help us form lasting memories, all of which we will compare to the Lego example.

	ASSOCIATION	EMOTION AND NOVELTY	REPETITION
Description:	Connecting new information to similar known information	Having emotion related to the new information	Learning information at different times and in different ways
Lego example:	Properly fitting new block onto existing blocks	Gluing the blocks together	Trying different bricks and orientations

We will cover each of the three mechanisms in more detail in the following pages.

Association

Imagine if you tried to build a Lego structure by just dropping some loose blocks onto a small structure you had already put together. Of course, the new pieces would not stay attached. This is like trying to remember ideas without connecting them to what you already know. Your memory for the new information will "fall apart."

If, instead, you properly fit the new Lego pieces to your existing structure, your final structure will be a lot more stable. Properly connecting new information to what you already know allows you to remember it much better. And, the better the new information fits with the old, the better you will remember the new information.

©Picsfive/Shutterstock.com

Association Strategy 1: Analogy

We used the example of Lego because that itself is an association technique called an analogy. An analogy is a comparison between two concepts, usually using one that is familiar to help explain one that is not. Most people are familiar with Lego. When we compare memory to Lego, you are associating the new information about memory to what you already know about Lego and how it fits together.

Good teachers *and* good learners use this technique all the time. For example, a biology teacher may compare the circulatory system to a road system and cars to blood cells. Most people can visualize how cars move through road systems, and then can better understand how blood cells move through the circulatory system. Research has shown that analogies significantly improve memory and learning.[1]

You will often find analogies right in the textbook and instructors are likely to use them in their lectures. Pay close attention to these analogies, and try to ask questions to find more similarities and differences between two compared concepts. If you are not given an analogy, create one yourself. Ask your instructor or peers whether it is a good analogy to use. Also, analogies that you can easily visualize in your mind—like our Lego example here—tend to work best.

Association Strategy 2: Chunking or Grouping

Another way to use association is to learn new information in chunks or groups. With Lego, this would be like getting a group of new Lego bricks already put together. You just have to attach the new group to your existing structure all at once, instead of one piece at a time. Several methods of chunking or grouping are explained below.

Chunking Methods

©nfsphoto/Shutterstock.com

- **Acronyms**

    An example of chunking information is the use of acronyms—using the first letter of each word to make a new word or group of words that you memorize. "Roy G. Biv" is a common acronym to remember the order of the colors of the rainbow: Red, Orange, Yellow, Green, Blue, Indigo, and Violet. It is much easier to remember one name than seven separate colors and their order. Your brain only has to associate the name Roy G. Biv to a rainbow.

- **Rhymes and Songs**

    Another way to group information together is through a rhyme or song. Almost everyone learns the alphabet by singing it as a child. The song groups the letters together so you only have to re-member the song rather than 26 separate letters. Also, the rhyming and rhythm helps you associate the words with each other, which is why you sometimes have to actually sing the alphabet back to yourself to remember the order of the letters.

- **Peg Systems**

    One more example of association is the peg system. This system involves memorizing, in advance, an easy list of words or objects. The words in the list are the "pegs" on which to "hang" new items you need to remember. Once you have your pegs memorized, you can associate (hang) many different lists to those peg words. Take a look at Link 5-36 for more information about how peg systems work.

Apply any of these association strategies to your studying. Find ways to group information together and associate it to what you already know. The key is to think of ways to connect information together in ways that fit well and make sense to you.

Association Strategies in Your Studying

1   **Analogies**: create a comparison of a new concept to what you already know. A visual comparison works well. *Example*: circulatory systems versus road systems

2   **Acronyms**: combine the first letters of key words you are learning to create a single word or phrase you can more easily remember. *Example*: Roy G. Biv

3   **Rhymes and Songs**: create rhymes and rhythm around important words and phrases from your studies. *Example*: the alphabet

4   **Peg Systems**: use a list of memory "pegs" onto which you can "hang" and remember new information. *Example*: see the webpage you read on peg systems

Emotion and Novelty

Emotion and novelty trigger our brains to release chemical signals that can improve memory. Think about the most memorable trip you have taken in your life. You may have had lots of excitement, fun, or maybe even a little fear of the unknown. You likely also saw and did things you never had before: your brain experienced novelty. The chemical signals produced by emotion and novelty act like a "glue" that helps make your memories stick together longer.[2,3]

Picture a Lego structure that is glued together and the glue is dripping out from between the bricks. You can also visualize the glue coming out of your head to glue the pieces together as you stare at it. The strangeness of that image is intended to be novel and create emotion—maybe amusement, maybe disgust. Either way, it helps "glue" together your concept of how memory works.

©David Brimm/Shutterstock.com

You can take advantage of emotion and novelty in your studying. As we did with the Lego image, create strange and unusual images related to the information you need to remember. You can even draw them in your notes. The images can be strange, funny, or even a little gross. You can also create unusual rhymes or acronyms, which then combines the association method with emotion and novelty.

Repetition

The most common method for learning and memorization is simple repetition. However, repetition is not very effective unless it is done a certain way.

Spaced repetition is when you review or study the same information with significant time in between. This is much more effective than repeating the information over and over in a single study session. In other words, cramming is usually a bad idea.[4] So, how much time should you take between reviewing the information? A good approach is shown below.

Repeat Learning at Different Times

1. **First time**: take notes while listening to lecture or reading text.

2. **Second time**: review and revise notes later the same day. This is a great time to come up with questions about the material to ask your instructor or in a study group. You can also use your memory techniques here—create analogies, acronyms and emotional cues related to the material.

3. **Third time**: do a quick review or group study session up to one week later, such as in a weekly review session. You can also visit your instructor to get your questions answered.

4. **Fourth time**: do this the week before the exam as part of studying for the exam. This is a good time to try some practice questions, quizzes or tests so you can see where you may need to strengthen any weak areas.

Repeat Learning in Different Ways

Another important thing to remember about repetition is that you should try to repeat the information in different ways. Just re-reading the information is **not** effective. Remember that novelty is what helps with memory. If you try to build Lego by repeatedly pressing the same Lego brick onto your structure in the exact same way, you may not build a very solid structure. If, instead, you try different bricks and orientations, you are more likely to build a solid, lasting structure. So what are the different ways you can repeat the information? A good approach is shown below.

1. **First time**: taking notes while listening and reading

2. **Second time**: editing and adding to notes—both with words and by drawing information visually

3. **Third time**: discussing the information with someone else, try teaching it to a peer

4. **Fourth time**: quizzing yourself with flashcards, practice tests, or other methods

Memory Activity

Let's try to apply all three memory helpers right now while watching a video about feats of memory. Before starting the video, carefully read and think about the three points below. You can even pause the video and re-read the points to help you remember them as you watch.

1. Make a conscious effort to associate the ideas presented in the video to what you have already learned. You can do this by trying to identify to which of the three factors (association, emotion and novelty, or repetition) each tip in the video belongs.
2. Make an effort to be engaged in the video. Get excited to hear his story and be interested in how he tells it. Remember that emotion comes from how you react to things, not the things themselves.
3. The video will repeat many of the points made already in this section on memory. However, they will be repeated in different ways. If you want, you can even take a "study break" right now and watch the video later today if you want to space things over time a little more.

OK, ready to start the video? You'll find it at Link 5-37.

MEMORY JOURNAL

Just like taking notes after a lecture, the journal entries in CollegeScope allow you to summarize (*repeat*) what you have learned so you can better remember it. We also try to get you to *associate* concepts with your personal experience and maybe elicit some *emotion*.

For this journal, we want you to write what you learned about memory techniques. Use the following questions to help guide your response.
- What are some tricks you can use to help you remember what you learn?
- What makes those tricks work?
- What piece of information from this section stands out the most for you? Explain.

SECTION 4F: WRITING

Write for the Senses

The reader should SEE, HEAR, SMELL, TASTE, TOUCH what you are writing about whenever possible.

"Don't tell me the moon is shining; show me the glint of light on broken glass."

– ANTON CHEKHOV

One way to really get your reader's attention is to appeal to his or her senses. In other words, make sure he or she can SEE and HEAR what is happening in your writing. Don't forget about SMELL, TASTE, and TOUCH. When relevant, let the reader smell, taste, and feel what you are writing about.

©Sofi photo/Shutterstock.com

FIVE SENSES WRITING

Think of an event that happened to you in the past week or two. Close your eyes and see yourself back then. See yourself reliving the whole event from beginning to end. Focus your attention on what you can SEE all around you. Then repeat focusing on each of your other senses. Write notes for each sense in the spaces below.

I see...

I hear...

I smell...

I feel...

I taste... (you might need to be creative)

Write with a Clear Purpose

Another important part of writing is to define your purpose. Is it mainly *expressive*, *informative* or *persuasive*?

Writing Purposes

Expressive

Informative

Persuasive

- writing to express **personal experience**
- usually conveys **emotion and inner thoughts**
- often written in the **first-person** ("I")

Examples: journals, personal stories, and poetry

- writing to **explain** something or **inform** others
- usually uses less emotion but can be very **descriptive**
- often written in the **third-person** ("he", "she", "they", "it")

Examples: news articles and textbooks

- writing to **convince others** of an idea or to **take action**
- often written in the **second-person** ("you")

Examples: editorials, opinion pieces, essays, or speeches

These three writing styles can certainly overlap. For example, a fictional novel could be a blend of expressive and informative writing. Many speeches, including the Steve Jobs Stanford graduation speech, are a mix of expressive and persuasive. Some writing can even be a blend of all three, but there should still be a clear goal for your writing.

Audience

Whenever you write, keep your audience in mind. You would not choose the same words to speak to a group of third-grade students as you would college students. Your word choice will be driven, to a great degree, by your audience. Likewise, your tone and the voice behind your writing will change depending upon your audience.

Would you send the same text to a close friend as you would to a prospective employer? Probably not. Not only would the subject likely be very different, but your attention to word choice, grammar and punctuation would be different as well.

It is never OK to use "chatspeak" (see Link 5-38 for a definition) in academic writing.

Academic Essays

At some point in college, if you haven't already, you will have to write an academic essay. You will likely have to write many. You may have written a few in high school, but the expectations generally increase in college. There is a high standard of writing expected, regardless of the course in which it is required. It may be physics, nursing, art history or psychology—the standards are high for each.

However, don't be too intimidated. If you follow some general guidelines, you should do well.

As mentioned before, it is crucial to know your purpose and your audience. This is important for all writing. For academic essays, here are some additional guidelines:

Academic Essay Guidelines
- Introduction with a thesis statement
- Body paragraphs that follow a logical order and include explanations and examples
- Conclusion that includes a summarizing statement and leaves a little extra to think about, such as considering the future
- Transitional words that take us smoothly from one point to the next within paragraphs and to connect paragraphs (for instance, first, next, last, after, meanwhile, also, another, finally)
- Very few errors, if any, in grammar, punctuation and spelling

Consider the following paragraph:

When planting flowers, there are three important points to keep in mind. First, consider the size of the flowering plants and the size of the container. If you are planting into a pot, make sure the pot is about twice as large as the plant, leaving room for growth. Second, be sure you know how much sun that particular type of flower needs in order to thrive, and consider the amount of sunlight where you are going to put the plant. For example, petunias need six to eight hours of sun each day. On the other hand, impatiens can do beautifully with three or four hours of sunlight per day and live well in places that are shady much of the day. Finally, be sure the flowers will get enough water, either by rain or by your watering it, or a combination of the two. A little thinking ahead will definitely be worth your while, and you will have blooms to enjoy for a long time to come.

ELEMENTS OF A GOOD ACADEMIC ESSAY

Take a look at the guidelines for an academic essay and the sample paragraph. While the paragraph is not a full essay, it does contain many of the elements needed for a good academic essay. In the spaces below, identify those elements.

What is the thesis?

What are two explanations and two corresponding examples?

What transition words are used to make the sentences flow from one to the next?

What is the conclusion?

Grammar and Punctuation

What about correct grammar and punctuation? Does it matter? In general, if you are writing for a college class, then accuracy is quite important. Likewise, if you are writing to apply for an office job, incorrect grammar, punctuation or spelling could result in your application being rejected. Remember that if the person you are writing to does not know you personally, then that person will be making judgments about you solely on the basis of what you have written. Clearly, if you are trying to present a good image, then you will want to make sure your writing is free of errors.

"The difference between the almost right word and the right word is really a large matter—'tis the difference between the lightning-bug and the lightning."

– MARK TWAIN

For more tips, read the list of items to improve your writing at Link 5-39. Always consider word choice, word clutter, and the importance of writing with active verbs.

©Alena Hovorkova/Shutterstock.com

MY WRITING

Think about the writing tips in this section and describe two actions you can take to improve your writing.

SECTION 4G: STUDYING AND TEST TAKING

Learning Objectives

- Identify methods for studying that are effective and ones that are not
- Understand strategies to maximize performance on tests

Be Prepared

While we titled this section Studying and Test Taking, this whole chapter has discussed studying and test preparation. Studying for a test includes thinking about learning style, using critical thinking, listening, taking notes, reading, and memory techniques. In other words, the best strategy for doing well on a test is to *be prepared* by having good study habits from the start. Being prepared not only gives you the knowledge to respond to questions on the test, it reduces stress simply because you feel more prepared. The earlier you begin preparing for the test, the less you have to cram the night before and the less stressed out and tired you will be on test day.

While being prepared is the most important tip we can give you, here are some other tips that can help in the time leading up to the test itself.

- **Study in small groups.** Big groups tend to get sidetracked more. Two to four people is plenty. Focus your time on quizzing each other and explaining concepts to each other in different ways. Also, discuss what kinds of questions you think you may be asked. Review previous tests, assignments and lecture notes to discover what your instructor tends to focus on.
- **Create a one-page summary sheet** of the key ideas, equations, procedures, etc., that you might need to know on the test. If the test is closed-book, know what's on the sheet. If it's open-book, bring the sheet with you.
- **Set a second alarm and leave early.** You never know when something will go wrong with your first alarm or your commute to the exam. Being late or missing your exam would be a massive waste of all that preparation you did.
- **Have everything you need for the exam packed the night before.** Going to sleep feeling fully prepared will help you sleep better and ensure you don't forget anything.

"I've always considered myself to be just average talent and what I have is a ridiculous insane obsessiveness for practice and preparation."

– WILL SMITH

Test Time

Here are some more tips that can help you during the test:

- **Scan the whole exam before beginning**. Take note of how it might be divided into sections and the overall length. This can help you with pacing. Also, sometimes questions can give you clues on how to answer other questions, earlier or later in the exam. If it is a long multiple-choice test, don't try reading every question at the start—you can always go back to a question if you discover a clue later on.
- **Keep your momentum**. If you get stuck on a question, take your best guess and make an obvious mark next to the question so you know to come back to it at the end.
- When appropriate, **show your work**, even when you can do the problem in your head.
- **Attempt every question**. Some questions may look intimidating, but never leave the answer blank—especially multiple-choice questions. For long-answer questions you may be able to get partial credit. Also, you may remember more information once you get started with an answer.
- **Write neatly**. Losing credit because the instructor could not read your answer is a shame.
- **Read over your answers when you are finished**. Mistakes happen. You may even catch a question you forgot to answer!

Multiple-Choice Tests

Most students prefer multiple choice, but don't get overconfident when you see that the test is all multiple choice. Some instructors can make things tricky. Here are some tips to help you perform your best.[1]

- **It is OK to change your first answer**. It is a myth that your first answer is the best answer. A study in 2005[2] showed that when students change their answer, they change it from wrong to right twice as much as they change it from right to wrong.
- **Look for the response that is MOST correct**. Sometimes there may appear to be more than one correct answer in multiple choice. If selecting more than one is not an option, choose the one that is most correct. Some response options may be partially correct or correct in exceptional circumstances, but that means they are partially wrong too. Make sure you carefully read all the options to determine which one is best.
- **Be wary of absolute words**. Words such as "only," "never," and "always" often make response options incorrect. Most things tend to exist in states of in-between, such as "usually," "sometimes," and "mostly." However, just like most things, there are exceptions and absolute words can be part of a correct response. Just take a little extra caution when selecting a response with an absolute word.
- **Watch out for negatives**. Missing one little word such as "not," "false," or "incorrect" in the question can make you select the wrong response even when you know the right one. You may have noticed that CollegeScope uses many quiz questions with the word "not" to make you think deeply about what doesn't belong. Some test makers (the trickiest ones) will even add extra negatives in the response options to create double negatives when combined with the question. Read slowly and underline negative words as you come across them to increase your awareness of them.
- **Think of an answer before you read the response options**. During a test there is so much information being consciously processed that you may get confused when you read all the response options—especially if the test maker created good *distractors* (response options that seem reasonable but are wrong).

If you have a good idea of the answer before you read those distractors, you are less likely to be thrown off by them.

- **Don't play the odds**. Test makers generally do NOT try to evenly distribute correct answers between "A," "B," "C," and "D." The correct answers may be four "A"s in a row and there may be no "C"s correct in the entire test. Stick to choosing the best response for each individual question and don't assume there are any patterns in the answers.

Essay Questions

Many students get nervous about essay questions. They require deep understanding of the subject and the ability to communicate that understanding clearly. However, with good preparation and a few handy tips, you can perform well on the most demanding essay questions.[3]

- **Practice essay responses BEFORE the test**. This may seem like a lot of extra work, but you can make it easier on yourself by doing it verbally or in point-form if you prefer. If you meet with a study group, think of potential essay questions and talk through what your responses might be. Think of a series of points you would make and organize them on paper. It is probably worthwhile to also discuss what you should not include in your response.

- **Underline or highlight each key part of the question**. This is to ensure you completely answer the question. Also pay attention to any guidelines for how you need to frame your response.

- **Write down main points before writing your complete essay**. Once you are in the exam, have read the essay question and underlined the keys parts of the question, quickly write down your main response points—similar to how you practiced before the exam. Make sure you address every part of the question. Go through all the parts you underlined in the question and ensure you have at least one point in your response that addresses each item you underlined. Once you are sure you have enough points, organize them into an essay. Don't spend too much time on the points before you begin to write, however. You should spend most of your time on the essay itself.

- **Don't use filler**. Instructors usually expect nice flow and transition in regular essays, but for test essay questions, they usually want you to be more brief and to the point. Stick to the point-form outline you created at the start and don't add extra information just because it is floating around in your head. You also do *not* need a fully developed introduction or conclusion. Being brief will also save you time to review your response and clean it up or add anything you missed.

TIPS FOR TESTS

In this section we discussed tips before the test, general tips during the test, multiple-choice tests and essay questions. From each of those four categories, pick one tip that stands out for you. Pick some that you think will make the biggest difference for you when you try them. If you can't find one in this section, do a web search and find one. Describe the four tips below.

SUMMARY

This marks the end of the chapter on learning and productivity. We realize this is a lot of information. Don't expect to memorize every detail and don't expect to become super effective overnight. Developing your ability to learn and be productive is a lifelong pursuit. Just remember it all starts with effort and motivation. Then you can develop the ability to use your learning and productivity skills.

One of the key takeaways you should get from this chapter is that sometimes slowing down and paying close attention to what you are doing can actually save you time and effort in the long run. We saw that theme for critical thinking, metacognition and other study skills. It also helps to reflect on your thoughts and actions after you do them, especially if there is little time to reflect during the activity, such as during a test. When you reflect carefully on your thoughts and actions, it is much easier to analyze them and compare them to suggested tips and strategies. You can then begin to make plans for what you will do better next time.

Don't get caught in the trap of repeating the same behavior and expecting things to get better just because it is the second or third time you are doing it.

The chapter quiz is next. Make sure you go back and re-read any pages that you need to review before starting the quiz.

"Improvement begins with I."

– ARNOLD H. GLASOW

CHAPTER 5 QUIZ

Learning and Productivity

This quiz covers all of the topics from this chapter on learning and productivity. Before you answer any questions, scan them and return to review any pages you need to be confident in your answers.

1. Which of the following has **NOT** been shown to improve learning and productivity?
   a. delayed gratification
   b. happiness
   c. wanting it
   d. grit

2. What term is most closely related to self-control?
   a. mindset
   b. delayed gratification
   c. metacognition
   d. intrinsic

3. A key to boosting confidence and motivation is:
   a. gratitude
   b. putting others down
   c. only doing easy tasks
   d. focusing on extrinsic motivation

4. Which of the following is **NOT** a critical thinking skill?
   a. getting the relevant information
   b. being aware of bias
   c. using every source available
   d. communicating clearly

5. Which of the following is **NOT** part of metacognition?
   a. reading quickly to cover a large variety of topics
   b. using a variety of learning strategies
   c. matching learning strategies to the situation
   d. thinking aloud

6. When it comes to technology in education, which of the following is **TRUE**?
   a. technology should focus on convenience to enhance learning
   b. it is usually best to have the latest technology
   c. technology skills are only needed for IT positions
   d. you should use critical thinking skills to evaluate the technology you use

7. Which of the following is **FALSE** about effective note-taking?
   a. try to understand the information as you are recording it
   b. make sure to copy the information word-for-word
   c. different note-taking systems work better in different situations
   d. visual-oriented people should take notes

8. Which of the following is **NOT** part of the SQ3R method for reading?
   a. Skim
   b. Question
   c. Reverse
   d. Review

9. Which of the following is usually **NOT** good to use as a source in your research?
   a. a blog
   b. an academic journal article
   c. the *Wall Street Journal*
   d. a book recommended by your school librarian

©Piotr Marcinski/Shutterstock.com

10 Which of the following is **NOT** one of the three main mechanisms of memory for learning?
   a. sensing
   b. association
   c. emotion and novelty
   d. repetition

11 Which of the following is **NOT** recommended for academic essays?
   a. a thesis statement

   b. using examples to support statements
   c. quick changes in topic
   d. a conclusion that summarizes the essay

12 Which of the following is **NOT** part of deep processing when studying?
   a. thinking about similarities between concepts
   b. thinking about differences between concepts
   c. memorizing the exact wording of concepts
   d. relating concepts to personal experience

LEARNING AND PRODUCTIVITY

This is a quick survey to measure what you know about this chapter topic, both before and after you complete the chapter. Just be honest and rate how much each of the following statements applies to you. Give yourself a score of:
1 for Not a bit • 2 for A little • 3 for Some • 4 for Mostly • 5 for Definitely

AFTER CHAPTER

		Not a bit 1	A little 2	Some 3	Mostly 4	Definitely 5
1	I can describe mindset, grit, self-control, motivation and how they affect achievement in school and work.	○	○	○	○	○
2	I understand the difference between extrinsic and intrinsic motivation.	○	○	○	○	○
3	I know several proven strategies to improve motivation.	○	○	○	○	○
4	I know the most common ways motivation can be decreased and how to avoid them.	○	○	○	○	○
5	I know what critical thinking is and how to develop my ability with it.	○	○	○	○	○

6	I can describe my preferred learning styles and strategies to accommodate them.	○	○	○	○	○
7	I know what metacognition is and how to develop my ability to use it.	○	○	○	○	○
8	I know the pitfalls of technology and how to ensure it benefits my education.	○	○	○	○	○
9	I know where to go for help with technology if I need it.	○	○	○	○	○
10	I know several good listening techniques.	○	○	○	○	○
11	I know several note-taking strategies and when to use them.	○	○	○	○	○
12	I know good research-supported reading techniques.	○	○	○	○	○
13	I know the steps and where to go to perform good research and information analysis.	○	○	○	○	○
14	I can describe several effective memory techniques and why they work.	○	○	○	○	○
15	I know the expectations for good writing in college and how to meet those expectations.	○	○	○	○	○
16	I can describe several effective studying and test-taking strategies.	○	○	○	○	○

Add up your scores to determine your **After Chapter** total and write it down here:

Write your **Before Chapter** total here:

Compare your Before and After scores to see how your knowledge of this chapter topic has changed.

CHAPTER 5 FEEDBACK

Congratulations, you've completed Chapter 5! To conclude your learning in this chapter, consider and note the following:

What parts of this chapter were most helpful to you?

How would you improve this chapter?

6 COMMUNICATION, COLLAB-ORATION, AND LEADERSHIP

COMMUNICATION, COLLABORATION AND LEADERSHIP

©arka38/Shutterstock.com

This is a quick survey to measure what you know about this chapter topic, both before and after completing the chapter. Just be honest and rate how much each of the following statements applies to you. Give yourself a score of:

1 for Not a bit • 2 for A little • 3 for Some • 4 for Mostly • 5 for Definitely

BEFORE CHAPTER

		Not a bit 1	A little 2	Some 3	Mostly 4	Definitely 5
1	I know what emotional intelligence is and how it relates to communication.	○	○	○	○	○
2	I can explain the benefits of good communication skills.	○	○	○	○	○
3	I know how to speak with confidence in front of other people.	○	○	○	○	○
4	I know how to be an active listener.	○	○	○	○	○
5	I know how to read and use nonverbal cues effectively.	○	○	○	○	○
6	I know how to select the best form of media to communicate a message.	○	○	○	○	○
7	I can describe several benefits of effective collaboration.	○	○	○	○	○

8	I can select the best tools for collaborative tasks.	○	○	○	○	○
9	I can describe several characteristics of an effective collaborator.	○	○	○	○	○
10	I can list the warning signs that a conflict is developing.	○	○	○	○	○
11	I know effective strategies for remaining calm and resolving conflict within my team.	○	○	○	○	○
12	I can explain why leadership experience is valuable.	○	○	○	○	○
13	I can list the characteristics of good leadership.	○	○	○	○	○
14	I know how to persuade others to support my vision.	○	○	○	○	○
15	I can name the five development stages of group dynamics.	○	○	○	○	○
16	I can describe several leadership opportunities available to me in college.	○	○	○	○	○

Add up your scores to determine your **Before Chapter** total and write it down here:

Key Questions

1. Motivation Check: How does emotional intelligence relate to communication and collaboration?

2. What are good communication skills?

3. How can I collaborate successfully with others?

4. How can I recognize and develop good leadership skills?

©alphaspirit/Shutterstock.com

CHAPTER PREVIEW

In this chapter you'll learn about the benefits of effective communication, collaboration and leadership. You'll identify a variety of media and methods for communicating, cooperating with and leading others. You will also determine how to select the best approach in a variety of circumstances, and learn strategies for avoiding and resolving potential conflict situations.

Among the key ideas to take away from this chapter:

- Meaningful communication requires the use of your eyes, ears, mouth, and brain
- Empathy and an open mind are two of your greatest assets when relating to and leading others
- Opportunities for leadership experience are readily available and can serve you well, now and in the future

We will also discuss a concept called emotional intelligence and how developing it can lead to better communication, more effective teamwork and greater opportunities for influencing people in a positive way.

MOTIVATION CHECK

Emotional Intelligence

"Any person capable of angering you becomes your master."

– EPICTETUS

You may know your IQ, but do you know your EQ? What is EQ? EQ (which stands for Emotional Quotient) refers to a person's *emotional intelligence*. It is defined as the ability to identify, use, understand, and manage emotions—your own and other people's—in positive ways.

©Sofi photo/Shutterstock.com

A TIME OF STRESS

Think about a time when you've been really stressed, angry or upset with someone. Maybe you were relying on them for something important and they let you down. Perhaps you were blamed for something that wasn't your fault. Or maybe someone hurt your feelings badly. Write a couple of lines about the circumstance you were faced with and describe what you did.

How did you handle that situation? If you lost it and reacted by shouting or crying or telling them off, don't worry! Your reaction was typical.

For a humorous look at how *not* to react during a conflict, check out the video at Link 6-1.

Going on the offensive or bursting into tears is a pretty common reaction when people find themselves under pressure in a highly charged situation. But wouldn't it have been much nicer if you could have held it together, remained cool, and found a way to turn that difficult situation into something positive?

People with a high degree of EQ are able to do just that. They're able to recognize what they're feeling, control their emotions and react in a constructive way. They can also read other people's emotions and influence their behavior. They do this by identifying with the other person, understanding their point of view, and treating them with patience, sensitivity, and trust.

Think about it: if you react aggressively during a disagreement and the other person feels like they're under attack, they're likely to become distressed and react defensively. Then the situation risks becoming even more combative. But if you approach a potential conflict calmly and rationally, with composure, self-awareness—and, importantly, with *genuine empathy* for the other person's thoughts, feelings and perspective—it defuses the pressure. Once you accomplish this, both of you will be in a position to converse in a reasoned, respectful manner.

That's the secret power of EQ. Become proficient with it and you will enjoy richer, more effective communications in all aspects of your life. You will be better prepared to manage conflict and more capable of influencing other people in a positive way. The greatest thing about it is, emotional intelligence is something we can all learn and develop. It just takes practice.

If that sounds familiar, it's because the same concept applies to developing your multiple intelligences. Just like multiple intelligences, emotional intelligence can be learned, strengthened, and refined. In fact, two of the multiple intelligences—*intrapersonal* (understanding yourself) and *interpersonal* (understanding others)—are key components of emotional intelligence. So, as you improve your intrapersonal and interpersonal intelligences, you are also building your EQ.

Refer to the intelligence profile chart in your online *MI Advantage* report. What does it tell you about your level of emotional intelligence?

RAISING YOUR EQ

Read each statement below. If the statement describes a way to strengthen your emotional intelligence, select true. If not, select false.

		True	False
1	Work on my sense of humor and try to make people laugh.	O	O
2	Learn a new word every day to expand my vocabulary.	O	O
3	Spend more time in nature and learn the names of plants and animals.	O	O
4	Write out my thoughts and create a plan for self-improvement.	O	O
5	Think about life's purpose and humanity's place in the universe.	O	O
6	Get more exercise so that I will be more mentally alert.	O	O
7	Volunteer or get involved in charity work.	O	O
8	List a set of goals, from easy to difficult, to accomplish in the next year.	O	O
9	When trying to solve a problem, listen to music that helps me focus.	O	O

Answers:
1. True. Learning how to be funny in a positive way can improve your interpersonal intelligence. It requires the ability to read your audience well and deliver lines with precise pace, timing and clarity.
2. False. This may improve your linguistic intelligence, but it will not strengthen your emotional intelligence.
3. False. This may help expand your naturalist intelligence, but will not strengthen your emotional intelligence.
4. True. Reflecting on your thoughts, feelings and behaviors is a good way to improve your intrapersonal intelligence.
5. False. This may help to increase your existential intelligence, but will not strengthen your emotional intelligence.
6. False. This may improve your bodily-kinesthetic intelligence, but will not strengthen your emotional intelligence.

7. True. Service-oriented activities improve your ability to feel empathy and understand other people's points of view, and help you learn to communicate more effectively. All are excellent ways to develop your interpersonal intelligence.

8. True. As you achieve goals of increasing difficulty, your self-confidence will build and you will become more aware of your strengths and challenges—your intrapersonal intelligence improves.

9. False. This relates to your musical intelligence. It will not strengthen your emotional intelligence.

USING YOUR EMOTIONAL INTELLIGENCE

Use Link 6-2 to learn more about improving your EQ skills. Then return and complete the journal exercise.

Now that you know more about emotional intelligence, let's revisit that tough situation you dealt with at the beginning of this section. Think about your feelings at the time. What could you have said to yourself to release the negative emotions and change your perspective to a more positive one? Also consider the other person's position. Why do you think they treated you the way they did? What were they thinking, how were they feeling? How could you have expressed your point of view and encouraged them to discuss the situation with you in a non-threatening way?

SECTION 6-1: COMMUNICATION SKILLS

The Value of Good Communication Skills

"Talk is by far the most accessible of pleasures. It costs nothing in money, it is all profit, it completes our education, founds and fosters our friendships, and can be enjoyed at any age and in almost any state of health."

– ROBERT LOUIS STEVENSON

In this lesson you'll learn about the value of good communication skills and how to be an effective communicator (hint: it's not all about talking!).

In aviation, even a small error in communication can have catastrophic results. The world's deadliest aviation accident took place in 1977 on the island of Tenerife in the Canary Islands. Two 747 jumbo jets collided on a runway in dense fog, killing 583 people. Subsequent investigations revealed a series of misunderstandings between the flight crews and air traffic control had contributed to the mishap.

Transcripts show that the air traffic controller and the co-pilot of KLM Flight 4805 were using improper terminology, which caused some of their exchanges to be misinterpreted. In some respects, it was as if they were speaking different languages.

The KLM captain thought he was cleared for takeoff, but the controller had only intended to relay route clearance—instructions for the aircraft to follow once it was airborne. Meanwhile Pan Am Flight 1736 was on the runway, making its way through the heavy fog in an attempt to find the exit it had been assigned.

Anxious to get in the air and believing the controller had given him clearance, the KLM captain accelerated full-throttle down the runway through the fog, unaware that the Pan Am jet was directly in front of him. By the time both planes could see each other, it was too late to avert disaster.

As a result of the Tenerife accident, aviation authorities adopted a global system of standard aviation phrasing. Today, as part of their training, air crew and air traffic controllers all over the world are taught to communicate with each other using a specific protocol and terminology. They will often repeat back critical parts of the message to ensure they've received and understood the message correctly.

The Benefits of Effective Communication

Miscommunication doesn't always result in tragedy, but the consequences can feel pretty tragic when it happens to you. A lack of adequate communication skills can severely affect your ability to successfully navigate personal and professional relationships. Poor communication is blamed for ending careers, destroying marriages and ruining friendships. It can prevent you from getting a raise, qualifying for a promotion, and even from landing a job in the first place.

Here's a look at the advantages of communicating well:

©VLADGRIN/Shutterstock.com

- **Clarity**: Good communication gets your message across clearly and completely. It is simple, straightforward and easy to understand. There is no room for ambiguity or misunderstanding, which can lead to conflict, misdirection and frustration.
- **Productivity**: A well-communicated message can lead to enhanced efficiency, greater productivity and more overall success. People who know what they're supposed to do and how they're supposed to accomplish it will waste less time and effort trying to figure those things out for themselves.
- **Gratification**: The ability to make ourselves understood, and to understand others, adds to our sense of personal fulfillment. Sharing thoughts and feelings is a basic human desire. Successfully communicating with one another creates a stronger bond and makes us feel good about connecting.
- **Persuasion**: There is a "sales" element to communicating well. A good communicator is better able to persuade others to understand and accept things from their perspective. This can be particularly helpful in teamwork and leadership situations.
- **Negotiation**: With their ability to relate well to others, an effective communicator can act as an intermediary and use their skills to reconcile disputes between other people.

So, now that you know all the good things that can result from successful communication, how can you develop the skills you'll need to take the world by storm?

The Dos and Don'ts of Effective Communication

At its core, communication is simply the exchange of information, ideas or feelings. It happens in every aspect of life. We use it in our personal lives, in our interactions with friends and families. It's essential in the workplace when dealing with colleagues, supervisors, subordinates and clients. Even just walking down the street, we are communicating with those around us through body language and nonverbal cues.

How to Speak So Your Message is Understood

You may have heard of Toastmasters International. It's a non-profit organization that helps people all over the world learn how to improve their public speaking skills. A Toastmasters club

©Michael D Brown/Shutterstock.com

operates on a "learn by doing" philosophy. Members learn by preparing and delivering a number of speeches in front of the other members of the club.

Each speech builds on the previous ones in terms of difficulty and skills required. Immediately after each presentation, the speaker is evaluated by another member of the club. The evaluator offers constructive feedback and positive suggestions to encourage the speaker and help them improve their skills for the next speech.

While building their abilities within the supportive surroundings of the club, speakers develop in seven key areas:

The SV-COACH Approach to Speaking

- **Story** – use personal experience and stories to better connect with the audience
- **Voice** – pay attention to tone, pace, clarity and volume of your voice
- **Clear and concise** – express ideas in a clear and concise manner, avoiding fillers such as um, ah, and like
- **Own it** – own the message that is delivered—make others believe that you believe it
- **Audience**—keep the content appropriate and tailored to the specific audience
- **Comfort**—become comfortable with public speaking through practice
- **Humor** – use humor to hold the audience's attention and build your own confidence

Notice that the first letters of those areas spell out SV COACH, as in a speaker's voice coach. Use that acronym to remember the key areas as you work on any type of speech. If you do, you will improve your speaking ability.

But what if you're not making a speech?
- What if you're called upon to state your view during a meeting or need to convene a group to work on a project?

- What if you're sitting in a job interview and the interviewer asks you the dreaded, "Tell me why we should hire you" question?

Confidence, clarity, preparation and good content are still key. Once you've overcome the all-important fear factor and mastered the art of expressing your message in your own voice with self-assurance, you're well on your way to becoming an effective speaker in any situation.

Remember, effective communication is a two-way process. It ensures messages are sent and received as intended. This requires not only the ability to form and send a message appropriately, but also to receive—through listening, watching and interpreting—a message correctly.

MY PRESENTATION STYLE

Together with one or two others, have each person select one of the following topics: favorite sport, dream job, the perfect day, biggest pet peeve, or something else of your choice.

Taking turns, have each person speak about their topic for 60 seconds. After each presentation, discuss the performance in relation to the seven key areas described above.

- Did the speaker come across as knowledgeable about their topic?
- Did they look relaxed and comfortable or were they rushed and nervous?
- Did they use lots of filler words?
- What could they have done to improve their delivery?

If you really have trouble finding someone to do this with, you can take a video of yourself giving the presentation. Then, send the video to someone else to watch and get their feedback. As a last resort, watch the video and analyze yourself. *Note*: at some point, you will have to get used to the idea of presenting to others.

In the box below, write down your topic and describe what you learned about your presentation style. What would you do differently next time to improve?

How to Be an Active Listener

> *"If the person you are talking to doesn't appear to be listening, be patient. It may simply be that he has a small piece of fluff in his ear."*
>
> – WINNIE THE POOH

Here's a statistic that may surprise you:

Effective communication consists of about 20% talking and 80% listening.

It's true. If you want to have a productive conversation with someone, try listening more and talking less. Developing and habitually using your listening skills when communicating with others can help you avoid misunderstandings, resolve conflict and build stronger, more meaningful relationships.

©Olena Yakobchuk/Shutterstock.com

Being a good listener is not just about keeping quiet, however. It's about practicing *active* listening. That is, making an effort to understand, process and absorb what the other person is saying. This requires paying attention not only with your ears, but with your eyes and your brain too.

Look at the following comparison of a good listener versus an ineffective one. Use the comparison to pick up some important tips on how to be a good listener.

Good Listeners	Ineffective Listeners
• ignore any distractions such as incoming calls or texts • carefully observe body language, facial expressions and tone of voice • ask for more detail or ask questions closely related to what is being said • paraphrase or restate important points at natural breaks in the conversation to show they understand the speaker • make regular eye contact with the speaker	• say "Just a sec" while attending to their phone or another person • only listen to the words of the other person • say nothing at all or simply nod and say things like, "Uh-huh" • turn the conversation to themselves, or say things like "Sounds like when I...." or "If it were me...." • look away—at their phone or another person, for example

Always remember the 80/20 rule. If you're doing most of the talking, then you're not getting everything you should be from the conversation.

How to Use and Understand Nonverbal Cues

It's been estimated that nonverbal communication accounts for between 75 and 90% of all the communicating we humans do. That's a lot of communicating—even if not a single word has been spoken!

All of these are ways in which we communicate nonverbally with others:

- facial expressions
- eye contact
- gestures
- vocal tone and inflection
- the way we dress
- posture
- the physical space we put between ourselves and others

Unconscious, but Real

Because these are things we do unconsciously, nonverbal messages are often interpreted as the truest sign of a person's feelings or intentions, regardless of the words coming out of their mouth. Learning how to use these signals, and interpret them in others, can add a huge amount of information to our exchanges with other people.

People send out nonverbal cues all the time. Usually they're not even aware they're doing it. But these messages can have a huge impact on the way a person is perceived. Sending out confusing or negative signals can affect their ability to interact successfully with others. It may cause them to be disliked or mistrusted, even if they're unaware of it. That can have serious repercussions, particularly in the workplace.

NON-VERBAL COMMUNICATION

Read the following scenario about non-verbal communication and record your response to the questions below.

Imagine you've just started a new job and are meeting two of your colleagues for the first time. You walk into their office and say, "Hello, my name is..... I wanted to drop by and introduce myself. I'll be working in the office next door."

A man stands up and strides across the room toward you. He looks you in the eye, a friendly smile on his face, as he extends his hand. "Welcome aboard!" he says, and shakes your hand warmly. "My name is Charlie. And this is Andrea." He turns and waves his arm in the direction of a woman behind him. She remains seated at her desk, eyes fixed on the computer screen in front of her. At the sound of her name, her jaw tightens. She glances up at you with a tight smile and holds out her hand. You walk over and shake it.

"Nice to meet you," Andrea says briskly. As soon as you let go of her hand, the smile vanishes and her eyes dart back to the computer screen, a look of intense concentration on her face. Charlie, meanwhile, has walked across the room to stand next to you. "If there's anything we can do to help you get settled in, don't hesitate to ask," he says.

What are your impressions of Charlie? What are your impressions of Andrea? Whom do you think you'll approach if you need help? Explain.

Sending the Right Signals

While it's not possible to control your nonverbal cues, you can train yourself to project more of the "right" kind of signals—the sort that can help you convey confidence and credibility. Here are some tips from Forbes magazine:

Make good eye contact – it communicates your level of involvement, interest and warmth. Merely glancing at someone for a second or less conveys insecurity, anxiety, or evasion.

Have a firm, confident handshake – touch is an important form of nonverbal behavior. Shake up and down once or twice, coupled with a sincere smile and eye contact. Avoid the extremes of either a limp handshake or an overly aggressive one.

Use effective gestures – they can help to express an idea, opinion or emotion. Be sure the motions suit who you are and match your message. Try to avoid distracting movements such as finger pointing, tapping, or playing with your hair.

Dress the part – choose high quality, well-tailored clothes that convey professionalism. Avoid flashy accessories, tight garments and revealing necklines. Don't use perfume (in case people are sensitive), do control perspiration, and be sure your breath is fresh and your nails and hands are neatly manicured.

Consider your posture and presence – by standing up straight and tall, you send a message of self-assurance, authority and energy. Good posture conveys an attitude of leadership. Bad posture signals a lack of confidence.

Use appropriate facial expressions – facial expressions are closely tied to emotion, so they are often unconscious. Be aware of what your face is revealing and choose an expression that matches your intended message. If you want to look enthusiastic, for example, allow your face to become more animated. Practice in front of a mirror until it looks and feels natural.

Initiate interactions – be the first to make eye contact, offer your hand to shake, have an idea or solution, or enter a room to meet people.

©ChrisMilesPhoto/Shutterstock.com

Nonverbal Communication Tips
- Make good eye contact
- Have a firm handshake
- Use effective gestures
- Dress the part
- Consider posture and presence
- Use appropriate facial expression
- Initiate interaction
- Use appropriate tone
- Give full attention
- Watch for and respond to cues

Use appropriate tone – the quality of your voice and its pacing, pausing, volume, inflection, pitch, and articulation convey emotion and attitude. Think about what your voice communicates.

Give your full attention – face a person when you're speaking to them. Lean into the conversation; focus your eyes, ears and energy on them. Don't check e-mail, look at your phone or get distracted in any way. It shows disrespect and a lack of interest.

Watch for and respond to nonverbal cues – pay close attention to other people's body language and tone of voice. Their nonverbal cues can tell you if they have a question, want to say something, agree or disagree, or require more explanation. Use your emotional intelligence to convey suitable emotions and to recognize what the other person is feeling. With an appropriate response you can express confidence, sensitivity and empathy, which builds trust and understanding.

"Listen with the intent to understand, not the intent to reply."

– STEPHEN COVEY

Communicating with Different Media

Recently, about 18,000 employees of Microsoft learned via email (see Link 6-3) that their jobs were being eliminated. Instead of being informed ahead of time—preferably in private by their direct supervisors—they received the news in a corporate memo circulated company-wide to over 100,000 employees by the new CEO. Talk about insensitive.

If you've ever been fired by phone or dumped via text message, you know the feeling. Some messages are best communicated in person.

©violetkaipa/Shutterstock.com

Media richness theory describes how and why certain media (such as phone, face-to-face, email, flyers) are best for delivering a message. You can learn about it at Link 6-4. Essentially, it states that a medium's appropriateness is based on its ability to support:

- Sending multiple cues (such as body language and tone) simultaneously
- Timely feedback
- A personal touch (providing the ability to convey feelings and emotions)
- Natural language (the use of different words to assist understanding)

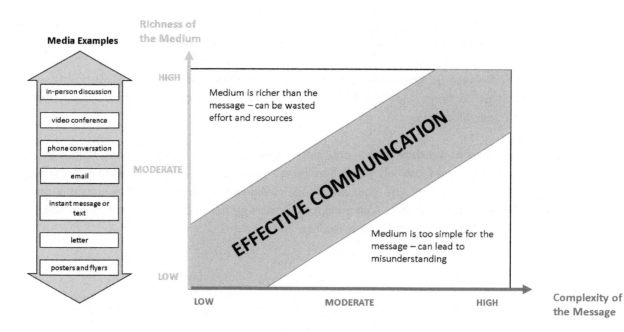

This means a "rich" medium is better suited to messages that could be misinterpreted, while lean media are fine for routine messages that are perfectly clear. For example, if you have a project strategy meeting with someone on the phone, they can't see your expression, gestures and other visual cues that could add meaning to the conversation. So the phone is a less rich medium in that instance than a face-to-face meeting or, say, a video call, which at least would enable you and the other person to see each other. On the other hand, if you're waiting for the electric company to tell you how much you owe this month, a bill in the post or an invoice via email is sufficient.

In simple terms, depending on the message, some forms of media are better than others for delivering it. Knowing which form is most appropriate for a particular situation, and how best to use it, can help you be a more effective communicator.

In-person

While it's becoming less and less common in a world dominated by electronic devices, there's still no substitute for good old-fashioned face-to-face communication. This is especially true when sharing important messages, where it's critical that they be discussed and understood. Sometimes, it's just a lot more soul-satisfying to interact with someone in person.

Discussing things in person provides an opportunity to ask and respond to questions (providing immediate feedback), and for both parties to see the other's body language, hear their tone of voice and pick up on other nonverbal cues. It makes it possible to employ our emotional intelligence—use our intrapersonal and interpersonal abilities—to read reactions, convey empathy, and connect on a deeper level.

Check out the funny clip at Link 6-5 for an example of the miscommunication that can occur without visual cues.

Not for Everyone

But wait—is it *always* more beneficial to communicate in person? Not necessarily. People with less-developed interpersonal skills might struggle to communicate as effectively in a face-to-face situation as someone who excels interpersonally. They may need time to compose their thoughts before speaking. That puts them at a disadvantage. Depending on the message, they might be more comfortable and have greater success expressing their ideas in writing or on the phone.

Voice

Of course, it's not always convenient—nor, as we've learned, always advantageous—to communicate in person. If required by distance, time or expense, or just due to individual preference, communicating by phone is often the favored option.

Think about some of the slogans used by telephone companies over the years:

Reach out and touch someone. • It's the next best thing to being there. • Can you hear me now?

Voice-based communication allows us to impart a personal touch to a message without physically having to be there to deliver it. When your intent is to build rapport and create a personal connection, a phone call really can be "the next best thing" to being there in person. It's quick, convenient and universal (do you know anyone who doesn't have a phone?). Plus, if you need to discuss things as a group but can't get everyone together, they can participate via conference call.

Making the most effective use of this medium requires being aware of the power of your voice. The voice is capable of tremendous influence. It's not only about the volume, pitch and emotion it carries. It's about the words you choose and the expressiveness, speed and skill with which you deliver them.

©Alena Hovorkova/Shutterstock.com

IMPROVE YOUR VOICE

The vocal techniques used by professional singers can be used by anyone who wants to train their speaking voice and improve their tone, range, pronunciation and diction. Check out the video at Link 6-6. Then return to this page and answer the questions.

List two things you learned from the video. Describe how you can apply these tips to improve your speaking voice.

Electronic Communications

Humans have been writing since ancient times. Email first appeared around 1993, making it a newbie in the history of writing, even though today it seems as ubiquitous as toothpaste. Technological advances have only sped up since then. A vast array of electronic media are at your disposal, from instant messaging and chat tools, social media, blogs and videos to discussion boards, voice-over IP, web conferencing, e-learning applications, wikis, and other online collaboration tools.

©sayhmog/Shutterstock.com

Perhaps their newness explains why many people don't know how to use electronic media most effectively. While they are incredibly convenient, they aren't equally suitable for every purpose. For example, email is great if you need to send a file to a group of people or you need a record of a message that you can refer back to later. But it's not the best option if your message is long and complicated or highly confidential. For those, a face-to-face discussion might be the best option. (You can use email to set up the meeting.)

The key with all electronic media is to keep it simple. Think about the most succinct way of accomplishing your goal. Here are some general guidelines to help you navigate your options:

- Think about the media richness chart and ask yourself, What's the most effective way to communicate my message? How can I ensure the recipient will understand it in the way I intended?
- Keep your message concise, direct and clear. If the topic is lengthy, discussion is necessary or there's room for misinterpretation, you might want to arrange a call or a face-to-face meeting instead.
- Be organized and complete. Think about what you want to say before you start. Don't ramble, don't be vague and don't trail off. Do pay attention to proper grammar and spelling.
- Be polite and keep it clean. Be respectful of the recipient's time and feelings. Don't joke around or be sarcastic. Such comments often fall flat and can be taken the wrong way in an online environment.
- Don't automatically judge others. If you're unsure about a person's meaning or the tone of a message, seek to clarify it with them. And remember, it's OK if their ideas, principles and outlooks differ from yours. You don't have to agree on everything.
- Weigh the need for privacy. If a message contains or requests confidential information, select a more secure method for transmitting it.
- If multiple people need to be involved in a discussion, consider options such as discussion boards or wikis to aid collaboration.

Don't be afraid to open up and share a little of yourself in your communications. Using descriptive words that describe how you feel about things and expressing your personal values, interests and attitudes can help others relate and form a picture of the "real you."

SECTION 6-2: COLLABORATION SKILLS

"Alone we can do so little; together we can do so much."

– HELEN KELLER

The Importance of Good Collaboration Skills

In this lesson you'll learn about the value of good collaboration skills and how to work well cooperatively with others.

At some point in your life, you're likely to find yourself sitting in a job interview being asked about your team-work skills. The question might sound something like this: "Tell me about a time when you worked on a project as part of a team." Or, "Describe a rewarding team experience you've had in the past." It might even be posed this way: "Give me an example of how you've dealt with a difficult team member."

What the hiring manager is trying to find out with these questions is how well you work with other people. An ability to work cooperatively with others is considered vital in most workplaces. If you can't demonstrate the potential to get along well with your prospective colleagues—or diplomatically handle problematic personalities who already work there—the manager might decide you're not a good fit for the job.

The Cost of Not Collaborating

It's an important consideration for an employer. Making a bad hiring decision can be extremely costly, especially for a small business. It's estimated[1] that disengaged employees cost the economy about $450 billion every year in lost productivity. When people don't work well together, it can[2]:

- **Damage a company's image.** If people are bickering in front of clients or badmouthing the company in public, it can seriously affect their employer's reputation and future prospects.
- **Harm working relationships.** In a dysfunctional team, individuals grow resentful. They may even sabotage the work of others to prove they aren't a good fit for the squad.

- **Hurt productivity**. Deadlines slide when a team is inefficient. Workers may put in long hours to catch up, fuelling further resentment.
- **Create a downward spiral**. When they don't meet deadlines or provide good service, companies lose business. They also lose good employees, who decide to seek more satisfying work elsewhere. This has a cumulative effect and can seriously hurt a company's ability to survive and thrive.

It's also important to consider the personal cost. People who aren't happy at work tend to get sick more often. They struggle with low morale and high stress levels and miss more days at work. The likelihood of injury on the job also increases when working relationships break down.

The Benefits of Working Cooperatively

Good teamwork means[3]:

- **Better problem solving ability**. If two heads are better than one, consider the problem-solving brawn of an entire group. Each person brings a unique perspective to the team. Their ability to work well together makes them more capable of arriving at the best solution.
- **Healthy competition**. Friendly rivalry within the group motivates people to try harder, which helps the team to excel.
- **Developing relationships**. People build bonds when they work together. Empathy, trust and understanding encourages socialization and helps avoid unnecessary conflicts.
- **Greater efficiency**. The harmonious blending of knowledge and abilities and the confidence to spark off one another's ideas helps the team to work more productively.
- **A sense of purpose**. People working together toward a common goal are more likely to feel motivated and fulfilled.
- **Personal growth**. Being willing to take risks and learning from others helps each individual develop and enhance their own skills.

A TEAM EXPERIENCE

Let's see how you would respond to that job interview question at the beginning of this section. Select one of the following options and answer the questions:

A. Think about an especially rewarding experience you've had as part of a team. Perhaps it was a work situation. Maybe it was a sports team you were on or a school project team. It might have been a volunteer project you worked on. Discuss why that time was so memorable. Was it the people you were working with? The accomplishments you achieved together? The fun of the steps involved? Did you feel pride, joy, laughter, satisfaction? Explain below.

OR

B. Think about an especially bad experience you've had as part of a team, one in which your involvement led to a solution. Perhaps it was a work situation. Maybe it was a sports team you were on or a school project team. It might have been a volunteer project you worked on. Discuss why that situation was so challenging. Did you feel anger, frustration, disappointment, resentment? How did you handle it and help to achieve a resolution? Explain below.

Individual Traits that Benefit the Group

The video at Link 6-7 takes a lighthearted approach, but we can still learn something from reflecting on it. For a group or team to collaborate, the individuals on that team need certain traits. An example of a trait for collaboration is empathy or awareness of others. Think about how quickly the characters in the video realized that one of their own was vulnerable and organized themselves in offering aid. What other traits did they exhibit that allowed them to collaborate so well?

©Alena Hovorkova/Shutterstock.com

TRAITS FOR COLLABORATION

Describe at least two traits that an individual needs to collaborate effectively.

SELECTING MEDIA

Below are some tasks that require collaboration. From the following list of options, choose the best tools to accomplish each.

A. In-person meetings and web conferences
B. Phone, email, text, and instant message
C. Wikis and collaborative document applications
D. Online forums and discussion boards
E. Project management tools and online spreadsheet applications

1. Create and share a planning document as a group

2. Hold a brainstorming meeting

3. Send a reminder about a group update meeting

4. Give a presentation to the rest of the team

5. Share, refine and track ideas to build consensus

6. Track each person's tasks and milestones

7. Touch base with a team member

©arka38/Shutterstock.com

Answers:

1C – Tools like wikis and collaborative document applications allow all team members to access, write and revise a single copy of the document.

2A – In-person and web conferences allow the group to communicate using their eyes, ears and brains. People also tend to be more motivated and focused when they can see each other.

3B – Phone, email, text and instant message are quick, convenient ways to send the same message to a specified group. Email is the best option because it can link to calendar and reminder options.

4A – In-person meetings and web conferences allow you to share visuals such as presentation slides, charts and diagrams. Some web conference applications also allow you to record and store presentations online.

5D – Online forums and discussion boards allow everyone to post, read, reply and comment at the same time. Exchanges are dated and organized as well.

6E – Online spreadsheets and project management tools have features that help you organize, sort and track information for quick reference. All team members can quickly and easily see what needs to be done, by whom and when.

7B – Phone, email, text and instant message provide a simple, direct way to contact the person and have a quick chat without all the effort it might take to arrange a meeting.

Sometimes your options will be dictated by circumstances. For example, if you're taking an online course or are part of a virtual work team, you may have few or no chances to discuss things with your group in person. If you're in a traditional classroom or office environment, you might have to designate roles within the team to manually handle tasks like document creation, meeting minutes, or task tracking.

It's always a good idea to become familiar with the tools used by your peers, on your campus and in your workplace.

What Kind of Collaborator Are You?

"Talent wins games, but teamwork and intelligence wins championships."

– MICHAEL JORDAN

Collaboration is all about working together to achieve shared goals. When done well, it can bring an enormous sense of satisfaction. But not everyone is born a great collaborator. Many people have to work at developing these skills. Start by identifying your strengths and challenge areas with this comparison chart[4]:

An effective collaborator...	An ineffective collaborator...
• Evaluates others' views with honesty and empathy	• Aggressively promotes their own opinion over other opinions
• Is dedicated to accomplishing the group's goals	• Puts their interests ahead of the group's goals
• Is enthusiastic and resourceful	• Is critical and pessimistic
• Retains a sense of humor, even when the going gets tough	• Is resigned to the inevitability of defeat
• Is receptive to new ideas	• Lacks tolerance for ideas that differ from theirs
• Can be depended upon	• Is unreliable
• Takes responsibility for their tasks	• Lets the others do most of the work

Do you see yourself in any of these characteristics? If you notice some matches in the right-hand column, that's OK! Identifying areas for improvement is the first step toward building better collaboration skills. Here are some tips for more successful group work:

Don't be married to your ideas – they could be accepted, modified or rejected. Be prepared for that, and don't take it personally.

Listen, don't judge – be open-minded about others' suggestions, even if you don't think they're very good.

Share credit – it doesn't matter who comes up with the "winning" ideas; in the end, they belong to the team.

Be clear about who's doing what – well-defined roles and responsibilities reduce the potential for confusion and duplication of duties.

If you screw up, admit it – everyone makes mistakes. Holding yourself accountable builds respect and prevents a culture of blame and shame.

Make a compelling point – you'll be more effective if you deliver a well thought out, clearly articulated suggestion.

Keep your eye on the ball – never lose sight of the goal. Focus, and don't get sidetracked.

Socialize outside of school or work – it's easier to empathize and build rapport when you see your teammates as real, fully dimensional people with similar issues, concerns and interests to your own.

Have a positive attitude – negativity is demoralizing and undermines the team. If problems arise, acknowledge them, learn from them, and move on.

Becoming a better team player isn't easy and it won't happen overnight. It requires tolerance, commitment and a willingness to change habits and preconceptions that you may have held for a lifetime. But if you can do it, the payoffs—stronger relationships, personal development, greater productivity and a sense of accomplishment—are well worth the investment.

BECOMING A BETTER COLLABORATOR

What are some simple steps you could take right now to become a better collaborator? What things can you work on longer term?

MANAGING CONFLICT

"You cannot compromise unless people talk to you."

–AUNG SAN SUU KYI

Rule No. 1: Avoid the Conflict Zone

Imagine that every group has a "group happiness" scale. Think of group happiness as the overall level of contentment the members feel as a result of being part of the group. When one person's level of happiness within the group decreases, it can bring down the level of happiness experienced by the others. Conversely, when a person's level of contentment within the group increases, it can boost the happiness level for the others. When group happiness is up, there tends to be no conflict. So, you can avoid most conflict by keeping group happiness up.

Check out the article at Link 6-8 for some tips on how to keep employees happy.

Step 2: Recognize When Conflict is Forming

Every group runs into trouble at some point. Differences of opinion are unavoidable when people work closely together, especially with the added influence of egos, deadlines and budgets. The key is to find positive ways of managing these disputes *before* they blow up into something bigger. Too often people avoid conflict by ignoring the warning signs that a conflict is forming. They put up with it until it becomes a serious problem for themselves and others. Dealing with the issue from the start would save a lot of time and effort and prevent damaging relationships.

Conflict Warning Signs

Here are some common indications that trouble is brewing on your team[5]:
* Ignoring or not speaking to each other
* Criticizing or disputing others' opinions
* Refusing to cooperate
* Splitting off into cliques to discuss things away from the others
* Left out of team meetings because they are considered to be "too difficult"
* Not interested in others' opinions, only in pushing their own agenda
* Using personal insults and aggressive language to intimidate others on the team
* Reacting defensively when someone dares to question their idea
* Avoiding seeking solutions to a problem, preferring to ignore it or talk around it
* Complaining to others about people on the team
* Assuming the worst about someone else's intentions

Things Have Reached Boiling Point. Now What?

Even when you have done your best with maintaining group happiness and catching conflicts early, trouble can go undetected and a major conflict can erupt.

Don't panic. Don't threaten. Don't blame. Don't issue ultimatums. Sounds like common sense, right? But in the heat of the moment, when stress builds and everyone is passionate about the outcome, things can deteriorate. Manners, respect—and yes, even common sense—can go out the window.

When emotions are running high, it's especially difficult to discuss an issue rationally. In order to reach a resolution that meets everyone's needs, it's vitally important to get past the anger. Giving in to emotional outbursts will only intensify the feelings and make things worse. Here are a few tips for turning a potentially negative conflict into a beneficial one[6]:

©AVAVA/Shutterstock.com

Control yourself: Resist the urge to vent or tell someone off (even if you think they genuinely deserve it). Nothing can be accomplished when people are upset. So take some time, let everyone cool off and agree to get back together when people are capable of discussing things more calmly.

Deal with people directly: If you have an issue with someone specific, don't complain about it behind their back and don't use email to make your point. Talk it over in person and work out a resolution together. A face-to-face discussion helps to keep people talking honestly and openly, improving the odds of finding a mutually agreeable solution.

Brainstorm: Everyone thinks their own idea is the best one. Challenging the team to do a little creative problem solving opens up the discussion and allows the group to work out a solution collectively.

Shut up and listen: Use your active listening skills to fully appreciate the others' point of view. Make sure you're clear on what people really need so you can work toward a solution that everyone feels is fair.

Make your point: To be understood correctly, you must express your comments clearly, concisely and constructively. Don't let emotions get the better of you or permit yourself to rile the others. Be straightforward, keep your message factual and address people with respect.

Keep an open mind and think the best of everyone: Always go in with a positive outlook and assume the others mean well too. A conciliatory attitude can go a long way in helping to settle differences and smooth the way for more productive exchanges in future.

MANAGING CONFLICT

Let's take a look at a couple of typical conflict situations. Select **one of the following two** to discuss:

A. You're at work: A colleague in the next cubicle makes personal phone calls all day long. You try not to listen, but it's impossible to block out the noise, especially when the conversations are punctuated with loud laughter. Your colleague refuses to acknowledge the problem and tells other co-workers that you're just "too sensitive." You have a heavy workload and this affects your ability to concentrate. It irks you that your colleague can spend so long on the phone and leave on time, but you have to work overtime most days just to keep up.

OR

B. You're at school: Your roommate constantly invites friends over to stay. They talk or party late into the evening, night after night. The visits interrupt your study time and disturb your sleep. Your roommate says getting together with friends is part of college life and laughs off your concerns, saying, "You can always study at the library." You find it infuriating. You feel like your privacy has been invaded and that you've lost the right to a space of your own. The lack of sleep and inability to study effectively are starting to affect your grades and you're ready to blow up.

What are the warning signs that conflict is developing? What can you do to defuse the situation before it gets worse? What can you say and how should you say it? Explain in the box below.

SECTION 6-3: LEADERSHIP SKILLS

Learning Objectives

- Understand the importance of leadership skills for success in college and career
- Recognize the characteristics of good leadership, no leadership, and bad leadership
- Know how to communicate vision, mission or purpose that encourages commitment and action in others
- Understand how to encourage positive group dynamics and democratic principles
- Know the opportunities to display and develop leadership while in college

The Value of Leadership

In this lesson you'll learn about the value of leadership, how to lead a team successfully and ways to gain leadership experience.

"If your actions inspire others to dream more, learn more, do more and become more, you are a leader."

– JOHN QUINCY ADAMS

Everyday Leadership

Are you a leader? When was the last time you influenced someone else's life in a positive way? Drew Dudley thinks everyone has what it takes to be a leader. In fact, he says, many people exhibit leadership qualities every day without even realizing it.

In Link 6-9, Dudley explains how it's within everyone's grasp to be a leader. Watch the video, then answer the questions.

WHAT IS A LEADER?

Does this video change your perception of what a leader is? Think about how you can use Dudley's message in your education and career. What are some ways in which you have exhibited leadership qualities or could use them in future? Explain.

Why You Should Take the Lead

If you think you'd prefer to be a follower and not a leader, you might want to reconsider. Leadership experience can help you build skills in planning, communication, negotiation, delegation, decision making, and team building. You'll gain self-assurance and others will grow to have confidence in your abilities. You'll learn how to be responsible not only for yourself but for the tasks, resources, budgets, and people you oversee. You'll develop a personal network of valuable professional contacts and have some first-rate experience to list on your resume. All of these things will serve you well through college and beyond.

Still not convinced? Let's zoom ahead and look at your career prospects.

People with leadership experience are more likely to...
* be hired
* be advanced in their job positions
* earn higher incomes than people with less leadership experience
* have more choice in which jobs they get
* influence others
* make a difference in other people's lives, helping them to pursue their dreams

The Good, the Bad, the Indifferent

There are good leaders, bad leaders ... and, sometimes, there is no leadership in evidence at all. As you learned at the start of this section, everyone has the potential to be a leader. But like nearly everything else in life, becoming good at leadership takes time, practice and commitment.

Good leaders share a number of key characteristics[6], such as:

Honesty and integrity: Setting standards and adhering to them influences others to act the same way. Earning their team's trust and respect also helps to establish the leader's authority and ability to take responsibility for the group

Enthusiasm: By exhibiting a passion for the work and an appreciation of their team's efforts, the leader keeps the members motivated and moving forward

Confidence and composure: A leader who is able to remain calm and cool and never lose sight of the goal, even in crisis situations, lends a sense of stability to their team. The leader's self-assurance helps to maintain morale and inspires others to feel confident too

Strength and optimism: A positive attitude helps to keep the team feeling energized and provides a sense of security and reassurance when times are uncertain

Ability to analyze: An ability to envision not only the overall goal but the smaller, manageable steps necessary to achieve it helps a leader to organize their team's efforts and lets the members experience plenty of "wins" along the way

Commitment: Dedication to achieving the goal and a willingness to work hard alongside the others earns the team's respect and influences them to adopt the same commitment and hardworking attitude

Communication skill: Frequent communication, clearly and concisely provided, encourages regular exchanges between a leader and their team and ensures everyone understands the vision and goals

Ability to delegate: A willingness to trust that others can do the work and an ability to identify team members' strengths and make the most of them helps to spread out the workload and allows everyone to share a sense of accomplishment

Sense of humor: Being able to laugh, even when guiding the team through difficult times, helps to maintain morale and keeps productivity high

All of these qualities can be learned, developed and strengthened. It just takes time and diligence to put them into practice.

Key Characteristics of Good Leaders
- Honesty and integrity
- Enthusiasm
- Confidence and composure
- Strength and optimism
- Ability to analyze
- Commitment
- Communication skill
- Ability to delegate
- Sense of humor

Everyone Benefits from Leadership

With good leadership, a company will reap the benefits of high morale, good staff retention, and long-term success. On the other hand, the effects of poor leadership—or no leadership at all—can be disastrous[7]. It can erode a company's productivity and have a ruinous effect over time.

A team takes its cue from the leader. If a leader is irresponsible or ineffective, the team members are less motivated to put in anything more than a minimal effort. If the leader makes bad decisions that affect the company's bottom line, morale suffers and employees worry about losing their jobs. Staff who have better options elsewhere are likely to leave rather than be dragged down by their employer's bad reputation.

A complete lack of leadership is no improvement over poor leadership. With no one at the helm, the team is left without direction or focus. There is no one available to organize, motivate and, well, *lead* the way forward.

Communicating Your Vision

"People I work with are open to leadership that has a vision, but this vision has to be communicated clearly and persuasively, and always, always with passion."

– ANITA RODDICK

The Vision of Nelson Mandela

One of the greatest visionary leaders of our era was Nelson Mandela. Arrested several times and eventually sentenced to life imprisonment, Mandela spent nearly 30 years in prison. Throughout that time, Mandela held tight to his vision[8] of a democratic, racially just South Africa in which all citizens would have equal rights and every adult would have the right to vote.

Upon his release from prison Mandela continued to pursue his vision, driven by an unwavering belief in equality for all. His determination to reconcile the races and free his country of apartheid, South Africa's system of officially sanctioned racial segregation, won him the admiration of people all over the world. He became an international symbol of equality, freedom, and justice, inspiring people to forgive, to be tolerant, and to put other's needs ahead of their own welfare.

In time, Mandela's resolve began to have an effect. In 1993, apartheid was abolished in South Africa. The following year, multiracial elections were established. Mandela was elected president, becoming his country's first black head of state and the first to be elected in a fully representative democratic election.

Clearly, Mandela's vision was one that evoked a strong emotional response within his own country and with supporters around the world. He possessed the courage and commitment to maintain his vision through many years of violence, strife, and great personal cost. His dignity, charisma, and self-sacrifice struck a chord with many. Perhaps most important, he had the ability to clearly and passionately communicate his vision to a wider audience, rallying national and global opinion in support of his cause and ultimately making his vision a reality.

Not everyone sets out to change the world. Your own "vision" may be a goal or direction for your team, a corporate mission or a purpose to accomplish. But every leader, regardless of their objective, must be able to convey their vision clearly and convincingly in order to motivate and inspire people to take action. Otherwise your vision will never make it beyond the dream stage.

Growing Leaders, a nonprofit that fosters the development of young leaders, suggests the following sequences of steps for developing and communicating your vision successfully.

> *"Leadership is the capacity to translate vision into reality."*
>
> – WARREN BENNIS

Establishing the Vision

A vision is not something you just dream up one day. It takes a careful process that ensures the vision will satisfy everyone's needs and will actually work. An effective process is illustrated in the following graphic. A good way to remember the process is to remember the four "ex"s:

Establish the Vision

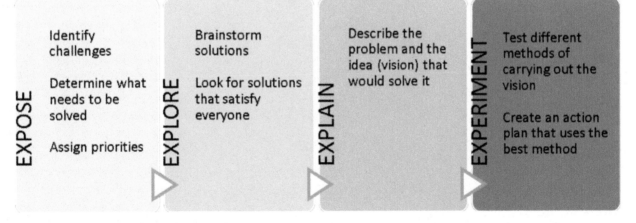

EXPOSE
Identify challenges

Determine what needs to be solved

Assign priorities

EXPLORE
Brainstorm solutions

Look for solutions that satisfy everyone

EXPLAIN
Describe the problem and the idea (vision) that would solve it

EXPERIMENT
Test different methods of carrying out the vision

Create an action plan that uses the best method

Once your vision is established, the absolute worst thing you can do is try to bully people into submitting to it. The VOTE sequence is a positive approach to attracting support for your idea. By delivering your vision in a logical, memorable way, you can persuade others to want to adopt it.

Get the V.O.T.E.

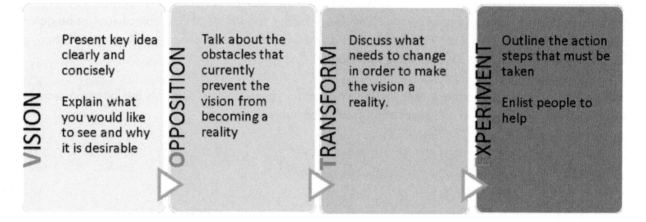

VISION
Present key idea clearly and concisely

Explain what you would like to see and why it is desirable

OPPOSITION
Talk about the obstacles that currently prevent the vision from becoming a reality

TRANSFORM
Discuss what needs to change in order to make the vision a reality.

EXPERIMENT
Outline the action steps that must be taken

Enlist people to help

As the leader, you should always be championing your vision. People around you will pick up on your enthusiasm for the idea and will look to you when they need direction or inspiration to do their part.

"You don't lead by pointing and telling people some place to go.
You lead by going to that place and making a case."

– KEN KESEY

YOUR PROJECT VISION

Think of a project you might *like* to do, even if you don't have time right now. Choose a project that requires vision and leading others. For example, you could organize a fund raiser, build or renovate a clubhouse for your club or sports team, start a business, organize a rally for a cause or policy change, or run in an election (student, civic or other). This is hypothetical—it doesn't have to be something you actually do.

Go through the questions below and provide a brief answer to each after giving each some thought. It should help to read through all the questions first, then begin to answer them one at a time.

Each of the questions and answers relates to an aspect of developing and communicating a vision. Keep these points in mind when you decide to carry out your vision, whether it is the one you chose here or another.

1. Using clear, concise, and dynamic language, what is your vision?

2. How does your vision fit with the goals of everyone involved?

3. What are some obstacles you may encounter and how might you deal with them?

4. What is the first step for making your vision happen?

Creating Positive Group Dynamics

The term "group dynamics" refers to how the people in a small group interact with each other. Each person's behavior influences the group and determines whether its dynamic is positive or negative.

Groups with a positive dynamic tend to be highly efficient. The members of the team communicate well, understand and respect each other, and have the ability to work together to mutually agree on the best decisions. In a group with a negative dynamic, the members' behavior and reactions clash. This interferes with their ability to work cooperatively, accomplish goals and make good decisions. Sometimes it prevents the group from agreeing on anything at all.

"Outstanding leaders go out of their way to boost the self-esteem of their personnel. If people believe in themselves, it's amazing what they can accomplish."

– SAM WALTON

According to theorist Bruce Tuckman, there are five stages[9] a group must go through in order to grow, face up to challenges, tackle problems, find solutions, plan work and deliver results. Here's a look at the stages Tuckman has identified and some ways in which you, as leader, can help your group successfully navigate them.

Forming

Forming takes place at the beginning, when the group is first established. Eager to be accepted and to avoid conflict, members tend to be courteous as they become acquainted with each other and start thinking about how to approach the task ahead.

5 Stages of Group Dynamics
- Forming
- Storming
- Norming
- Performing
- Adjourning

A good leader will exchange some personal information, get to know each person as an individual, get a sense of their strengths and challenges and see how they respond to pressure. You can use this information to assign roles and responsibilities that are best-suited to the individual and of greatest value to the team.

Storming

Storming happens when people's attitudes and behaviors start to clash. In any group, inevitably, differences will surface. Tension builds as members challenge others' ideas, question your leadership or struggle with what has been asked of them. Louder, more forceful personalities may intimidate or drown out others in the group. Some teams never develop beyond this stage.

A good leader will stress tolerance, defuse aggressive behavior, and encourage the members to respect everyone's views and opinions. Make sure all voices are heard and everyone gets an opportunity to participate. If people aren't clear on their responsibilities, you must clarify it for them.

Norming

Norming comes about as the tension softens, understanding grows, and the group begins to coalesce around a common goal. At this point members are more cooperative, sometimes giving up their ideas and agreeing with others in support of the group and its purpose.

A good leader will encourage the continued atmosphere of goodwill. It's essential to ensure that people aren't just agreeing for the sake of avoiding conflict. A commitment to making the best decisions in achieving the team's goal should remain of utmost importance.

Performing

Performing is a phase in which the group is working together smoothly and efficiently as a highly functional team. Motivated and capable, the members are able to make their own decisions and work toward the team's goal independently. Some, but not all, teams manage to reach the performing stage.

A good leader will step back from the need to direct the group's processes and focus more on helping each individual develop and apply their knowledge.

Adjourning

Adjourning is the final stage. The goal has been accomplished and the team is disbanded.

A good leader will reflect on the overall results of the group, individual strengths and challenges that have been revealed, and lessons that can be applied to future tasks. Don't forget to thank your team for their hard work and congratulate them on everything they have accomplished!

Watch the video about leadership at Link 6-10. Pay close attention to the stories told in the video as we will ask you to connect elements of those stories to the five stages of group dynamics and the recommendations for good leadership.

GROUP DYNAMICS AND GOOD LEADERSHIP

Describe **three examples** from the video that represent different stages of group dynamics or what a good leader does in one of those stages.

How to Be a College Leader

"Leadership and learning are indispensable to each other."

– JOHN F. KENNEDY

By now, you should be sold on the benefits of leadership! But how can you get started? In college there are many outlets in which to gain leadership experience, from teams, clubs, and political organizations to volunteering, tutoring, work experience, and school publications. Any opportunity you can take to get involved will be beneficial.

The website Let's Grow Leaders, at Link 6-11, describes nine ways to develop your leadership skills while in college.

Nine Ways to Develop Leadership Skills

Work hard

Leadership doesn't come naturally. Be prepared to work hard.

Take risks

Look for opportunities to do things that take you out of your comfort zone.

Think, write and speak better

Take classes that challenge you to organize and articulate your point of view. Consider an improv or other theater class. Get comfortable in front of people. If you hate public speaking, keep taking classes until you don't.

Learn who you are

Learn from all of your experiences, regardless of how things turned out. Keep reflecting on and refining your values.

Find mentors

Talk to professors, people in the community and experts in specific areas of interest -- who you look up to and ask them to mentor you. Volunteer and serve on their teams to watch, observe and learn.

Solve problems

Find something you're passionate about, gather a group and work together to solve the problem.

Expand learning

Take every opportunity to learn more than your degree requires. Attend free lectures. Take courses unrelated to your major. Talk to others about what they are learning.

Volunteer

Expand your horizons beyond the confines of the campus. Get involved with volunteer groups and spend time in the community.

Build a network

Get to know a wide range of people from all walks of life. Find your niche, but don't limit yourself.

©Alena Hovorkova/Shutterstock.com

DEVELOPING LEADERSHIP SKILLS

We have described how to develop your leadership skills, but you may still wonder what opportunities exist to actually *practice* those skills. Read through the list of college leadership opportunities in Link 6-12. Identify two opportunities that you would take part in. Feel free to also choose leadership opportunities outside of those mentioned on this list.

Each opportunity you choose should help you with some of the nine ways you can develop leadership skills. For each opportunity, identify the two ways that the opportunity will help you most.

Opportunity No. 1

Opportunity No. 1 will help me with

Opportunity No. 1 will also help me with

Opportunity No. 2

Opportunity No. 2 will help with

Opportunity No. 2 will also help me with

CHAPTER 6 QUIZ

Communication, Collaboration, and Leadership

This quiz covers all of the topics from this chapter on communication, collaboration, and leadership. Before you answer any questions, scan them and return to review any pages you need to be confident in your answers.

1 The more detail I provide in an email, the better my message will be understood:
   a. True
   b. False

2 The acronym SV COACH stands for:
   a. Skills, Variety, Choice, Over, Abilities, Complete, Help
   b. Skills, Voice, Clarity, Over, Audience, Comfort, Help
   c. Story, Voice, Clarity, Own, Audience, Comfort, Humor
   d. Simple, Value, Choice, Options, Advantage, Comfort, Help

3 Effective communication consists of about:
   a. 80% talking and 20% listening
   b. 50% talking and 50% listening
   c. 80% listening and 20% talking
   d. 80% face-to-face and 20% nonverbal

4 Which of the following is NOT a direct benefit of working cooperatively?
   a. Improved problem solving ability
   b. Higher wages
   c. Improved relationships
   d. Greater sense of purpose

5 An effective collaborator does all the following EXCEPT:
   a. Remains open to new ideas
   b. Admits to mistakes
   c. Shares the credit
   d. Lets others do a lot of the work

6 When team conflict is brewing, it's important to:
   a. Defend your ideas more strongly
   b. Meet again after some time to calm down
   c. Ban the difficult people from team meetings
   d. Call the troublemakers aside and give them an ultimatum

7 Leadership experience can help you do all the following EXCEPT:
   a. Make your work easier
   b. Make you a better negotiator
   c. Teach you to manage a budget
   d. Earn you a higher income

8 In the Norming stage:
   a. People become more cooperative
   b. People challenge each other's ideas
   c. People are just getting to know each other
   d. People are able to make their own decisions

9 Which is NOT a good way to communicate your vision to a team?
   a. Demonstrate how it would make a difference to people
   b. Provide reasons to explain why it's the right thing to do
   c. Find ways to align your vision with the needs and interests of others
   d. Present a detailed plan showing how it can be accomplished

10 Group dynamics describes:
    a. The action steps required to make your plan a reality
    b. How the people in a group interact with each other
    c. A sequence of steps for developing your vision
    d. How to become a better team player

COMMUNICATION, COLLABORATION AND LEADERSHIP

This is a quick survey to measure what you know about this chapter topic, both before and after completing the chapter. Just be honest and rate how much each of the following statements applies to you. Give yourself a score of:

1 for Not a bit • 2 for A little • 3 for Some • 4 for Mostly • 5 for Definitely

AFTER CHAPTER

		Not a bit 1	A little 2	Some 3	Mostly 4	Definitely 5
1	I know what emotional intelligence is and how it relates to communication.	○	○	○	○	○
2	I can explain the benefits of good communication skills.	○	○	○	○	○
3	I know how to speak with confidence in front of other people.	○	○	○	○	○
4	I know how to be an active listener.	○	○	○	○	○
5	I know how to read and use nonverbal cues effectively.	○	○	○	○	○
6	I know how to select the best form of media to communicate a message.	○	○	○	○	○

7	I can describe several benefits of effective collaboration.	○	○	○	○	○
8	I can select the best tools for collaborative tasks.	○	○	○	○	○
9	I can describe several characteristics of an effective collaborator.	○	○	○	○	○
10	I can list the warning signs that a conflict is developing.	○	○	○	○	○
11	I know effective strategies for remaining calm and resolving conflict within my team.	○	○	○	○	○
12	I can explain why leadership experience is valuable.	○	○	○	○	○
13	I can list the characteristics of good leadership.	○	○	○	○	○
14	I know how to persuade others to support my vision.	○	○	○	○	○
15	I can name the five development stages of group dynamics.	○	○	○	○	○
16	I can describe several leadership opportunities available to me in college.	○	○	○	○	○

Add up your scores to determine your **After Chapter** total and write it down here:

Write your **Before Chapter** total here:

Compare your Before and After scores to see how your knowledge of this chapter topic has changed.

CHAPTER SUMMARY

In this chapter, we talked about the benefits of effective communication, collaboration, and leadership. We identified a variety of media and methods for communicating, cooperating with, and leading others. We also determined how to select the best approach in a variety of circumstances, and learned strategies for avoiding and resolving potential conflict situations.

Among the key ideas to take away from this chapter:

- Meaningful communication requires the use of your eyes, ears, mouth and brain
- Empathy and an open mind are two of your greatest assets when relating to and leading others
- Opportunities for leadership experience are readily available and can serve you well, now and in the future

We also discussed the connection between emotional intelligence and your intrapersonal and interpersonal intelligences and showed you how developing these aspects can lead to better communication, more effective teamwork, and greater opportunities for influencing people in a positive way.

We hope you found the chapter interesting and feel that you can use some of the knowledge to help you in school, your career, and your personal life. Before you continue, make sure you have completed all the activities and journals in this chapter.

CHAPTER 6 FEEDBACK

Congratulations, you've completed Chapter 6! To conclude your learning in this chapter, consider and note the following:

What parts of this chapter were most helpful to you?

How would you improve this chapter?

CAREER READINESS: FINDING MY FIT

CAREER READINESS

This is a quick survey to measure what you know about this chapter topic. Just be honest and rate how much each of the following statements applies to you. Give yourself a score of:

1 for Not a bit • 2 for A little • 3 for Some • 4 for Mostly • 5 for Definitely

BEFORE CHAPTER

		Not a bit 1	A little 2	Some 3	Mostly 4	Definitely 5
1	I can describe what the value of failure or the "near win" is.	O	O	O	O	O
2	I can state three personal and three community benefits of work.	O	O	O	O	O
3	I can name five different types of experiences through which I can gain valuable work skills and expertise.	O	O	O	O	O
4	I know the difference between a fellowship, an internship, and a shadow program.	O	O	O	O	O
5	I can describe several strategies to use when searching for a work-experience program.	O	O	O	O	O
6	I can name three things that would help me make the most of a work experience program.	O	O	O	O	O
7	I have done some research on what to expect in a typical workplace.	O	O	O	O	O

©arka38/Shutterstock.com

8	I can name three rights and three responsibilities of employees.	○	○	○	○	○
9	I can name three rights and three responsibilities of employers.	○	○	○	○	○
10	I know where to look to determine exactly what violates work discrimination laws.	○	○	○	○	○
11	I know how to use Twitter, Facebook, and LinkedIn to advance my career.	○	○	○	○	○
12	I can clearly tell someone in 30 seconds or less what my brand and career goals are.	○	○	○	○	○
13	I have done a web search of my name and know how my online presence appears to others.	○	○	○	○	○
14	I have recently updated my resumé or have specific plans to do so.	○	○	○	○	○
15	I have up-to-date online profiles that will help advance my career.	○	○	○	○	○
16	I have a prepared elevator pitch that will help get me a job.	○	○	○	○	○

Add up your scores to determine your **Before Chapter** total and write it down here:

Key Questions

1. Motivation Check: How do I deal with failure on my career path?

2. What opportunities, besides school, can best prepare me for my career?

3. What can I expect in different workplaces and what environments work best for me?

4. How can I use technology to maximize my career potential?

5. What are the best practices for the job application process?

©Rawpixel.com/Shutterstock.com

CHAPTER PREVIEW

In this chapter we go beyond just knowing how to explore career options.

The first section will outline strategies to help you seek out and succeed in experiences such as internships, mentoring and volunteering. Experiences like these are invaluable in building your potential to be hired or blaze your own trail as an entrepreneur.

The second section describes the expectations of different workplaces so you can be ready to meet or even exceed those expectations and thrive at work.

In the final two sections, we look at how to use technology to promote yourself and how to use technology and other resources to apply for work.

MOTIVATION CHECK

How do I deal with failure on my career path?

One of the central themes in CollegeScope is the idea that life is just as much about the journey as it is about the destination. We saw this with intrinsic motivation (the journey) and extrinsic motivation (a destination). We also saw it in the Steve Jobs speech urging you to pursue your passions now—that you'll be able to "connect the dots" when you look back later. We're bringing up this theme once more, but in a slightly different way.

Soon after college, many people experience what they believe is a lot of failure. It may be failure to find work, failure to afford the things that they could afford before, or failure to accomplish certain life goals they had created for themselves. Instead of labeling these things as "failures," there may be a lot more value in labeling them as "near wins." And, instead of aiming for the sometimes elusive idea of "success," we should be aiming for "mastery." Watch the video at Link 7-1 to better understand what we mean.

THE NEAR WIN

Think about the message of the video as it applies to your career over your lifetime. The journal questions below provide some guidance as to how you can think about it.

1. According to the video, what are the benefits of the "near win"?

2. When you are applying for jobs, what would be a near win and what could you learn from it?

3. If you are seeking career advancement in your chosen field, what do you think seeking "mastery" looks like? Be specific to a career area that you have planned or are considering.

SECTION 7-1: WORK EXPERIENCE OPPORTUNITIES

Learning Objectives

- Understand the value of work-based experience
- Understand the similarities and differences between work-based experiences such as internships, shadowing and volunteering
- Know how to find and access work-based experiences that will provide the most benefit

Introduction

You've probably heard people joke about interns being a lot like "gophers"—they're the ones who "go for" the coffee, make the copies, do the grunt work, and so on. So many people have participated in internship that there is a sense of shared experience and interest in the topic—enough so that a movie was created with that title, The Internship.[1] You may also be familiar with TV shows such as The Office or The Apprentice, which address workplace or work experience topics. However, comedies and reality TV shows are not the best ways to understand work experiences.

Despite the negative depictions of internships and other work experiences, there are many benefits and even enjoyment to be had from those experiences.

PREVIOUS EXPERIENCE

Think about a life, work or volunteer experience in which you've learned a lot—maybe it was a babysitting job, a service project, or a part-time position. What did you learn from diving in and being "on the job"?

"Tell me and I may forget, teach me and I may remember,
involve me and I learn."

–BEN FRANKLIN

Work-based Experiences

There may be a variety of types of experiences that you will seek out to prepare you for your career path –- this may include volunteering, military service, internships, or a multitude of other experiences. Regardless of the type of experiences, the Ben Franklin quote above sums it up well.

There's nothing that teaches quite like getting involved. Before you do, however, it is important to know the benefits of being involved so you can realize those benefits. For instance, it is important to understand that work is not just to earn money or status. When you consider the other benefits of work, you will make the most of your opportunities. Here's a look at some examples.

Personal Benefits

- develop knowledge and skills not learned in school
- build credentials and experience
- earn income (sometimes)
- form relationships and a network of contacts
- learn firsthand what type of work suits you

Community Benefits

- produce engaged and happy citizens
- produce goods and services
- encourage a sense of responsibility
- provide a tax base for public programs and infrastructure
- create a sense of community

Types of Work Experience

We will describe a few types of work experience. There may be others that aren't listed here.[1,2] The type that you seek should depend on you and your career goals. Be sure to visit your college career center and your academic advisor to learn about all your options.

Internships

Internships provide an opportunity for you to reinforce academic and career objectives and personal values related to work, identify the skills you need to enter a given field, gain practical work experience to balance classroom training, and get an edge in a competitive job market over individuals with no relevant work experience.

Alison Greene, in *U.S. News and World Report*, describes it the following way.[3]

> "Internships have become a must for college students. Without the work experience they provide, the post-graduation job search is significantly more difficult."

Visit Link 7-2 for some tips on how to get the most out of your internship. Read through the advice and remember any tips you can use if and when you take part in an internship.

You also might want to check out Link 7-3 to search for internship opportunities in your area.

Apprenticeships

A Registered Apprenticeship program is a great way to train for a career. You can earn a paycheck and get hands-on experience while building up your skills. Check out Link 7-4 to view careers that offer apprenticeships. You can even search for apprenticeship opportunities in your state.

Co-ops (cooperative education)

Very much like internships, co-ops are usually paid, highly structured in nature, and directly related to your course of study. Typically, you must be enrolled in a cooperative education program at a college or university to participate. Many community colleges and state universities offer this type of experience.

Externships or Shadow Programs

These types of experiences allow you to spend anywhere from a day to several weeks observing a professional on the job. You'll gain an overview of a specific career field, and a perspective on the activities of a particular professional.

Volunteer/Community Service/Service Learning

Generally, unpaid work or service opportunities are common in the human service or non-profit sector. If you are interested in non-profit experience during the summer and cannot afford to participate in an unpaid internship, note that some schools offer grants to help subsidize an unpaid service-based internship. In addition, many schools offer service-learning classes that feature a service project as a course requirement.

Your school and community likely have local volunteering opportunities. You can usually just type "volunteer" and the name of your city or state into a search engine and find many opportunities. The site at Link 7-5 allows you to search nationally, but filter your results by location, interests and government agency.

Fellowships/Research

Fellowship or research opportunities allow you to receive income and do work in a particular area such as public policy, science, the arts, or education. Fellowships tend to be sponsored by specific organizations or agencies. Your school may sponsor undergraduate summer fellowships.

Finding Work Experiences

Here are some tips to help you get started.

1 Know what you want before you start searching

Think about the following questions to help guide your search:

- What type of internship or experience are you looking to acquire?
- What skills would you most like to develop?
- What type of organization and work environment would fit your interests and values?
- What qualities do you look for in an ideal supervisor?

©unpict/Shutterstock.com

2 Start your search early and get help

This is especially true if you want an internship with a large company. Many companies hire summer interns in September and October—eight months before the actual start date. Smaller companies post summer positions in January and February. Strategies for finding a good internship vary by field; to get insider tips for your industry, call and schedule an appointment with your career counselor.

The process of looking for an internship is not much different from looking for career positions. The three basic approaches are:

- **Apply**

  This consists of applying for established opportunities (things advertised in databases, on websites, in publications, etc.). Your school may have a job/internship database that contains thousands of opportunities. Ask at your campus career center. Or, you may have to look within a specific department, such as engineering or computer sciences. You can also enter "internship" in the search tool for your school's website. Some schools in a region combine to create a consortium of intern opportunities. There are also websites such as LinkedIn, Internships.com, and job sites like Monster.com.

- **Network**

  This is the process of utilizing contacts to learn about possible unadvertised positions. Think of some of the people you've contacted for the "Talk to Someone" sections and go for it!

- **Seek**

  In this approach, you send out unsolicited emails with resumés and cover letters to organizations for whom you'd like to intern. It might feel like "cold calling" but if there are certain companies or organizations you are especially interested in, go for it!

- **Ask Before You Accept!**

  Once you land an opportunity, be sure to *respectfully* ask three (or more!) critical questions before accepting an internship experience.

  - What type of training is provided for interns?
  - Who will supervise me and how would you describe his or her supervisory style?
  - Can you give me specific examples of the types of projects that I would work on and what types of skills I would develop through these projects?

While keeping in mind the tips above, remember that some of the best resources for finding opportunities are usually right on campus.

Your school may have jobs and other work experience opportunities available on and around the campus. You can also search for jobs on websites like the one at Link 7-6.

More Ways to Find Work Experience

CareerOneStop, at Link 7-7, is another great website for finding training programs.

Things You Can Do on CareerOneStop
- Find apprenticeship programs
- Learn certification requirements for different jobs
- Find other short-term training programs

CareerOneStop is a massive site that can help in many more areas than we have mentioned. We just focused in on a few that are relevant to this section. Feel free to browse around when you have the time.

During Your Work Experience

Below is a list of all the tips from a *Huffington Post* article.[4] Some of the tips restate the same basic idea. Use your critical thinking to identify three basic ideas or themes that are repeated in the tips. Record those ideas in the journal activity below the list.

1. **Check your ego.** No matter what you have been or done before, you are an intern in *this* situation.

2. **Fake it 'til you make it.** If you don't know how to do something, learn it as you go. Just don't tell people you know how to do things you don't. Be honest and tell them you will figure it out. People respect a "can do" attitude.

3. **Trust yourself.** Just because you are an intern, doesn't mean you can't have great ideas.

4. **Tell them what you are capable of.** People may assume interns don't know much, be sure to make them aware (without bragging) of what you can do.

5. **Be on time or early every day.** When and how you show up for work is like a first impression every day. No matter what your reason, it is pretty hard to overcome the bad impression of being late. Take every precaution possible to avoid being late.

6. **Do what you do with an enthusiastic attitude.** Attitude gets noticed. Even if a task feels mind-numbing, do it with a smile. Better yet, find a way to *make* it enjoyable.

7. **Put the phone away.** If your phone is pinging or you are checking it every 10 minutes—or even worse, checking it while someone is speaking to you or when you're in a meeting—you are basically saying, "I have more important things to do than this internship."

8. **Know your workplace policies.** If you are constantly asking others about things that are already documented somewhere, it will look like you didn't do your homework. Check with someone in HR if there is a handbook or website where you can read up on workplace policies and any other information that can help you know your way around the workplace.

9. **Don't rely on others to develop basic office skills.** If you don't know how to do something in Word or Excel, you can always Google it or use the "Help" function. This applies to other applications as well. Save your questions for topics that aren't easily answered by a web search.

10. **Be proactive.** If, at any time, you aren't busy with a directly assigned project, ask how you can help. Or, even better, offer to help with a specific task that you know you can do well, learn from, and use to make a lasting impression.

11. **Meet anyone and everyone.** Here is your chance to form a network of contacts that can help you get a real job, even if it is not where you are doing your work experience. Find ways to connect with people outside your department, over coffee for example. Just don't let your networking take priority over your assigned work.

12 **Focus on learning the position.** While you will learn other skills as a side-effect of your work experience, be sure to stay focused on what you were originally brought on to do. In the end, that is mainly what you will be judged on.

13 **We learn more by listening than by speaking.** You may be excited and have some great new ideas, but remember that there is a lot of experience around you. Your role as an intern is to learn and develop. Your ideas will still be around after your internship and by then, probably even better.

14 **Be grateful and appreciative.** Not only will this make you happier and enjoy the experience more, but it will also make others more likely to help you and teach you new skills.

15 **Remember that you were hired because of your potential, not your knowledge base.** While it is important you contribute when asked and in ways that gain respect from your new contacts, your primary purpose is to learn and improve. Throughout your work experience it is a good idea to journal what you learn.

16 **Speak up.** While humility and listening are important, you should also speak up when opportunities arise. It is better to be remembered as the person who, when asked, always had an idea rather than the one who never had ideas.

17 **If they don't give you work, make work.** Sometimes workplaces forget they have interns. But if you take the initiative to remain productive and find ways to contribute, it will be noticed.

18 **Never say you don't have a pencil or notebook.** It is bound to happen: you will be asked to take notes or write something down. If you have to run to your desk or fish something out of your bag, you will look unprepared.

19 **Remember that everything you do all pays off in the long run.** Sometimes it is the small things that count. Being friendly, saying hello, making copies, fetching coffee, suggesting ideas and answering phones all contribute to how people remember you. You can either be remembered as "that intern who did intern stuff," or you can be remembered as someone who was ambitious, a team player, and did a lot of things really well.

20 **Don't be afraid to reach out to people whose work you admire.** If you admire someone, it is probably because he or she is in a position that you would like to be in and has talents you would like to have. One of the best ways to achieve those things yourself is to have a mentor.

21 **Act as if you are part of the team.** While your role may be different from an actual employee's, you are still a member of the team. Don't isolate yourself or focus solely on your personal goals. If you contribute to the overall goals of the group, you will be seen as an important part of the team and possibly be asked to stick around once your work experience is done.

22   Be yourself, but... don't push the boundaries of the current culture too much. You're an intern, not the CEO hired to rock the boat. You might know things that more established employees don't know, such as new technologies. That said, don't be conceited. Even if you know how the latest social media tool works, your more established co-workers have the wisdom that comes with having experienced a lot more in the industry. You don't want to lose their respect by acting like a know-it-all.

23   It's not only acceptable to ask questions, it's expected. Not only are questions a great way to learn the knowledge and skills you are trying to develop, they can make you look interested and eager. Try to ask intelligent questions. It might be a good idea to do a little research on your question before you ask it. Then you can frame your question with what you learned already, impressing others with the fact that you have "done your homework."

24   Make a case for a job at the end. Remember the earlier tip about journaling what you learn and the contributions you've made during your work experience? If you can write up a brief report of your experience using those notes, your supervisor will be impressed. Also, you will have an ideal addition to your resumé that should impress future employers.

©Alena Hovorkova/Shutterstock.com

MAKE THE MOST OF YOUR WORK EXPERIENCE

From the list of tips, identify three main ideas or themes for being successful in your work experience. Record the three themes in the space below, then check your response.

Your response may differ in the wording slightly, but you should have something similar to these themes:

- show humility
- take initiative
- communicate and connect to people
- be professional
- be ready to learn

Earn Credit While Gaining Skills

While developing skills and advancing your career options, you also may be able to earn credit for certain career or life experiences. Many colleges offer credit for internships or other work experience programs. Participating in a military training program, a corporate training program, or seeking a professional license (for instance, FAA pilot or respiratory therapy technician) can count toward a college degree or certificate.[4] The American Council on Education (Link 7-8) provides tips on how to earn credit while also gaining experience and offers a free National Guide to College Credit for Workforce Training.

Make sure you find out if any work you have done or will be doing can count toward your diploma.

SECTION 7-2: WORKPLACE EXPECTATIONS

Learning Objectives

- Understand some general dos and don'ts regarding workplace expectations
- Gain awareness of employment laws, rights, and responsibilities

Workplace Expectations

No workplace is exactly the same as another. Workplaces are as varied as the people who work in them. The environment and expectations in any given workplace will depend greatly upon the leadership, the industry, the location, the culture, the job expectation, and much more. As a simple example, the physical workplace of a miner would be very different from that of a dentist. The culture, norms and expectations will vary as well.

©Rawpixel.com/Shutterstock.com

Differences aside, there are certain things that are common from place to place—such as employee rights and responsibilities. In this section, we seek to help you understand what your rights include and what they do *not* include.

RIGHTS IN THE WORKPLACE

Think about the following quotation:

"My right to swing my arm ends at the tip of your nose."

The quotation obviously refers to a right, but it also hints at a *responsibility*. It is the responsibility of knowing where your rights end and where someone else's rights begin.

Rights and responsibilities tend to be more clear for physical boundaries such as our body and our property. What about the right to free speech?

Do you think the boundaries for free speech are as clear? Explain.

What can people and organizations do to define boundaries and ensure that rights and responsibilities are clear to everyone?

This particular section is guided by the following:

- What to expect, and what not to expect or do, in the workplace
- My rights and responsibilities as an employee (the worker)
- The rights and responsibilities of my employer (the entity that hires you)
- Adapting—we've talked about that in other lessons

While some of the topics here should be taken seriously, especially the ones about rights and responsibilities, let's start with a humorous look at some basic workplace expectations and how one fictional office environment dealt with people who didn't meet certain expectations.

The video at Link 7-9, while fiction, does reveal some reasonable expectations for the employees of a company. What about expectations for the employer? Take a look at the video at Link 7-10 to see what one well-known company provides as an employer.

Now that you have seen some extreme, and perhaps entertaining, examples of workplace expectations, let's look at a very realistic example. While expectations will vary in different workplaces, the following list includes some very common expectations that apply to just about every workplace.

Sample Workplace Expectations[1]

- **Get to work on time.**
  You've been hired to do a job, and as the one who pays your wages, your employer has a right to expect you to show up on time. If you're going to be delayed, contact your manager in advance to let them know.
- **No skiving off.**
  Sometimes there are good reasons to miss work. But a reason that seems good enough to you may not wash with your employer, and frequent absences could jeopardize your job. So if you need to be away from work, it's important that you discuss it first with your manager.
- **When you're at work, do your job.**
  If you have personal calls to make or other private business to attend to, do it on your own time. When you're at work, your focus should be on performing your professional duties.
- **Wear suitable attire.**
  While many workplaces employ a "smart casual" dress code, some may require more formal clothing while others may have an "anything goes" approach. Look around. How do your colleagues dress, especially those who work in similar positions to yours? If you're unsure, talk to your manager about the company's dress code.
- **Mind your manners.**
  Never forget that, when at work, you are acting on behalf of your employer. It's important that you conduct yourself in a calm, professional manner, even if you're dealing with difficult situations or people who push your patience to the limits. For advice on remaining composed in challenging circumstances, check out the article at Link 7-11.

- **Take pride in your work and do it to the best of your ability.**
  Whether you're washing dishes in a restaurant or running a Fortune 500 company, the quality of your work will reflect on you. By taking pride in what you do and doing it well, you'll make a better impression, potentially improve your chances of promotion and gain greater satisfaction from doing your job.
- **Don't let problems fester.**
  If something is bothering you at work, don't leave it unresolved: deal with it as soon as possible. If the issue is with a colleague, start by trying to talk it over with them. They may not realize there's a problem, and may appreciate the opportunity to discuss it with you and help to reach a resolution. If necessary, take the issue to someone higher up.
- **Respect your employer's need for discretion.**
  You may not even be aware of it, but you may have access to information that is not generally available as a result of being in your job. Typically this would be sensitive material relating to your employer or their customers, and sharing it could have serious consequences for both your employer and you. Be aware that spilling such details could cost you your job—or worse. In many situations, employees have faced criminal charges for disclosing information that should have remained private.

While the recommendations above may seem obvious, everybody is human, can forget where they are and break from their professional selves. For example, people sometimes mix up personal rights with employee rights. It is your *personal* right to speak poorly in public about a company and its practices—as long as it isn't defamatory (see Link 7-12 for a definition if you don't know what this means). However, it is NOT an employee right. If you work for that company, you can legally be fired for speaking poorly about the company or its employees.

It is important to understand the difference between personal and employee rights. Generally, workplace expectations can provide a guide as to where your employee rights end and your responsibilities begin.

Employment Law

Employment law, or labor laws, are designed to mediate the relationship between workers (employees), employers, trade unions and the government. Government agencies enforce these laws. In the United States, employment law is the responsibility of the Department of Labor (DOL). The DOL maintains a website with a summary of the major laws regarding employment. The site includes information about compensation, whistleblower protection, veterans' rights and training, family and medical leave, plant closings and layoffs, and workplace health and safety guidelines. You can find it at Link 7-13.

There is also the National Labor Relations Board (NLRB) which focuses on the "rights of most private sector employees to join together, with or without a union, to improve their wages and working conditions." The NLRB has a site that summarizes employee rights covered by the National Labor Relations Act. You can read it at Link 7-14.

The U.S. Equal Employment Opportunity Commission (EEOC) enforces federal laws prohibiting employment discrimination. The EEOC has a page that summarizes the rights of employees and job applicants. Check it out at Link 7-15.

Open a browser and scan the three webpages noted above. Look for information that you didn't know before and that is likely to apply to you in the future. You will be asked to summarize that information in the journal activity below.

EMPLOYMENT LAW

Briefly describe two things you learned from the webpages above about employment law or rights.

Rights and Responsibilities of Employers

Just as employees and job applicants need rights to protect their safety and well-being, employers need rights to protect their interests as well. Below are some examples of employer rights. Earlier we stated that rights come with responsibilities. Often an employer right comes with an employee responsibility. As you read each employer's right, think of the employee's responsibility that would come with it. Then go on to read the explanation.

Rights of an Employer

- Set requirements for job positions.
  Employee responsibility: meet all requirements to be considered a candidate for the job
- Set wages and work hours (in accordance with the Fair Labor Standards Act).
  Employee responsibility: accept wages and work assigned hours until changed through negotiation
- Obtain certain information about employee background that could impact role (for example, criminal and academic records).
  Employee responsibility: be truthful about background records as it pertains to request from employer and job role
- Create and enforce contracts for work obligations.
  Employee responsibility: fulfill all the requirements of the work contract
- Set policies and standards of conduct for the workplace and, in some cases, for outside the workplace.
  Employee responsibility: follow policies and standards of conduct wherever and whenever they apply
- Keep trade secrets and certain information private.
  Employee responsibility: maintain confidentiality regarding company products, processes, customers and other proprietary information
- Terminate employment under certain conditions.
- Employee responsibility: accept termination when lawful and required conditions are met

Just as an employer's rights translate into their employees' responsibilities, employees' rights translate into the employer's responsibilities. It is a give-and-take relationship that benefits both parties. Viewing the employer-employee relationship this way is healthy and usually results in a happier and more productive environment.[2]

The idea of rights and responsibilities being bound together is not limited to work environments. It is a basic principle of a cooperative society. You may notice that theme in the chapter on communication, collaboration and leadership. Basing your behavior and interaction with others on a balance of rights and responsibility can help you have a happier and more productive life.

"But we must create in each person a sense of responsibility in order that each one of us can have the right to enjoy all his rights."

–FEDERICA MONTSENY

SECTION 7-3: PROMOTING YOURSELF

Technology is Transparency

One of the major impacts of technology in recent years is the availability of information. Accessibility to personal information, in particular, has increased with social media becoming more and more a part of people's lives. Information that was previously considered private has become publicly available or more "hackable." Take a look at the video at Link 7-16, which hints at just how public our private lives have become.

While the video has a scary message, the good news is that you have control over your online presence and you can use it to promote yourself rather than put yourself at risk. In this section, we want to help you learn what you should and should not do with technology in order to maximize your chances of getting the job you want.

The reality is that recruiters, admissions officers, and employers are checking you out online before deciding to meet you in person.

Your Online Presence Gets Noticed

- 27% of college admissions officers look up students using Google[1]
- 26% of college admissions officers look up students on Facebook[2]
- 93% of employment recruiters check candidates' social media postings[3]
- 1 in 10 people aged 16 to 34 have been rejected for a job because of online comments[4]

POSITIVE ONLINE PRESENCE

The best way to prevent a *negative* online presence is to actively build a *positive* online presence. Briefly describe one or two things you can do to build a positive online presence.

Don't worry if you had a hard time thinking of ways to build a positive online presence. This section will provide you with tips to do exactly that. The following questions indicate how this section is organized:

* What types of media are common to the professional environment?
* How can you maximize your personal brand?
* What are some things you should *avoid* in order to maintain a positive online presence?

In the next section we'll get into more specific details about how to apply for work by creating a professional resumé, online profiles, and an elevator speech.

Media for Your Online Presence

Online media make up a significant force—we saw some a demonstration of this in the 2014 ALS Ice Bucket Challenge (see Link 7-17 for information about this event). Just as the Ice Bucket Challenge used media to advance awareness for its cause, you can use technology and media to advance your career.

Trying to keep up with all the different social media tools can be daunting. New words have to be invented just to describe what these tools do and how they are classified.

We have listed just a few media tools below, but don't feel pressured to use all of them or only them. They are listed in order of importance for helping you get your career started—the first ones are most likely to have the biggest impact. Some career goals may be better served by other, very specific media tools, but these should work for most career areas. It is a good idea to have a presence on more than one tool, and you can usually copy or replicate a lot of what you create across different tools, which will speed up the process. You likely already have at least one profile started in the media listed below—that would be a good place to start.

LinkedIn

LinkedIn (Link 7-18) has 93 million users in the U.S. and 313 million worldwide.[5] While it is not the largest site in terms of users, it is most popular for those focused on career development and networking. LinkedIn can be described as an online resumé and networking tool. LinkedIn allows you to:

- Establish your professional profile complete with experience and skills
- Stay in touch with colleagues and friends
- Find experts, ideas, and opportunities in specific areas of interest

Creation of a profile is free, though certain upgrades and specialized tools require a subscription fee. One of the nice things, if you choose to start with LinkedIn, is that there are plenty of help guides to walk you through the process of creating a LinkedIn profile and resumé, along with launching your career search. One such help guide is the video at Link 7-19. The video is very brief and only scratches the surface in terms of getting you started. Once you begin creating your profile, you will see more in-depth help for taking your profile to the next level.

Twitter

Twitter (Link 7-20) has 284 million active users each month.[6] It can be used for a wide variety of purposes. It can motivate, question, convey thoughts and beliefs, and engage your followers. It is a great tool to learn, and, when you share what you are doing, it can amplify your impact in the professional realm. Be sure to make a good impression (with your handle and profile), determine a few key hashtags (#) you'd like to use and follow, use the retweet function, and don't forget to link to and share videos, podcasts, and photos.

There's a good article at Link 7-21 about using Twitter to enhance your personal brand.

Google+

It is free to create a Google+ (Link 7-22) account, and Google has many tools beyond just the social media piece. Having a Google account allows access to many free tools such as office productivity, email, calendar, online storage, voice and video chat, website authoring, and much more. However, one of the biggest advantages of having a Google+ account is that it helps position you in Google's search engines more favorably. By hosting over two-thirds of all online searches, Google is still the most popular search engine by far.[7]

Add people to your circles to expand your network and your search engine visibility even further. You'll find the getting started page for Google+ at Link 7-23.

Facebook

While many people use Facebook (Link 7-24) socially, and you may be one of them, don't forget that many businesses, non-profits, schools, and foundations are on Facebook. So, be sure to like, follow, and stay connected with organizations and people that are a good fit for you. We will talk more about what to post and not to post later. As a start, imagine your future boss, colleagues and customers seeing your Facebook page. Keep that in mind when you post comments and pictures to Facebook.

Here are four ways to take your social-focused Facebook profile and make it work for your career:

1. **Complete the work and education sections of your profile.**
   Many Facebook users neglect these parts of their profile. There are sections to put your accomplishments and some of your work history—use them.

2. **Group your friends.**
   You have the option in Facebook of creating different friend lists. Create one for "education," "work," or any other label that groups your friends into categories that will help you find certain types of work. Don't forget to have a group with just social contacts. Some of your Facebook contacts may belong to more than one group, and that is fine. Then, when you do updates, you can target a specific group. Pictures of your last vacation can go to just your social contacts, while the update of a training course you just completed can go to your professional contacts.

3. **Post updates that promote you and respond to others.**
   Post updates about your education, job status, extracurricular activities and anything you think a potential employer might see as a positive. Pay special attention to contacts you placed on your professional lists. Reply to their updates and make comments that are relevant and show that you know something about that topic. Don't be a know-it-all, just show enthusiasm for the topic. And, don't forget to be supportive and positive. Think about what type of person you would want to hire and reflect that personality in your posts.

4. **Make new connections.**
   Facebook suggests new connections based on your current connections. Pay attention to these and focus on the ones that seem to be related to your professional plans. You may also find these connections through company profiles and certain group associations in Facebook. Facebook has profiles for just about any group you can think of, from dental hygienists to painters to engineering. You can even connect to a specific organization if your goal is to be hired by that organization or a similar one. When your connections see your interest in a professional area, you are more likely to get noticed and expand your network in that area.

Pinterest (Link 7-25) is a free website where users can upload, sort, and manage images and video in the form of "pins." You can browse other people's pins or pins from websites and choose to "pin it" to save a pin on your "board"—the site where you store your pins. You can have multiple boards to organize your pins. Businesses very often create virtual stores by having boards and pins to reflect what they sell. As of July 2013 Pinterest had 70 million users.[8] Experts say that Pinterest has grown significantly since then.

Using Pinterest to promote your career may not be obvious. You'll find a good article at Link 7-26 to help you understand how.

Job Posting Sites

The sites we named above are focused on being social media sites. That is, they connect people to each other. Job posting sites, on the other hand, focus on connecting people to actual jobs. However, the lines have blurred between the two and many job posting sites allow you to create complete profiles and carry on conversations with others.

Typically, a job posting site is not as robust in terms of being social and allowing you to develop a network of people who can help you get that job. Instead, a job posting site can help you find an actual job. The best approach is to use both. Start with the social media sites to develop your brand and professional presence. Then, sign up for some job posting sites and look for jobs and employers to show off that professional presence you worked so hard to develop.

Most job posting sites allow job seekers to:
- Create an online profile that includes a resumé
- Search job postings that match specific criteria
- Be notified when an employer views or shows interest in your resumé
- Send your resumé and other information to employers who have posted a job

Below is a quick list of some job posting sites. This is not meant to be a complete list, but just a sample of a few sites.
- Glassdoor (Link 7-27)
- CareerBuilder (Link 7-28)
- Monster (Link 7-29)
- Workopolis (Link 7-30)
- Indeed (Link 7-31)

PROMOTING YOURSELF ON SOCIAL MEDIA

Pick one of the media listed above or a different one that you feel can promote your career. It can be a social media tool that you already use or one you have not yet joined. Get started with some of the suggestions above. In the space below, record the tool you used and what you did to help promote your career with that tool.

Your Brand

What is meant by "brand"? Brand is how people perceive something. It is a presence and can be good, bad or a combination of both. It is a marketing professional's job to establish and promote brands for products and services that will motivate people to buy those products and services. A brand may be promoted as clean, edgy, sophisticated, sexy, reliable, safe, valuable or any number of other adjectives.

Nowadays, brand is very much driven by technology. As we learned in the previous pages, people have the means to access information on just about anything at any point in time. Brands now apply to much more than just products and services. All that information we get through technology influences our decisions to buy something, watch a movie, travel somewhere, choose a college, join a gym, join a movement, donate money, decorate our homes, or even cook a recipe.

Technology also adds the ability to establish relationships based solely on common interests and written messages. Contrast this to the past, where relationships were mostly based on location and family ties. Through connections on Facebook, Twitter and other technologies, we now have digital relationships with people and organizations all over the world.

"Personal" and "professional" brands are brands that belong to people rather than things. These relatively new terms now apply because social media has made it possible to broadcast information about you to the entire world. Often, the message that you broadcast can be unintentional. Every time you use a search engine, click "like," post a photo, or even just visit a webpage, information about you is being gathered and analyzed. Most often, this information is being used to figure out what you might buy. Together with the information you purposely broadcast, it forms *your* brand.

YOUR BRAND

For this mindset activity you will doing web searches on your name. You may have done this before, but it is good to check often.

Before you do any searches, make sure you are logged out of any social media accounts—you want to see results that are open to the public. When you do the searches, try using your full name and any nicknames you use. If your name is a common name, try adding the name of your city, community, school, or anything else that will narrow your results.

Use all three of the following search engines:
* Google (Link 7-32)
* Bing (Link 7-33)
* Yahoo (Link 7-34)

Browse the results for each of the search engines listed and try to get a sense of what others might think your brand is just based on the results list. You may need to open up a few of the links (such as Facebook or LinkedIn) in your results to get more information. If you end up finding nothing, that's OK. It's easier to build from zero than it is to start with a negative online presence.

Based on your search results, write a brief description of what someone else might identify as your brand.

It takes time to establish a brand—online and otherwise. Get started with the suggestions on the previous pages that explain the social media tools. Most importantly, you want to build an *authentic* presence. This means you want to be true to who you are and your strengths. Don't sell yourself as something you are not. Also, don't over-hype your strengths. Be confident but honest. For some specific tips on building your brand, look at the following lists of what to do and what *not* to do.

Building Your Brand—What To Do

- Focus on platforms that reflect your strengths. Business professionals likely benefit most from platforms like LinkedIn while an artist may benefit more from Instagram or Pinterest.
- Focus on your headline. The most-read words of your profile will be your headline. The second most read will be the very first sentence. Invest your time accordingly.
- Be professional but don't be a robot. Add a few personal elements that make you human and more memorable. Pick personal items that best reflect who you are as a person. You are more likely to get along with the employer that is drawn to the personal elements in your profile.
- Present your current self. Only talk about the past in terms of how it has influenced your development into who you are and what you can do.
- Content is king. Create content that you'd be interested in yourself. Think of your future colleagues as your target audience, not just your friends or the entire online community.

Building Your Brand—What NOT To Do

- DON'T say "I don't need an online presence." You do!
- DON'T post inappropriate pictures on social media. In a survey of the grad class of 2013, 90% report being cautious about online posts. *However*, 35% have posted profanity and 30% have comments or pictures about alcohol.[1] While you can have fun, employers want to know if you have judgment.
- DON'T forget to proofread what you write and pay attention to grammar.
- DON'T post multiple profiles on the same site.
- DON'T be too wordy—make your point quickly.
- DON'T rely on privacy settings to protect certain pieces of information.
- DON'T have a messy presence. Not taking great care with social accounts, blogs or personal sites, is like inviting guests to a dirty house.
- DON'T spend so much time worried about your online presence that you forget to network face-to-face!
- DON'T forget to Google yourself occasionally.

THE BRAND YOU WANT

We already asked you to do an online search of your name and note the online brand that you seemed to have now. What do you *want* your online brand to be? Think of what your core goals and values are. It might help to think about what you determined your purpose to be in Chapter 1.

SECTION 7-4: APPLYING YOURSELF

We hope CollegeScope has helped you learn more about who you are and where your best career fit will be. There are a lot of potential jobs out there. You probably have a lot of different interests and skills. Putting together your resumé is a good way to review which jobs might suit you. Doing so forces you to summarize your education, skills, traits and experience—the things that make you *you*—and helps you start to see which jobs might be a good fit.

Your Resumé

Your resumé might be the most important tool for getting you a job. It usually provides a potential employer with their first impression of you. Before we dive into all the tips and strategies for your resumé, let's take a look at some statements that were pulled from actual resumés and cover letters.[1]

- "I am very detail-oreinted."
- "I have a bachelorette degree in computers."
- "Graduated in the top 66% of my class."
- "I worked as a Corporate Lesion."
- "Served as assistant sore manager."
- "Objective: To have my skills and ethics challenged on a daily basis."
- "Special skills: Thyping."
- "Special skills: Experienced with numerous office machines and can make great lattes."
- "My contributions on product launches were based on dreams that I had."
- "Thank you for your consideration. Hope to hear from you shorty!"
- "It's best for employers that I not work with people."
- "I am superior to anyone else you could hire."

Some of those statements are funny and some are embarrassing. In either case, what do you think is the first impression the employer had when reading these resumés? Do you think these candidates were called for interviews?

Try to think of your resumé as your entire professional self condensed down to one or two pages. If you think that is a lot of condensing, you are right. That means you have to make every tiny detail as good as it can be. As you see above, one small little error can grab a lot of attention and end up becoming your whole fist impression...sorry, that's *first* impression.

Whether you choose to start with a traditional resumé and then your online profile (such as LinkedIn) or the other way around, it will be important to think through and summarize your goals, your strengths and information all in one place. If you already have a resumé and an online profile, maybe there can be some work done to align the two. If a potential employer reads your resumé and then searches for you online, it will look good to have a consistent message.

Keep It Short

We already mentioned that you should keep your resumé to about one or two paper pages in length. It can be difficult to keep things that brief. It will require some effort, but the last thing you want is for someone reading your resumé to lose interest or get frustrated with the length.

Most employers have to read through many resumés before selecting a candidate. And, if your resumé makes it past the initial screening, employers often refer back to it several times to find specific pieces of information. The shorter and better organized your resumé is, the easier it will be for employers to find what they are looking for. If employers have to take any extra time to search through your resumé, they will likely move on to the next one in the hope that it will be easier to read.

Don't fool yourself into thinking short means easy. It takes time to create a short, high-quality resumé. You will have to work at saying much with few words—be sure to put in the effort.

"I would have written you a shorter letter,
but I did not have the time."

–BLAISE PASCAL

Keep It Organized

A good resumé is easy to read. It uses lots of white space and a font size larger than 10 point. Your strongest features should be listed near the top of the resumé.

There are hundreds of formats for a resumé, but most are organized into the following sections:

- Contact information. The top of your resumé should include your contact information: name, address, phone number, and e-mail address. If you have a longer resumé, CV, portfolio or similar online, you can include the URL for that here. This information is the title of your resumé. Print your name in a larger font size or in bold so that it stands out. Remember, you want to make it easy for an employer to contact you!
- Goal statement. A goal statement defines what type of work you are looking for. It demonstrates that you have a clear purpose in your job search and can be used to feature key strengths. Your goal statement should be short, usually just one sentence. Your goal statement might say, "To secure a position that will allow me to use my web design skills," or "To find a role as an educator where organizational skills, experience working with children, and a strong work ethic are assets."

If you are including a cover letter with your resumé, your goal statement will be part of the cover letter. In that case, your goal statement should be very specific to the job for which you are applying.

- **Education.** In this section, list in point form your best grades, courses, and any academic degrees, certificates, recognition or awards. If you have other training, such as CPR or project management, list these as well. Employers prefer to hire achievers.
- **Experience.** In this section, list any paid or volunteer jobs or internships you've held. Describe each position briefly using bullet points. You can also list school or community activities or volunteer service, especially if these activities show your skills or your responsibility and dedication. Employers prefer to hire active people.
  - Use short, clear points rather than complete sentences.
  - Use action words.
  - Use numbers and percentages to quantify your accomplishments.
  - Mention any skills or credentials specific to the job you are seeking.
- **References.** A reference is someone the employer can contact who knows you and the type of person you are. A reference could be a professor, a former employer, a supervisor from a volunteer position, or someone else with whom you have worked. Include your references' titles next to their names, to help the reader understand their background. Three references are all you'll need. Be sure to ask your references' permission before you put their names on the resumé!

Other Resumé Tips

- Avoid using the word "I": it's easier than you think and sounds more professional.
- Don't be shy: the resumé is a "brag sheet" that shows someone else your best work.
- List your resumé categories in order of your strengths. For instance, if your education is stronger than your experience at this stage, begin with that.

The Elevator Pitch

Famously named after the short time you would have in an elevator to pitch an idea to someone, the elevator pitch now refers to any short speech or conversation in which you have to get your message across fast. An elevator pitch can be a very useful tool for getting noticed by potential employers or people who can *connect* you to potential employers.

Once you have an elevator pitch, you can use it at career fairs, conferences, when you are introduced to certain people, chance meetings, and even in an elevator. Having an elevator pitch ready not only ensures that you deliver the right message, it also gives you more confidence in approaching people who can help you get a job.

The previous section talked about personal brand, and that is the perfect place to start in creating your elevator speech. You want to make sure your speech reflects your brand—both in content and in the way you deliver it.

Check out the video at Link 7-35 on how to perfect your elevator pitch.

Remember that your pitch should only be a conversation starter, approximately 30 seconds to two minutes long. If the other person is willing, exchange contact information with them. It's especially important to get their details so you can follow up with a longer conversation—and possibly your resumé!

YOUR ELEVATOR PITCH

A recommended speed for speech is about 150 words per minute.[2] A 30-120 second elevator pitch should then be about 75-300 words.

Using the recommendations above and what you've learned from the video, write an elevator pitch that would work for you. Don't worry if it is not perfect. Consider the one you write here to be a rough draft that you can work on over time.

Job Interviews

If you need to prepare for a job interview, congratulations! You have made it past at least the first round of screening. If you are nervous, that's OK. Being nervous means you care about getting the job and the employer will know that. Just don't let your nerves prevent you from clearly and confidently communicating the message that you will perform the job well.

One way to deal with nervousness, and also learn more about the job field, is with **informational interviews**. Do this BEFORE you land an actual job interview. An informational interview is not a job interview, and you will not be offered a job following one. However, there are enough similarities between the two, so that doing the former can help you with the latter. An informational interview reverses the role so that you are the interviewer. You find a professional in your desired field and interview that person to learn what it is like to work in that career. For some great advice on how to conduct and get the most out of an informational interview, check out Link 7-36.

Conducting a few informational interviews will arm you with valuable information to prepare you for actual job interviews. There are several other things you should do to help you prepare for a job interview.

Preparing for an Interview

- **Learn about the organization.**
  Go online, find their website and head straight for the "About Us" page—most organizations have one. You may also find pages on the history, company philosophy and leadership team. If you can't find a website, or any information on one, look for news articles or other third-party sources for information.
- **Create an inventory of the skills you have that match the job.**
  From the job posting and any other sources of information on what the organization is seeking, create a list of skills needed for the job. Then, for each skill, think of specific examples of times in which you have demonstrated or developed that skill. Write it all down and memorize that list.

  When you are in the interview, however, don't recite them back the way you memorized them. Instead, work them naturally when answering relevant questions. For example, most interviewers will ask questions such as "What skills do you have?" or "What can you offer our organization?" The interviewer may ask specific questions such as "Tell me about a time when you had to work with a difficult person." If the scenario involves skills from your list, you will be ready with a great answer.
- **Be ready for different types of interviews.**
  There are variations in how you should handle the different types of interviews. You'll find a great page with tips for each type of job interview at Link 7-37.
- **Prepare some responses for typical questions.**
  Many interviewers ask very similar questions. You can probably expect some of the questions listed below. Read each question and practice your response. To simulate interview conditions, have a friend ask you the questions and respond the way you actually would in a real job interview. Get some feedback from your friend and work to improve your answers leading up to the interview.

- Tell me about yourself.
- Why are you interested in working for this company?
- Tell me about your education.
- Why have you chosen this particular field?
- Describe your best/worst boss.
- In a job, what interests you most/least?
- What is your major weakness?
- Give an example of how you solved a problem in the past.
- What are your strengths?
- How do others describe you?
- What do you consider the most important idea you contributed or your most noteworthy accomplishment in your last job?
- Where do you see yourself in three years?
- Think about something you consider a failure in your life, and tell me why you think it happened.
- How do you think you will fit into this operation?
- If you were hired, what ideas/talents could you contribute to the position or our company?
- Give an example of a situation in which you showed leadership and initiative.

During the Interview

It's the big day and you've done all your preparation. Here are some tips to leave a great lasting impression on your interviewer.

1. Dress professionally, even if the job normally does not require it. It is better to dress up a little too much than to appear too casual.

2. Smile, look everyone in the eye and give firm handshakes. Address the interviewer by his or her title (Mr., Ms. or Dr.) and last name, unless prompted to do otherwise—this shows respect.

3. Bring your resumé (another copy, just in case), letters of reference and a work portfolio with samples of your work, if appropriate.

4. Bring a notebook and a pen to record any key points during the interview that you might want to include in a thank-you letter.

5. When you arrive, turn off your phone or disable any of the alert functions.

6. Bring any ID or licenses that you may be required to show.

7. Keep your answers short and to-the-point. Answer the questions completely but don't ramble on with extra information.

8. Listen carefully to the questions and watch the interviewer for non-verbal cues during your responses. Try to "read" the interviewer as best you can.

9. Remember to ask the interviewer any questions you would like answered. Ensure that these are questions that continue to make you look like a good candidate.

As soon as you arrive home, write your thank-you letter (or email) and send it. Do not use your phone or send a text. Write it, spell check it, proof it, and have someone else check it if you can. Do not skip this step! If there are other candidates who have performed as well as you up to this point, a thank-you letter can give you that last push over the top. Think of it as a sprint to the finish.

Your thank-you letter should include:
* Addressing the interviewer by title and last name.
* Appreciation for the opportunity.
* Further expression of interest in the job. Refer to something brought up in the interview that piqued your interest, if you can.
* A very brief restatement of your skills most relevant to the job.
* One extra thank-you for the opportunity to interview.

JOB INTERVIEW PRACTICE

Pick two of the sample interview questions on this page and come up with answers to those questions. Record both the questions and your answers below.

Interview question and answer 1

Interview question and answer 2

CHAPTER 7 SUMMARY

Before we close, it is important to emphasize two things.

1 Keep the big picture in mind. The following quote is from Susan Adams, who writes about career advice websites, lists and resources for Forbes.

> *"As we launch the lists, I feel compelled to say, as I've written numerous times before, that no job seeker should spend all day on the internet, reading career advice and sending resumés into the black hole of online postings. Rather, the web should be a place where you can get help and advice on job search basics like writing a resumé and LinkedIn profile, preparing for interviews and salary negotiations and researching and mulling over job options. If you're in job search mode, coaches recommend that you spend no more than 10% of your time online. The rest of the time should be devoted to pursuing leads, networking, researching companies where you want to work and getting out and meeting people in person."*

2 **Maintain a long-term perspective**. Job seeking can be a tough grind. It is normal to face rejection many times before landing that job you want. Surround yourself with supportive family and friends and, most importantly, don't give up!

Continue to improve and apply the skills learned in this lesson after every rejection and even after you get that first job. Throughout your life you will want an updated resumé and an elevator pitch about who you are and what you have to offer. It will get easier over time. We wish you the best and good luck!

> *"The biggest hurdle is rejection. Any business you start, be ready for it. The difference between successful people and unsuccessful people is the successful people do all the things the unsuccessful people don't want to do. When 10 doors are slammed in your face, go to door number 11 enthusiastically with a smile on your face."*

> –JOHN PAUL DEJORIA

The chapter quiz is on the next page. If you need to review any previous sections, now is a good time to do it.

CHAPTER 7 QUIZ

Career Readiness: Finding My Fit

This quiz covers all of the topics from this chapter on career readiness. Before you answer any questions, scan them and return to review any pages you need to be confident in your answers.

1 In seeking mastery it is helpful to experience the "near win" because
   a. it means the road to success is almost complete
   b. you are far from last place
   c. it motivates you to keep practicing
   d. all of the above

2 Which of the following is LEAST likely a benefit of a work experience program?
   a. you can get paid
   b. you can earn credits toward your degree or diploma
   c. you can expand your network of contacts
   d. you can graduate faster

3 Which best describes the way you typically get an internship?
   a. I need to be placed by an instructor or professor when I enroll in a course
   b. I need to search for and apply for an internship
   c. I need to be approached by a company who offers the internship
   d. I will be placed by my college career center

4 Which of the following is NOT something you should do during an internship or other work-experience program?
   a. act like you are one of the regular employees
   b. do "grunt" work such as make copies or get coffee
   c. focus on learning workplace skills
   d. communicate and network with others
   e. all of the above are things you should do

5 If an employee complains about discrimination, they can be fired for complaining:
   a. true
   b. false

6 The following is NOT an example of an employee right:
   a. right to fair wage for hours worked
   b. right to a safe workplace
   c. right to freedom of expression
   d. right to be free from discrimination

7 Employer rights include
   a. set standards of conduct
   b. conduct reviews of employees
   c. terminate employees for insubordination
   d. all of the above

8 Which of the following is NOT recommended when using technology to promote yourself and find a job?
   a. spend about 75% of your job search time doing work online
   b. focus on just one social media site to promote yourself
   c. post personal pictures to your profile to create a friendly and down-to-earth brand
   d. NONE of the above are recommended

9 Which of the following social media sites is most focused on career development?
   a. LinkedIn
   b. Twitter
   c. Facebook
   d. Pinterest

©Piotr Marcinski/Shutterstock.com

10. Your personal brand can best be described as
    a. the career you are interested in
    b. the strengths and characteristics that distinguish you
    c. your favorite commercial or company
    d. all of the above

11. According to Simon Sinek, people are more motivated by hearing WHAT you do than hearing why you do it.
    a. true
    b. false

12. Which of the following is typically not on a resumé?
    a. goal statement
    b. the wage/salary at your last job
    c. education
    d. experience
    e. contact information

13. Which best describes an elevator pitch? the first five minutes of an interview
    a. a career path for technicians
    b. a complete description of your experience and skills
    c. a brief explanation of who you are and what you offer

CAREER READINESS

This is a quick survey to measure what you know about this chapter topic. Just be honest and rate how much each of the following statements applies to you. Give yourself a score of:
1 for Not a bit • 2 for A little • 3 for Some • 4 for Mostly • 5 for Definitely

AFTER CHAPTER

		Not a bit 1	A little 2	Some 3	Mostly 4	Definitely 5
1	I can describe what the value of failure or the "near win" is.	O	O	O	O	O
2	I can state three personal and three community benefits of work.	O	O	O	O	O
3	I can name five different types of experiences through which I can gain valuable work skills and expertise.	O	O	O	O	O
4	I know the difference between a fellowship, an internship, and a shadow program.	O	O	O	O	O

5	I can describe several strategies to use when searching for a work-experience program.	○	○	○	○	○
6	I can name three things that would help me make the most of a work experience program.	○	○	○	○	○
7	I have done some research on what to expect in a typical workplace.	○	○	○	○	○
8	I can name three rights and three responsibilities of employees.	○	○	○	○	○
9	I can name three rights and three responsibilities of employers.	○	○	○	○	○
10	I know where to look to determine exactly what violates work discrimination laws.	○	○	○	○	○
11	I know how to use Twitter, Facebook, and LinkedIn to advance my career.	○	○	○	○	○
12	I can clearly tell someone in 30 seconds or less what my brand and career goals are.	○	○	○	○	○
13	I have done a web search of my name and know how my online presence appears to others.	○	○	○	○	○
14	I have recently updated my resumé or have specific plans to do so.	○	○	○	○	○
15	I have up-to-date online profiles that will help advance my career.	○	○	○	○	○
16	I have a prepared elevator pitch that will help get me a job.	○	○	○	○	○

Add up your scores to determine your **After Chapter** total and write it down here:

Write your **Before Chapter** total here:

Compare your Before and After scores to see how your knowledge of this chapter topic has changed.

Congratulations, you've completed Chapter 7! To conclude your learning in this chapter, consider and note the following:

What parts of this chapter were most helpful to you?

How would you improve this chapter?

MONEY, HEALTH, AND TIME MANAGEMENT

MONEY, HEALTH, AND TIME MANAGEMENT

This is a quick survey to measure what you know about this chapter topic, both before and after completing the chapter. Just be honest and rate how much each of the following statements applies to you. Give yourself a score of:
1 for Not a bit • 2 for A little • 3 for Some • 4 for Mostly • 5 for Definitely

©arka38/Shutterstock.com

BEFORE CHAPTER

		Not a bit 1	A little 2	Some 3	Mostly 4	Definitely 5
1	I know several types of financial aid and the differences between them.	O	O	O	O	O
2	I know where to apply for financial aid and how to maximize my chances of getting what I need.	O	O	O	O	O
3	I know how to avoid accumulating too much debt in college.	O	O	O	O	O
4	I can describe proven money management tips that will be useful over my lifetime.	O	O	O	O	O
5	I know what behaviors lead to poor spending habits.	O	O	O	O	O
6	I can describe the importance of health when it comes to school, work, and personal life.	O	O	O	O	O6

7	I can describe behaviors that lead to good nutrition and behaviors that lead to poor nutrition.	○	○	○	○	○
8	I know what the latest research says about the benefits of exercise.	○	○	○	○	○
9	I know what the latest research says about stress and how my beliefs about stress are important.	○	○	○	○	○
10	I can describe at least five benefits of proper sleep and what behaviors lead to good sleep patterns.	○	○	○	○	○
11	I know of at least two free sources of excellent information on financial aid.	○	○	○	○	○
12	I have searched for scholarships to find out which ones I qualify for.	○	○	○	○	○
13	I can describe at least one time-management strategy.	○	○	○	○	○
14	I have used a strategy to help me prioritize various tasks.	○	○	○	○	○
15	I know what causes procrastination and have thought of ways I can overcome it.	○	○	○	○	○
16	I am confident that I can effectively manage my money, health, and time while in college.	○	○	○	○	○

Add up your scores to determine your **Before Chapter** total and write it down here:

Key Questions

1. Motivation Check: Do I follow the path to happiness or the path of happiness?

2. What are the different forms of financial aid and how do I access them?

3. How do I avoid financial difficulty in college and after college?

4. What should I do, and what should I avoid, to achieve optimum health?

5. How can I make the most of the little time I seem to have available?

©Sabphoto/Shutterstock.com

CHAPTER PREVIEW

In this chapter we cover three important, yet often ignored, topics: money, health, and time.

We say "ignored," but we really mean disregarded until it is too late. Many people only snap to attention when they realize they have too little money, their health becomes poor, or there is not enough time. You may even feel you are in one or more of those situations already. CollegeScope can't perform miracles, but we can provide proven strategies to help you avoid those difficult situations.

MOTIVATION CHECK

Do I Follow the Path to Happiness or the Path of Happiness?

In discussing money, health, and time, many people end up talking about how they have too little of each. How much is enough? That is a question every individual must answer for themselves. Some people may seem driven to make lots of money, be super fit, and have plenty of leisure time. Others may seem content with little money, average health and little to no leisure time. Neither situation is right or wrong. The key is to continue to strive toward your goals for all three while finding happiness in the moment.

"The best way to pay for a lovely moment is to enjoy it."

–RICHARD BACH

As we saw in the chapter on learning and productivity[1], not only does happiness in the moment help you achieve your goals, it also allows you to experience happiness before and after you achieve your goals.

This chapter will not tell you how to make tons of money, become the fittest human on the planet, or travel through time. Instead, we will focus on how to make the most of what you have available. We will also show you how to save a little more money, maintain good health, and make good use of your time. The video at Link 8-1 demonstrates one method for making the most of what you have by showing you how to find the "happiest" route to where you are going, literally.

THE PATH OF HAPPINESS

The video demonstrated an app that can literally show you the happiest route somewhere. If you listened carefully at the beginning of the video, and used your critical thinking skills, you will realize there is a larger metaphorical message too. Read the closing quote from the talk.

I would like to end with this thought: do you remember The Truman Show? *It's a media satire in which a real person doesn't know he's living in a fabricated world. Perhaps we live in a world fabricated for efficiency. Look at some of your daily habits and, as Truman did in the movie, escape the fabricated world. Why? Well, if you think that adventure is dangerous, try routine. It's deadly.*[2]

What do you think the quote means?

SECTION 8-1: FINANCIAL AID

Introduction

Previous chapters discussed personal, college and career awareness. One of the topics in this chapter is money awareness. Many people *think* they have good money awareness, but the statistics show otherwise.

The 2014 Consumer Financial Literacy Survey of U.S. Adults[1]

- 32% do not save any money for retirement or "rainy day" type funds
- 34% carry credit card debt from month to month
- 41% give themselves a grade of C or worse on their knowledge of personal finance
- 73% agree that they could use professional advice and answers to everyday questions about finances

To be successful in college and in life, you need to know how to get, manage, and spend money wisely. Two of the top reasons for students dropping out of college are that they cannot pay for their education or they have to work so much that they have no time for school.

If you remember the chapter on career awareness, you know how education can significantly increase your future earnings. Figuring out how to pay for school might feel difficult, but the evidence shows that it will pay off in the long term. Also, college is a good time to practice managing money so that you are prepared for the time after graduation.

Take this quick quiz to test your financial literacy. Think of your response before you read the answer.

1. If you have $100 in a savings account earning 2% interest a year, how much will you have in five years?
   - $102
   - $110
   - more than $110
   - don't know

Answer: Savings accounts earn **compound** interest. Let's assume the interest compounds annually. In one year, the $100 would earn 2% of $100, which is $2. The next year the 2% would apply to $102, not $100, so the interest would be slightly more than $2. After five years, the total would be **more than $110** because the interest earned in years 2-5 is more than $2 each year.

2   Imagine that the interest rate on your savings account is 1% a year and inflation is 2% a year. After one year, would the money in the account BUY more than it would today, exactly the same or less than today?
  * more same less
  * don't know

Answer: It would buy **less** than it would today. Inflation represents how much value is lost from money over time. A 2% inflation rate means that what used to cost $100 a year ago now costs $102. If you kept $100 in a piggy bank for a year, it would not be able to buy as much at the end of the year. Even if you invested it at 1% and gained $1 for a total of $101, you still would not be able to buy as much as you could have at the start of the year.

3   Which of the following types of borrowing usually has the highest interest rate?
  * mortgage
  * student loan
  * credit card
  * car loan

Answer: Credit cards, hands down. Typical rates range from 20% to 30%. Imagine you had a credit card balance of $5,000 with an interest rate of 20%. If, each month, you paid off all the new charges you've put on your card and paid an *extra* $150 toward that $5,000 balance, it would take you over four years to clear your credit card debt! Also, you would end up paying $7,500 for that debt of $5,000. Interest rates for mortgages, student loans and car loans typically range from 0% to 7%.

4   If you spent $3,000 on a credit card, which of the following repayment options would cost you the least?
  * paying it back all at once
  * paying $500 a month
  * making the minimum payments
  * the total would be the same in each case

Answer: For debts that carry an interest rate, the total you pay back is almost always lower when you pay it off quickly. A couple of exceptions are mortgages and car loans, which sometimes charge a fee if you pay them off too soon. Credit cards, however, always allow you to pay off the balance entirely—so, in this case, paying it back all at once would be the smartest option.

5   Which of the following offers the greatest return on investment?
  * a high-interest savings account that earns 2% interest
  * a savings bond at 3% interest
  * a mutual fund with an average return of 5% and a management expense ratio of 2%
  * paying off a loan that has a 4% interest rate

Answer: In this example, paying off a loan that has a 4% interest rate will provide the greatest return on investment (ROI). ROI is not just about investing money; you can achieve a return by paying off debts too. Imagine you have $100 to put toward one of the four options. In the savings account, that $100 would grow to $102 after one year. The savings bond would be worth $103. The mutual fund would also be worth $103, because the management expense ratio is deducted from your earnings. By paying off the loan, you would reduce your debt by $104 at the end of the year. While the first three investments would allow you to gain $2 or $3, the last option would let you save $4. Therefore, it offers the greatest ROI.

6　Which of the following types of financial aid do you have to pay back?
- grants
- scholarships
- student loans
- none of the above

Answer: Of course loans have to be paid back. Did you know that grants may also have to be paid back if you drop out before the end of the semester?

7　What is the difference between merit-based and need-based aid?

Answer: Grants and government loans are usually *need based*—they are based on income, parents' income, and a few other factors related to your ability to access money. Private loans are usually accessible, regardless of need. Scholarships are mostly merit based—they are distributed based on academic, athletic, and other types of performance. Some scholarships also require you to be a member of a specific group or organization.

8　True or false: Paying for financial aid services increases your chances of getting financial aid.

Answer: False. Your chances of receiving aid are based on your level of need or merit. Some services may help you identify more options and assist you with the application process; however, they cannot change your circumstances regarding need or merit. Also, with so many freely available services and websites to assist you, paying for help could end up costing more than it is worth. Your school and many government-based websites can help you at no cost. And finally, be wary of services that ask for your banking or credit card information. They may be a scam.

How did you do? If you knew all the answers, congratulations! You are more financially savvy than most people. Don't worry if you didn't know all the answers. This section and the next will help you understand the topics covered by these questions and more.

Types of Financial Aid

Financial aid can come in many forms, but the main ones are loans, grants, scholarships, and work-study programs. Loans must be repaid over time. Grants and scholarships do not have to be repaid except in some cases when you do not finish the semesters for which you received the money. The difference between grants and scholarships is that usually grants are need based while scholarships are merit based. Work-study programs allow students to earn part or all of their financial aid by working in community service positions.

The table below provides an overview of the major forms of financial aid. Use the links in the right-hand column to find further information about each.

Financial Aid Overview

AID TYPE	HOW TO APPLY	BASED ON	CONDITIONS	AMOUNT	REPAYMENT	MORE INFO
GRANTS AND SCHOLARSHIPS						
Federal Pell Grant	FAFSA	financial need	undergraduate students only	up to $5,775 for 2015-16	only if you do not finish semester	Link 8-2
Federal Supplemental Educational Opportunity Grant (FSEOG)	FAFSA	financial need	only some schools offer this	$100-$4,000 /year	only if you do not finish semester	Link 8-3
TEACH Grant	FAFSA	financial need	must enroll in teacher training program and agree to work as a teacher with specific conditions	up to $4,000/year	only if you do not complete obligations of grant program	Link 8-4
Scholarships	varies by scholarship— usually you have to apply separately for each scholarship	academics, sports, talents, service, memberships, gender or other traits	scholarships may affect the amount of other aid you receive	some are very small and some are very large	none	Link 8-5

LOANS						
Direct Subsidized	FAFSA	financial need	undergraduate students only	up to $5,500— depends on your need and school costs	payments and interest begin at six months post-graduation or dropping below half-time student status	Link 8-6
Direct Unsubsidized	FAFSA	cost of attendance	undergraduate or graduate students	depends on costs of your school	interest begins immediately; payments begin six months after graduation or dropping below half-time student status	Link 8-7
Direct PLUS	FAFSA	cost of attendance and can be affected by credit rating	graduate and professional students only	depends on costs of your school	payments and interest begin im-mediately upon receiving loan	Link 8-8
Direct Consolidation	StudentLoans.gov	have an existing loan in a grace period	may have to make specific arrangements with your current loan servicer	depends on existing loans	usually begins two months after consolidated loan is paid out	Link 8-9
Federal Perkins Loan	FAFSA	financial need	not available at all schools—the school is the lender	depends on costs of your school	varies by school	Link 8-10
Private Loans	apply to the company offering the loan	you or your cosigner's credit rating	most require a minimum credit rating or cosigner	dependent on compa-ny and your credit rating	most private loans begin to accrue interest immediately and require payments immediately	Link 8-11

Federal Work-Study Program (FWS)	FAFSA and for the job itself through your school	financial need	work should be a "community service" position and be related to the student's program of study	the wage is dependent on the job, but must be at least minimum wage	none	Link 8-12

Financial Aid Strategy

When

If you are in college, you have likely already heard about and even applied for some form of financial aid. The best time to start is in high school. However, it is definitely not too late once you are in college. Financial aid is available for multiple years in college and you should look at your options each year. In fact, there are some forms of financial aid that are *only* available in your later college years. Many scholarships, for example, require that you be in your junior year or later. Most scholarships have deadlines that range from late January to mid-summer. There are exceptions and some have deadlines at other times of the year. It's a good idea to do some research on deadlines for various forms of financial aid and put those dates on your calendar for each year you are in college.

What

Start with getting a good background on all the forms of financial aid—exactly what this page is providing. Be sure to check out the More Info links in the table above. Once you have an idea of the different forms of financial aid, you should apply for as many as is reasonably possible. You don't *have to* accept all financial aid, especially the kind you have to repay, but it is nice to have it available if you need it.

- **FAFSA:** You should definitely complete the FAFSA, if you haven't already. You can find it at Link 8-13. As the chart above reveals, it allows access to multiple forms of financial aid. That FAFSA link also provides more information on deadlines, what you will need to complete the FAFSA, and a calculator that will estimate the amount you may be eligible to receive.
- **Scholarship search:** Scholarships are **free money**...almost. You really earn scholarships in advance through your previous efforts in school, sports, arts or other activities. You usually have to show excellence of some kind. There are over 7,000 scholarships in just one database at CareerOneStop (see Link 8-14), so chances are pretty good you have shown the right kind of excellence for at least one of those scholarships. Apply to scholarships that you think you have even a remote chance of getting. That "free money" is worth the effort of submitting your application.
- Your school is an important information source for, and a place to access, financial aid. Be sure to visit the financial aid office at your school at least once while in college. They will likely provide information and access to aid that you cannot find anywhere else.

- **Federal Work Study program:** Your school also has access to information about work-study programs that you cannot find anywhere else. You have to apply to work-study programs through your school. Even if you think you will not have any time for additional work in college, ask questions of the people in the financial aid office. You may find that a work-study program is a better option than your current job because it is aligned with your program of study. It never hurts to ask.
- **Tax credits.** While technically not financial aid because you only get money back after you spend it, tax credits can leave you (or your parents) with significantly less debt after college. Learn more about these at Link 8-15. Be sure to file a tax return for every year you are in college, even if you don't make enough money to require it. You (or your parents) should claim your college expenses while you are enrolled. You can then claim the tax credits later, when you are out of college and making more money. You can also claim the interest you pay on your student loans.

The list above does not cover every option. There are some private loans and scholarships that are not listed on any website or at your school's financial aid office. Ask around. Talk to relatives to find out if the companies they work for offer scholarships or grants. Sports organizations, clubs, and other institutions sometimes have scholarships and bursaries for past and current members; be sure to check with any organizations in which you have been a member.

> *"What counts is what you do with your money,*
> *not where it came from."*
>
> – MERTON MILLER

How Much

A good strategy is to get as much as you can while borrowing the minimum you need. This means you want to maximize the amount from grants, scholarships and sources that you do not have to repay, while only taking out loans for what is leftover and what you absolutely need. You want to graduate with as little debt as possible.

In filling out or updating your FAFSA, just be complete and honest. There is no special trick to it, and the website will help you along the way. When you apply to scholarships and some private grants, however, there are things you can do to maximize your payout.

Maximizing Your Scholarships

- **Get involved.** We've said this before in regards to developing skills and forming networks, and here is another reason. The more teams, clubs, and extracurricular activities you engage in, the more opportunities you have for scholarships and grants. Stick with groups and activities that truly interest you. Don't involve yourself in something just to get access to scholarships. Get involved as early as possible, but remember it is never too late. New scholarships become available each year of college. Also, even if your involvement in a certain group doesn't win you a scholarship for that group, remember that many organizations look at your overall involvement when making award decisions for scholarships.

- **Do your research**. Find as many scholarships as you can, and apply to any for which you meet the eligibility requirements. Use multiple searches—both online and by contacting organizations that are likely to offer scholarships. Some useful online searches include: CareerOneStop Scholarship search (Link 8-16), Scholarships.com (Link 8-17) and InternationalScholarships.com (Link 8-18). Don't forget to check with the financial aid office at your school.
- **Treat your application submission seriously**. Whether the application is a form, essay, video or any other type of media, keep it neat and professional. Also, read the instructions for the application very carefully! It might help to create a checklist of what you should include and go through it with someone else as you review your application. Again, your school's financial aid office can help. It may seem like a lot of work to create new applications for each scholarship, but you should be able to re-use some elements each time. Just be sure to make each application specific to the target audience, like you would with a job application.
- **Think of the payoff**. If the work of completing multiple applications feels overwhelming, think of it as being like a high-paying job. In the 2011-2012 academic year, the average grant and scholarship payout was $9,740 at four-year institutions and $4,480 at two-year institutions.[1] Even if you spend 20 hours working on your applications, you would earn an average of $487/hr at a 4-year college and $224/hr at a 2-year college. Those values only include payouts from public funds such as Pell Grants and TEACH Grants. If you add private scholarships, such as the ones found in the scholarship search tools, the payouts would be even higher.

Use Caution with Loans

Education is a good investment. However, borrowing more than you need can cause problems later on. Try to get as much aid that you do not have to repay as you can. If you still need to take out a loan to help pay for college, estimate how much you will need for your essentials such as tuition, school fees, books, housing, and groceries. Only borrow what you know you will need.

Federal aid programs typically calculate what you need based on your expected family contribution (EFC) and the cost of attendance (COA) for your particular program. Also, federal aid programs are paid to directly to your school on your behalf so the money can't be misspent. However, private loans and other aid that comes in the form of a check or bank deposit have the potential to be spent on things not necessarily needed for your education. Don't be tempted by the sudden availability of cash that comes with some aid. College is a time when it can be difficult to repay loans and other debts. The longer it takes to repay loans and other debts, the longer those debts accumulate interest and the more you have to pay back.

More Information

There is no shortage of information out there on financial aid. Use caution, however, as some companies are motivated by profit and may not have your best interests in mind. Some companies claim to guarantee scholarships and grants while charging a fee. You should **never** have to pay to apply for financial aid. Some companies will charge you a fee to help you find financial aid and complete application forms, and that may be of some help. However, think carefully about the value of that when there are government and school-based services that will do the same for free. Below is a list of useful sites which offer some of their services for free.
- Federal Student Aid (Link 8-19)
- U.S. Department of Education (Link 8-20)
- FinAid.org (Link 8-21)
- And, of course, your school's financial aid office. You may also find information on your school's website.

"There was a time when a fool and his money were soon parted, but now it happens to everybody."

–ADLAI E. STEVENSON

SCHOLARSHIP SEARCH

Open the scholarship search at 8-16 and find two scholarships that you have a decent chance of getting. You can use the search filters to help narrow your results. Make sure you meet all the requirements of the scholarships you choose. Record the names of the two scholarships and their application deadlines below. Later, be sure to actually apply!

SECTION 8-2: MONEY MANAGEMENT

Learning Objectives

- Describe effective techniques for creating a budget
- Know several common overspending mistakes and how to avoid them
- Describe money-saving techniques for specific personality types and situations

"A wise man should have money in his head, but not in his heart."

–JONATHAN SWIFT

Introduction

As we stated earlier, money management is something that needs to be practiced over a lifetime. Money can be a source of depression, joy, and everything in between. When you manage money well, it helps you feel positive emotions.

Money management can be divided into two major categories: income and spending. Most students don't have much income, other than the financial aid sources discussed in the previous section, so we will focus on *spending* in this section. Check out the infographic below from ApartmentGuide.com on college student spending habits.

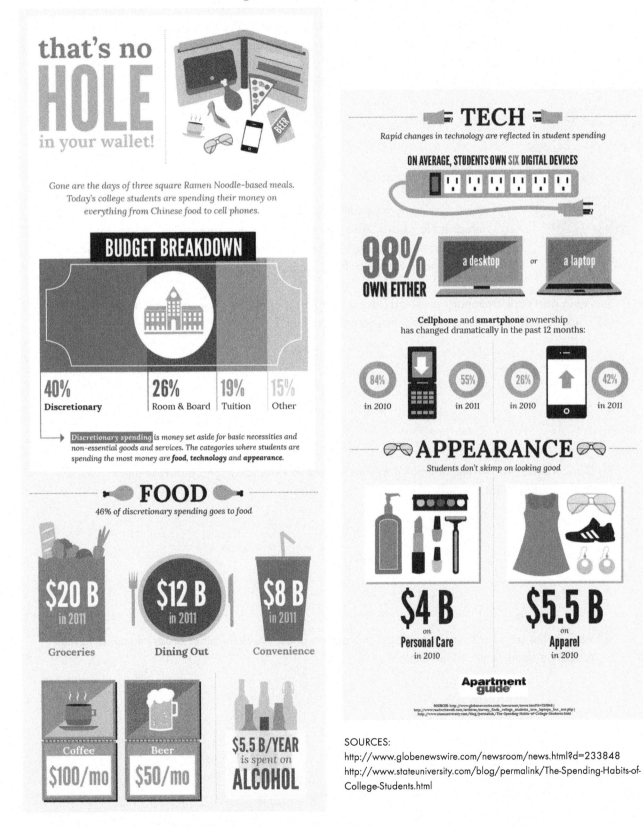

that's no HOLE in your wallet!

Gone are the days of three square Ramen Noodle-based meals. Today's college students are spending their money on everything from Chinese food to cell phones.

BUDGET BREAKDOWN

| 40% Discretionary | 26% Room & Board | 19% Tuition | 15% Other |

Discretionary spending is money set aside for basic necessities and non-essential goods and services. The categories where students are spending the most money are **food**, **technology** and **appearance**.

FOOD

46% of discretionary spending goes to food

$20 B in 2011 — Groceries
$12 B in 2011 — Dining Out
$8 B in 2011 — Convenience

Coffee $100/mo
Beer $50/mo
$5.5 B/YEAR is spent on ALCOHOL

TECH

Rapid changes in technology are reflected in student spending

ON AVERAGE, STUDENTS OWN SIX DIGITAL DEVICES

98% OWN EITHER a desktop or a laptop

Cellphone and **smartphone** ownership has changed dramatically in the past 12 months:

84% in 2010 → 55% in 2011 · 26% in 2010 ↑ 42% in 2011

APPEARANCE

Students don't skimp on looking good

$4 B on Personal Care in 2010
$5.5 B on Apparel in 2010

Apartment guide

SOURCES: http://www.globenewswire.com/newsroom/news.html?d=233848 | http://www.readwriteweb.com/archives/survey_finds_college_students_love_laptops_but_not.php | http://www.stateuniversity.com/blog/permalink/The-Spending-Habits-of-College-Students.html

SOURCES:
http://www.globenewswire.com/newsroom/news.html?d=233848
http://www.stateuniversity.com/blog/permalink/The-Spending-Habits-of-College-Students.html

The graphic focuses on spending in college. What about after college? Many people spend money on things that they don't really need. Sometimes this causes difficulty when it comes time to pay for things they *do* need. You may not have a problem with overspending right now, especially if you don't have much to spend. However, the best time to learn about overspending is before you actually do it. Once you graduate and are working full time, money will likely be more plentiful than it is now and you want to use it wisely. Check out the video at Link 8-22, which discusses one way to prevent overspending.

SPENDING HABITS

Think about your spending habits and compare them to the statistics in the infographic above. Also, think about the message in the video. Be honest with yourself and consider whether you are spending all your money wisely. Answer the questions below.

1 A big part of discretionary spending is food. Are you spending money wisely in this area? What could you do to save money (and maybe eat healthier)?

2 Do you overspend on technology? In what ways do you feel you might spend too much? Or, how are you able to *not* overspend?

3 Besides the areas of food, technology and appearance, are there other areas of spending that would be useful to examine? Explain.

Why Do We Overspend?

The previous page demonstrated that many people spend too much. Knowing why can help prevent further overspending. Here are some common reasons.

- **Keeping Up with Others.** While most people won't admit it, we are heavily influenced by peers and social media. Also, we tend to notice people who have more than us, rather than people in similar financial situations. It's natural to aspire to having more. This aspiration often pushes us to buy things that others have but we cannot afford so we can at least feel like we have more.[2]

- **Using Credit Cards.** Our brains are wired to understand sacrifice and reward. With cash, we can physically see and feel the loss of something we had and we weigh that against what we are buying. With a credit card, there is no physical evidence of losing something, only the gain of what we buy.[3]

- **Maintaining Previous Lifestyle.** Some life changes, such as starting school, having children, getting divorced or retiring come with an increase in expenses, a loss of income or both. Most people have a hard time adapting their lifestyle to fit their reduced finances. They want to continue to do and have the things they did before the change and this causes them to live beyond their means.

- **Impulsiveness.** We have all felt it. You are at a store and notice the latest phone, a nice pair of shoes, or a delicious-looking cookie and you *have* to have it. That feeling is normal; 57% of shoppers say they spend more than they planned to spend on any one shopping trip.[4] It is your actions that follow the feeling that count. The gratification that you get from buying that desired object usually doesn't last long. Instead, it is usually followed by guilt.

- **Convincing Yourself that You or Someone Else Deserves It.** A new job, graduation, a birthday, or any number of holidays typically cause a big increase in spending for many people. There are all kinds of reasons we use to justify spending on ourselves or others. It feels like those special occasions require that a certain amount of money be spent. The only problem is that the short-lived happiness gained in that moment becomes long-term difficulty from the debt created by it.

- **Underestimating Regular Expenses.** Expenses like rent, gas money, coffee, gym memberships, and cell phone bills seem small individually. Added together, however, they can get quite large. Because the bills are regular and repeated, we tend to take less notice—they become background noise. Then, we think we have more money than we actually do, and we spend it on other things.

- **Debt Has Been Normalized.** Governments do it, businesses do it, why shouldn't people do it? The short answer is that businesses and governments spend nearly all of their money on investments that generate some kind of return. People spend most of their money to maintain a certain lifestyle, so the money that we borrow is not bringing the future return that it does for businesses and governments. There are also so many different ways to be in debt now—student loans, credit cards, car loans, store credit, and more—that the total of all our different debts becomes less obvious to us. In the 1950s the total U.S. household debt was almost zero. By 2008 it had risen to almost $14 trillion! The recession woke people up enough to cause that number to drop to about $13 trillion by 2012. As of the end of 2014, it had risen back up to $13.5 trillion.[5] There are times in life where debt can be a good investment, such as with student loans. However, carrying debt over the long term results in profit for the lender and less money for the borrower.

Now that you know some common reasons for overspending, you should more easily recognize when you are doing so yourself. This should make it easier to correct the habit and perhaps spend your money more wisely. The following activity describes seven solutions to the seven problems stated above. Match each problem to the right solution.

SOLUTIONS TO OVERSPENDING

Read the solutions to overspending below. For each, choose the overspending problem that it would best solve. Think about your responses before reading the answers.

Use a Shopping Budget. Whenever you go shopping, calculate how much you can afford to spend and only spend that amount. If you know you have weak willpower, take only cash and leave the credit and bank cards at home.

Create Credit Card Barriers. First, try to stick to having only one credit card. Keep that one card inside a mini-notebook or sleeve on which you record each expense as you make it. This forces you to see how much you are spending each time you use it. Keep a running total on that same sheet. Don't use an app or rely on looking up your statement. A small slip of paper that you *have* to look at each time you take out your card makes your spending more obvious. Every billing cycle, change out the sheet of paper. Don't forget to keep a small pencil handy too. If you are buying one or two large items that aren't necessities, get out the paper before you approach the register as it may affect your decision to buy at all, which is a good thing.

Calculate all the Interest. Look at at your debts—credit cards, loans, and any others—and calculate the total interest you pay on your debts. Think about what it would be like if you didn't have to pay that interest every month. It may be a struggle to pay off your debts in the short term, but once you do, you will enjoy having more cash available for spending rather than paying interest.

Get Comfortable in Your Financial Skin. Just as we all have different looks, personalities and interests, we all have different financial situations. Getting comfortable in your own situation can be difficult no matter what the difference is. Remember that real friends support each other regardless of their differences. Anyone who pressures you to spend beyond your means is not acting like a true friend. Be honest and open with people about your situation and try to connect with others in similar situations. Do a web search of "financial peer pressure" and browse articles until you find one that helps you feel more comfortable or has advice that seems to work for you.

See Value Outside of Money. Unfortunately, there is a stigma that the value of things and experiences is based on how much they cost. Think about the following moments and their value to you: time with family and friends, a heartfelt letter or note written to you, your first kiss, or a time you worked really hard and achieved a goal. Most people would place a lot of value on those things, but they likely didn't cost much money. Gifts to others and yourself can be valuable without costing very much. It may take some thought, time and effort, but that is what makes the gift valuable—not only for the recipient, but for the giver as well. If you need some ideas, just search "inexpensive gift ideas" on the web.

Track All of Your Expenses. You can do this with a spreadsheet, specialized apps, or simple pencil and paper. While this may feel time consuming at first, you can develop a routine and make it pretty easy. Create categories for expenses such as food, rent, school, clothing and entertainment. You will quickly realize where you are spending more money than you thought. Once you have seen where you spend, create a budget that limits spending in areas that are not as necessary, such as entertainment and eating out.

Get Help to Deal with Change. There is no shame in seeking help for dealing with life changes, especially ones that significantly impact your finances. However, help in the form of gifted money is not long-term help. Instead, you should seek the gift of moral support and understanding. Coping with change psychologically will help you learn to adjust to your new lifestyle. Talk to family and friends or seek professional help. You can start with a search online, but be sure to think critically about which sites you use and remember that it is just a place to start. Reading articles can't replace making personal connections with others and feeling like you are understood.[6]

Answers:
Use a Shopping Budget: Impulsiveness
Create Credit Card Barriers: Using Credit Cards
Calculate all the Interest: Debt has been Normalized
Get Comfortable in Your Financial Skin: Keeping up with Others
See Value Outside of Money: Convincing Yourself that You or Someone Else Deserves It
Track All of Your Expenses: Underestimating Regular Expenses
Get Help to Deal with Change: Maintaining Previous Lifestyle

Money is a Resource

Just like oil or water, money is a resource that needs to be managed and used wisely. When money is plentiful, it is tempting to spend more, but you never know when a resource will become scarce. Think carefully about what you do with your money and ask yourself important questions each time you spend it. "Do I really need or want this? Will spending this amount bring me happiness over the long term, or will it cause me difficulty in the future?"

There are many articles full of financial advice for students. Browse around a little to find some tips that work for you. One particularly good article is available at Link 8-23.

"Money is only a tool. It will take you wherever you wish, but it will not replace you as the driver."

–AYN RAND

WHAT YOU DO WITH YOUR MONEY

Choose two money tips from this section that you think you can use. Identify the tips and describe how you can apply them in your life.

SECTION 8-3: MAINTAINING HEALTH

Introduction

Education is an investment in the quality of life of individuals and society in general. Investing in your health also improves quality of life for you and the people around you. Remaining healthy enough to play with your future grandchildren will take a little luck, but it also takes some investment in your health today. Everyday choices such as what you eat, how much you exercise, when you sleep and your mindset all have a big effect on your long-term health.

One way to think about health is to consider how long you will live, which usually gets people's attention! Take a look at the life expectancy calculator in Link 8-24, which uses statistical information to estimate how long you are likely to live.

After you complete the questions in the calculator and see your results, check all the boxes and click the button to "analyze health risks." You will see exactly how much each of those factors affects your lifespan. Notice that nearly all of the analyzed factors are things that you can control.

Some of the questions in that calculator may not have been a surprise. But, we often forget controllable factors that affect our health and our lives. For example, many people don't think about sleep affecting their lifespan. Sleep also affects things such as likelihood of a car accident, memory impairment, heart disease, obesity, depression, and skin conditions.[1] People have control over more health factors than they realize. Stress can have very different effects depending on how we view it. This section will provide more detail about factors that affect health and how to optimize it.

> *"Good health is not something we can buy. However, it can be an extremely valuable savings account."*
>
> – ANNE WILSON SCHAEF

Nutrition

Diet affects more than just your health and weight. Mood, academic performance, athletic performance and your overall energy levels are affected by what you eat. The following top 10 nutrition tips come from the *ChooseMyPlate* site provided by the U.S. Department of Agriculture.[9]

Top 10 Tips for Healthy Eating

- ### Add More Vegetables to Your Day
  Choose vegetables with bright colors such as red, yellow, orange, green, and purple. Don't cook vegetables until they are soft and dull in color, which can destroy the nutrients. Better yet, don't cook them at all. Here are some tips to make it easier to get veggies in your diet: try frozen or canned veggies if your fresh veggies tend to go bad, buy prepackaged salads with lots of veggies in them, plant a garden, buy vegetable soup, and cut up a lot of veggies when you have time so they are easy to grab later when you are in a rush.

- ### Make Half Your Grains Whole
  To eat more whole grains, substitute a whole-grain product for a refined product—such as eating whole wheat bread instead of white bread, or brown rice instead of white rice. Look for whole grain as the first ingredient on the label, not multigrain, 7 grain, bran, or cracked wheat. This applies to bread, pasta, tortillas, and cereals. If gluten or wheat present a problem for you, there are many substitutes such as buckwheat, millet, oats and more.

- ### Start Healthy Eating at the Store
  Once you bring home that bag of chips or ice cream, it is far more difficult to resist. Be choosy when you are shopping and resist the urge to buy those unhealthy items.

- ### Drink Healthy
  It does no good to eat healthy and then spoil it by drinking soda and other sweetened drinks. Many drinks are simply extra calories without much nutrition. There are many temptations: specialty coffee drinks, energy drinks, sports drinks, soda, chocolate milk, cocktails, and even too much fruit juice is not good for you. The best drink you can have is water. Low-fat milk is also a good choice. You will get all the nutrients and protein you need if you eat healthy and drink milk. If you don't drink milk, find another way to get calcium and vitamin D.

- ### Take the Time to Enjoy Your Food
  Eating too fast or when your attention is elsewhere may lead to eating too many calories. Pay attention to hunger and fullness cues before, during, and after meals. Use them to recognize when to eat and when you've had enough.

- ### Eat Certain Foods Less Often
  Cut back on foods high in solid fats, added sugars and salt. They include cakes, cookies, ice cream, candies, sweetened drinks, pizza, and fatty meats like ribs, sausages, bacon, and hot dogs. Use these foods as occasional treats, not everyday foods.

- **Compare Sodium in Foods**

  Use the Nutrition Facts label to choose lower sodium versions of foods like soup, bread, and frozen meals. Select canned foods labeled "low sodium," "reduced sodium," or "no salt added."

- **Avoid Over-Sized Portions**

  Most restaurants serve more food than is healthy for a single meal. Use a smaller plate, bowl and glass. Measure portions before you eat. When eating out, choose a smaller size option, share a dish, or take home part of your meal. You can save money, too.

- **Enjoy Foods from Many Cultures**

  Eating foods from a variety of cultures ensures you get many different nutrients and can make eating more enjoyable. Different cultures tend to use different herbs and spices, which can add flavor without adding calories and sodium. Try cooking the recipes yourself or with someone familiar with the culture and food. The meal will become more of an experience, and you will become more conscious of what goes into your food.

- **Balance Calories In and Calories Out**

  Check out the calorie calculator at Link 8-25. If you are not at a healthy weight, enter what a healthy weight would be for you. Look at the calorie figure and use that as a guide to achieve and maintain a healthy weight. Ultimately, it is calories that determine your weight, no matter how healthy or unhealthy you eat. You can still be unhealthy at a healthy weight, which is why you need to eat healthily AND balance your calories.

The *ChooseMyPlate* program provides a visual guideline for what a healthy and balanced meal should look like. Examine the picture on the right to get an idea of how much space the different food groups should occupy on your plate, and in your overall diet. The pages that follow go into further detail about each of the food groups. Each section describes how to recognize healthy choices for each of the food groups and the health benefits that each group can provide.

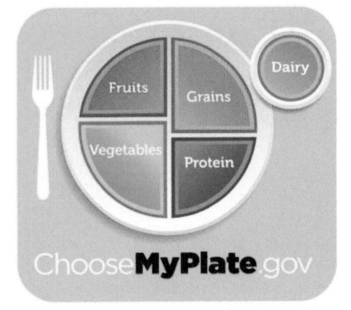

Much of this nutrition information will sound familiar, but most people don't stick to healthy eating all the time. It's OK to indulge a little sometimes. However, many people indulge too often because they don't have a good sense of how much or what they actually eat. That may sound strange. How can someone not know what they are eating? Research shows that many people underestimate how much they eat and overestimate how much physical activity they engage in.[2]

There are other reasons for not eating right, exercising enough or doing other things that aren't healthy. We procrastinate, make excuses, forget or lose willpower. We know what we should be doing to stay healthy, but we don't always do it. A good way to overcome those hurdles is to record the things that impact your health, such as diet and exercise. Keeping a record allows you to see exactly what you are doing—no over- or underestimating. It also keeps you thinking about your health when you might otherwise forget or lose your willpower. The U.S. Department of Agriculture has an online tracker that can help you plan, analyze, and track your diet and physical activity. The tracker is an excellent free tool that can help you, regardless of how healthy you are right now. Go to Link 8-26 to get started.

There are many other tools available that will perform similar functions: apps for smartphones, paper calendars or health consultants. Use some caution, however, as some tools can be pretty expensive and others may be using your personal information in harmful ways. Start with the government-sponsored tracker to learn what works for you. Then you should be able to make better decisions if you need to choose another health-maintenance resource.

Exercise

You should be physically active every day.

There are two basic forms of exercise: cardiovascular (aerobic) exercise, and strength and flexibility training.

In aerobic activity, you maintain elevated heart rate and therefore train your heart and lungs to become stronger. As you develop your aerobic fitness, you can exercise harder and for longer periods of time. This helps reduce the risk of diseases of the heart and lungs.

Strength and flexibility training includes exercises such as lifting weights and stretching. This helps to maintain strong muscles and bones, which delays the signs of aging and various diseases associated with muscle and bones.

Benefits of Exercise
- Improves endurance and strength
- Helps maintain a healthy weight
- Lowers risk of heart disease, cancer and diabetes
- Reduces anxiety and depression
- Is good for mental health and well-being
- Promotes strong bones, muscles, and joints

In order to maintain a regular exercise routine, choose activities that you enjoy. However, make sure you engage in **both** forms of exercise as you need both to gain the full health benefits associated with exercise.

New federal guidelines suggest the need for 30 to 60 minutes of moderate to vigorous physical activity each day. Activities are determined to be moderate or vigorous based on the extent to which they raise your breathing and heart rate. Light activities such as regular walking, shopping, and light household chores do not count toward physical activity recommendations.

Participating in vigorous physical activities allows you to meet recommendations in about half the time that would be required for moderate physical activities. See the lists below for some examples of moderate and vigorous physical activities.[3]

Moderate Physical Activities

- Walking briskly (about 3.5 mph)
- Bicycling (less than 10 mph)
- General gardening (raking, mowing)
- Dancing
- Golf (walking and carrying clubs)
- Water aerobics
- Canoeing
- Tennis (doubles)

Vigorous Physical Activities

- Running/jogging (5 mph)
- Walking very fast (4.5 mph)
- Bicycling (more than 10 mph)
- Heavy yard work, such as chopping wood
- Swimming laps
- Aerobics
- Basketball (competitive)
- Tennis (singles)

Stress

Most people immediately think of stress as being negative—that stress is bad for you and can cause health problems. This is only partially true. To understand stress better, first we need to define it.

Stress is the body's reaction to a stimulus or challenge causing it to move out of a normal balanced state.

Levels of stress can vary. The stress of being late for class differs from the stress of dealing with the death of a loved one, for example. Another type of stress is experienced when a person is ill, competing or in danger. In these last three situations, the body undergoes a "stress response," in which the heart and breathing rates increase and the body releases adrenaline and other hormones. A stress response is your body's way of helping you deal with a situation, and there's no risk to your health if it's of a short duration. Stress can become a problem when the pressure is constant. The way in which you view stress can also determine whether it has a negative impact on you. Watch the video at Link 8-27 to understand this idea better.

"The greatest weapon against stress is our ability to choose one thought over another."

– WILLIAM JAMES

©Alena Hovorkova/Shutterstock.com

HOW YOU VIEW STRESS

Did you view stress as a negative thing before watching the video? Think of some situations in your own life that cause you stress and describe two things you can do to make your stress a helpful response rather than a harmful or negative one.

"Sleep is a golden chain that ties our health and bodies together."

–THOMAS DEKKER

Sleep

Many students miss out on sleep when studying late for exams, going out with friends, and holding down a job outside of school. Unfortunately, sleep is extremely important for being successful in school. Lack of sleep can impair memory, and cause other learning difficulties.[4] Sleep deprivation can also cause problems with your immune system, mood, and your metabolism.

Enough Sleep

So, how much sleep do you need? Everyone has different requirements. To find out, think about how long you sleep when nothing wakes you up in the morning for about a week, such as on a vacation. After several days of not having to get up, your body will fall into its natural sleep rhythm. Don't count the first few days when you may sleep longer to catch up after being sleep deprived—as many of us are. Most people need between seven and eight hours.[5] More is not necessarily better. Current research shows that getting more than eight hours can paradoxically cause tiredness and other health problems.[6]

How to Sleep Better

Lying in a bed for eight hours does not necessarily mean you are getting a good sleep. The quality of your sleep is just as important as the length of your sleep. If you wake up after seven or eight hours and are still really tired, you are probably not getting quality sleep. There can be many reasons for poor sleep quality, from sleep apnea (Link 8-28) to a poor bedtime routine. Follow the list of sleep tips below to improve your overall quality of sleep.

Sleep Tips

- **Avoid caffeine, alcohol, nicotine, and other stimulants six hours before sleep**. These drugs not only inhibit your ability to fall asleep, they disrupt the quality of the rest you get when you finally manage to nod off. Some people believe alcohol helps them fall asleep. While this may be true, alcohol disrupts REM sleep (Link 8-29), which is important for overall sleep quality.
- **Have a relaxing bedtime routine**. Your body needs time to wind down at the end of the day. Avoid exercise, strenuous work or studying right before bed. Activities such as light reading—avoid thriller or horror novels—listening to relaxing music, a bath or shower, or simple conversation are good routines. Avoid anything that brings about stress or strong emotions. Dim the lights and allow the bedroom to cool a little before you go to bed. Sleep quality improves when the room temperature is a few degrees below the normal daytime temperature. Also avoid any large meals or rich foods before bed. It is better to snack in the afternoon and have a light supper than to stay hungry all day and gorge at night. Once you are in bed, get the room as dark and quiet as possible. Don't watch the clock as you fall asleep or if you wake up in the middle of the night; it will only stress you out more. You are better off turning the clock away from your bed.

- **Keep your bedroom focused on sleep only.** This is the one people most commonly neglect. Watching TV, using the computer, and studying are activities that stimulate the brain to stay awake and focus. As best you can, try to limit these activities to another room, even in the middle of the day. Your brain should associate your bedroom with sleep, not work or entertainment. A small exception to this is the light reading mentioned earlier. Reading in your bed is OK, but stick to light reading.

- **Invest in a good bed.** We spend a third of our entire life sleeping. This is more than the average person spends driving, on the phone, online, eating, in the bathroom, and watching TV—combined! Yet, many spend less time and money buying a mattress than they do on buying an outfit for a date. Do a little research and spend at least 20 minutes lying on a mattress before you decide to buy. Many places also have a money-back guarantee within a certain timeframe. Take advantage of this and trade in your mattress if you find you are not completely comfortable in your sleep. Also think carefully about your pillow and sleeping position, as these can have a big impact on your sleep. Check out the article at Link 8-30 for advice about sleeping and pillows.

- **Get light and exercise during the day.** Regular physical activity during the day (at least three hours before bedtime) improves the quality of your sleep at night. Also, getting a healthy dose of sunlight during the day, especially in the morning, helps with sleep. On cloudy days or if you are stuck inside, try brightly lit rooms and being near windows. Light, especially sunlight, helps naturally regulate melatonin, which is an important hormone for our sleep-wake cycles. See Link 8-31 to learn more about the role of melatonin.

- **Keep the same sleep-wake hours every day.** This one can be especially tough for students, who tend to change their sleeping patterns between the weekend and midweek. Our internal clocks take days to adjust to new sleep patterns. If you've ever traveled across time zones, then you've probably experienced jet lag. If you change your sleeping hours every few days, your body is in a constant state of jet lag. Shift workers experience this and very commonly have sleep problems. If you stay up late and go out with friends once every few weeks, you probably won't be affected too much. To offset the effect, if you happen to be up late one night, *don't* sleep in the next morning. Try to wake up at the same time every day. Your body will adjust the next night by going into a deeper sleep to catch up. If you are up late and sleep in every weekend, you're probably finding you are more tired than you should be during the week.

- **Stick to the plan.** Many people are already aware of these tips, but fail to follow through. Use techniques that you know will help keep you on track. Use reminders on your phone, plan together with your roommate, post reminders on your fridge—whatever it takes. After a few weeks of sticking to your plan, you should notice a difference in your energy levels, your ability to focus, and even your mood.

"Laugh and the world laughs with you;
snore and you sleep alone."

– ANTHONY BURGESS

TWO TASKS FOR YOUR HEALTH

Based on what you just learned about nutrition, exercise, stress, and sleep, describe two things you will do in the next few weeks to improve or maintain your best health.

SECTION 8-4: TIME MANAGEMENT

We have covered many topics and offered much advice up to this point. You may be asking, "How can I do all these things in the limited time that I have?" Luckily for you, we are going to finish with *time management!*

"The key is not to prioritize what's on your schedule, but to schedule your priorities."

–STEPHEN COVEY

©Sofi photo/Shutterstock.com

SCHEDULE OR PRIORITIZE?

Think about the quotation above. Describe what you think it means in your own words.

Introduction

Time could be considered our most precious resource. It is the only resource that we cannot renew. It is also the only thing that everyone gets the same amount of each day. It is what we do with the time available that makes us different. What we do with our time is called time management. There are lots of strategies and methods for managing time, many of which come from the business world. To a business, time is money.

In this section, we will discuss a few time management strategies and how to avoid one of the biggest "time eaters": procrastination.

ABC Analysis

ABC analysis is one of the older and simpler forms of time and resource management. It involves analyzing the things you have to do and assigning them one of three priorities: A, B, or C.

* **A items:** important and urgent (need to be done soon)
* **B items:** important, but not urgent
* **C items:** not important

The key to this strategy is the distinction between urgent and important. **Items that are important help contribute to your goals**. Items that are urgent need to be done very soon or the opportunity will be missed. Did you notice how we neglected to say whether C items are urgent or not? That is because urgency does not matter if it is not important. Many people run into time management problems because they focus so much on the urgency of items and forget about the importance of them. We get distracted by phone calls and texts because they feel urgent—we need to respond quickly. But, are all of your calls and texts important? A TV show, sporting event or dinner out with friends are opportunities we often don't want to miss, and they can be healthy recreational activities. However, when they interfere with tasks that contribute to your goals, you are not practicing good time management.

The activity below is a simplified way to practice ABC analysis.

ABC ANALYSIS

Imagine you are a student in the dental assistant program. Your primary goals are to graduate with a grade of 85% or higher, to graduate with no debt and to build a network of contacts who can help you find work. Look at the list of activities and label them as A, B, or C priorities. Then check your answers.

1. Study for an exam happening this week

2. Check out travel options for the summer

3. Meet with the career counselor about job opportunities after graduation

4. Get tickets for a concert that is almost sold out

5. Attend a school-organized luncheon tomorrow which local dentists are invited to attend

6. Fix your bike and get a transit pass so you can sell your car

7. Practice a song you have been working on with your guitar

8. Complete your online profile on LinkedIn

9. Select some extracurricular activities that will help you qualify for scholarships next year

10. Apply to a job posting for part-time work at the school health clinic

11. Make it to the one-day sale at your favorite clothing store

Answers: 1, 5 and 10 are A priorities. 3, 6, 8, and 9 are B priorities. 2, 4, 7, and 11 are C priorities.

If you scored perfectly in that activity, congratulations. If you missed a few, make sure you read through all of the feedback statements to understand what makes something an A, B, or C priority.

When you understand how to sort your priorities, it becomes easier to make decisions about what you should or should not do right now. You also need to determine *how much time* you spend on a task. If you have five A priorities, you should assign a level of priority within the A group. For example, if you have to study for a quiz worth 5% of your grade and have a paper due that is worth 20%, which should you spend more time on? That is an easy comparison. Comparisons get more difficult when you have to compare completing a resume for an upcoming job application or working on a paper that is due around the same time. You may have to find time by cancelling a regular scheduled activity related to one of your lesser goals. As you may have guessed, you need to clearly understand your goals to do this.

Typically, you want to focus on your A priorities first. When you have those out of the way you should work on your B priorities. Only when you have taken care of all the A and B priorities, should you work on C priorities. C priorities are typically recreational or simple "have fun" activities. Now, if you find that you are always working on A and B priorities, and never C, you may need to reevaluate your goals. You may have too many or you may have set unreasonable timelines for your goals. This can lead to burnout. Like many things in life, it is important to keep things balanced.

You need a balance of work and play. One approach that can help is choosing A and B activities that truly interest you. If you have selected your goals properly, they should already be aligned to your interests and other personal attributes. And, your A and B priorities should be aligned to your goals. If you find your A and B priorities all feel like chores, you may need to reevaluate your goals. There will always be priorities that feel more like work than play. For example, writing a math exam that is a required part of the dental assistant program probably does not fit in the "fun" category. However, there should be courses in your program that are interesting to you, and that should help make some of your A and B priorities more enjoyable.

Refer back to the quotation at the beginning of this section. Many people struggle to prioritize everything in their schedule because there are items in their schedule that are not A and B priorities. You need to *start* with identifying what your priorities are and only schedule those items. It may be difficult at first. It can make you feel productive to be working on many things at once. But, if you are not working on things that contribute to your goals, are you really being productive?

"How did it get so late so soon? It's night before it's afternoon. December is here before it's June. My goodness how the time has flewn. How did it get so late so soon?"

–DR. SEUSS

The last page discussed time management from the perspective of priorities. Once you know what your priorities are, there is still the matter of actually doing what needs to be done. Good time management means getting things done without becoming distracted and not procrastinating.

Procrastination

Everybody at some point in their lives is guilty of procrastination. Some people more than others. Take a look at your results in your online *Do What You Are* profile. Review the part that refers to the dimension of personality called judging and perceiving (JP). A person with a judging personality is not judgmental—they simply feel better after decisions have been made and like to do things in a methodical, planned-out manner. Perceivers like to keep their options open, often delaying decisions. They prefer to act in a more spontaneous manner—dealing with matters as they arise.

Remember that the dimension of judging or perceiving refers to how structured we prefer our lives to be.

No matter where you are on the JP scale, you can procrastinate or act decisively at different times. In fact, perceivers often act like judgers when they have to be decisive, such as in a leadership role or with an important deadline—it is just not their natural or preferred state. However, perceivers are *more likely* to procrastinate because of their personality type.

WHEN DO YOU PROCRASTINATE?

Think carefully about your *Do What You Are* results and your actions in the past. Be honest and think about whether you are prone to procrastinate. Describe situations in which you might procrastinate or what you think might cause you to procrastinate.

Procrastination has a few negative effects. The most obvious is that tasks don't get completed. For the procrastinator it also causes increased anxiety and illness.[1]

People know procrastinating is bad. So why do we do it? Let's take a look at the common reasons people procrastinate.

- **Belief that you will somehow be able to handle the task better in the future.** Of course, this belief is often misguided. In fact, problems are created and tend to get worse the longer a task remains incomplete.[2]
- **There is a short-term relief from not having to deal with a task right now.** This short-term relief comes at the expense of long-term suffering when the deadline approaches or the consequences of not completing the task finally occur. A common misconception is that procrastination results from having too much time. The opposite is actually true. Procrastinators have less time available than non-procrastinators, but falsely believe they can create time by putting things off until later.
- **Failure to find meaning or something positive in a task.** Chronic procrastinators are very good at finding the negatives in a task. Non-procrastinators are good at finding positive aspects in doing the same task. It is not about the task itself, it is about how a person views it.
- **Allowing distractions to hold your attention**. As new technologies present more potential distractions, this problem is becoming more common. Most distractions can be prevented: we can turn our phone off, close the email application, throw out that bag of chips, or go to the corner of the library to study instead of the middle of the campus quad. However, we often fail to prevent potential distractions. One reason may be the easy or quick rewards of those distractions, such as attention from others and sugary foods. A non-procrastinator can stay focused on the long-term rewards, such as good grades and a healthy body, that come with following through on a task.

- **The assumption that someone else will do it.** Very often, the other person is a parent, roommate, or romantic partner. This problem gets worse as the other person keeps covering for the procrastinator.
- **Getting caught in a cycle of guilt.** Procrastinators tend to suffer from feelings of guilt, especially those who procrastinate a lot. The guilt leads to a depressed mood, which results in further procrastination for the first and second reasons: procrastinators believe they should handle the task later, when their mood improves, and they get a quick mood boost by putting off the task.[3]

"Doing something that is productive is a great way to alleviate emotional stress. Get your mind doing something that is productive."

–ZIGGY MARLEY

So, how do you overcome these reasons and stop procrastinating? The first step is recognizing the reasons. If you can catch yourself delaying a task due to one of the reasons we've mentioned, you know you are procrastinating. This increased awareness helps you recognize that a reason to delay something is not really a reason but an excuse. The hard part is admitting the real reason for not doing a task. Try the journal below as an exercise in recognizing procrastination and doing something about it.

OVERCOMING PROCRASTINATION

Think of a task that you need to do but are putting it off. You may have just decided to delay doing it, or it may be something you have put off for weeks. It may be something small, such as cleaning the fridge out, or it may be something much more significant such as breaking up with your significant other. Answer the following questions based on delaying that task.

Reflect carefully on your reasons for procrastinating. Is it one of the reasons listed above? Is it another reason that will do more harm than good? Explain.

Based on the reason you chose for question 1, how do you think you can overcome your procrastination and get the task done?

CHAPTER 8 QUIZ

Money, Health, and Time Management

This quiz covers all of the topics from this chapter on money, health, and time management. Before you answer any questions, scan them and return to review any pages you need to be confident in your answers.

1. Which of the following offers the greatest return on investment?
   a. a mutual fund with an average return of 7% and a management expense ratio of 2%
   b. paying off a loan that has a 4% interest rate
   c. high-interest savings account that earns 3% interest
   d. a savings bond at 4% interest

2. Which of the following is most likely to have the highest interest rate?
   a. a federal unsubsidized student loan
   b. a private student loan
   c. a credit card
   d. a Pell Grant

3. Which of the following is one of the best ways to improve your chances of getting scholarship money?
   a. get involved in extracurricular activities
   b. hire a private service online
   c. focus your effort and apply for only one scholarship
   d. wait for a financial aid officer to contact you

4. A good way to know how much you are spending each month on small items is to
   a. get rid of your credit cards
   b. find value in things that cost less money
   c. track your expenses in a spreadsheet
   d. set up a budget before you go shopping

5. Which of the following is **not** a good way to maintain a healthy weight?
   a. make about 50% of your plate fruits and vegetables
   b. consume diet drinks
   c. focus on enjoying your food
   d. choose whole grains when eating breads and cereals

6. Which of the following is true about exercise?
   a. you can choose either aerobic exercise or strength training
   b. it reduces anxiety and depression
   c. you should do about 15 minutes every day
   d. light activities such as walking around the mall count as exercise

7. Which of the following is most important in determining whether stress has a negative impact on your health?
   a. the type of stress you experience
   b. the level of stress you experience
   c. how long you experience stress
   d. how you think about the stress

8. Which of the following is recommended to help you sleep better?
   a. sleep in when you don't have to be up in the morning
   b. exercise right before bed so you tire yourself out
   c. have a drink before you go to sleep
   d. get plenty of sunlight in the morning

9. In ABC analysis of priorities, a B priority is
   a. important and urgent
   b. important but not urgent
   c. urgent but not important
   d. neither urgent nor important

10. Which of the following is a common reason people procrastinate?
    a. their goals change
    b. they believe they will handle it better later
    c. nobody will help them
    d. they have too much time available

MONEY, HEALTH AND TIME MANAGEMENT

©arka38/Shutterstock.com

This is a quick survey to measure what you know about this chapter topic, both before and after completing the chapter. Just be honest and rate how much each of the following statements applies to you. Give yourself a score of:

1 for Not a bit • 2 for A little • 3 for Some • 4 for Mostly • 5 for Definitely

AFTER CHAPTER

	Not a bit 1	A little 2	Some 3	Mostly 4	Definitely 5
1. I know several types of financial aid and the differences between them.	○	○	○	○	○
2. I know where to apply for financial aid and how to maximize my chances of getting what I need.	○	○	○	○	○
3. I know how to avoid accumulating too much debt in college.	○	○	○	○	○
4. I can describe proven money management tips that will be useful over my lifetime.	○	○	○	○	○
5. I know what behaviors lead to poor spending habits.	○	○	○	○	○

6	I can describe the importance of health when it comes to school, work, and personal life.	○	○	○	○	○ 6
7	I can describe behaviors that lead to good nutrition and behaviors that lead to poor nutrition.	○	○	○	○	○
8	I know what the latest research says about the benefits of exercise.	○	○	○	○	○
9	I know what the latest research says about stress and how my beliefs about stress are important.	○	○	○	○	○
10	I can describe at least five benefits of proper sleep and what behaviors lead to good sleep patterns.	○	○	○	○	○
11	I know of at least two free sources of excellent information on financial aid.	○	○	○	○	○
12	I have searched for scholarships to find out which ones I qualify for.	○	○	○	○	○
13	I can describe at least one time-management strategy.	○	○	○	○	○
14	I have used a strategy to help me prioritize various tasks.	○	○	○	○	○
15	I know what causes procrastination and have thought of ways I can overcome it.	○	○	○	○	○
16	I am confident that I can effectively manage my money, health, and time while in college.	○	○	○	○	○

Add up your scores to determine your **After Chapter** total and write it down here:

Write your **Before Chapter** total here:

Compare your Before and After scores to see how your knowledge of this chapter topic has changed.

CHAPTER 8 FEEDBACK

Congratulations, you've completed Chapter 8! To conclude your learning in this chapter, consider and note the following:

What parts of this chapter were most helpful to you?

How would you improve this chapter?

RIGHTS, RESPECT, AND RESPONSIBILITY

THE 3 'R'S OF COLLEGE: RIGHTS, RESPECT, AND RESPONSIBILITY

This section will help you learn about your rights on campus, respecting others' rights, your college's responsibilities, and federal regulations intended to protect you.

Think you know your school pretty well? Let's find out. Do you know:
*   The name used by your school's athletics teams?
*   Your school mascot's name?
*   Your school's official colors and motto?
*   The name of the student newspaper?
*   What time the library closes?
*   The best place to get pizza late at night?

Too easy? OK, let's try some more questions. This time, let's see how much you know about campus crime, your rights and responsibilities at college—and those of your school.

RIGHTS, RESPECT AND RESPONSIBILITY - - - - - - - - - - -

This is a quick survey to measure what you know about rights, respect, and responsibility. Just be honest and select the response that is most appropriate, then read on for further information.

BEFORE CHAPTER

1   My school has a non-discrimination policy and I know what it covers.

True   **False**   **Unsure**

Did you know that all colleges are required to have a non-discrimination policy to receive federal funding? You will learn about this ahead.

2 If a student complains about discrimination, the school can kick them out.

True   **False**   **Unsure**

False. Federal law protects people who complain about discrimination. You will learn more about this ahead.

3 I know how to contact my school's Title IX coordinator.

True   **False**   **Unsure**

Did you know that all colleges are required to have a Title IX coordinator?

4 Colleges don't have to follow up on every complaint of sexual harassment.

True   **False**   **Unsure**

False. The school is required to follow up every complaint according to a published procedure. You will learn more about this ahead.

5 My school provides information about how to prevent sexual violence.

True   **False**   **Unsure**

Colleges are required to provide this information to students. You will learn more about this ahead.

6 If a student gets drunk and ends up having sex when they didn't want to, it's their own fault.

True   **False**   **Unsure**

Not true. In fact, the perpetrator could be criminally charged.

7 No serious crimes ever happen at my school.

True   **False**   **Unsure**

Unfortunately, there is an epidemic of serious crimes on U.S. campuses. Steps are being taken to mitigate the problem, but there is a long way to go.

8 Victims of sexual assault are required to change their living arrangements on campus.

True   **False**   **Unsure**

False. They are only required to be *told* that they have the *option* to change things if they want to.

9 I know the procedure for reporting a crime at my school.

True   **False**   **Unsure**

Did you know that all colleges are required to make known the procedure for reporting a crime?

10   I know what to do if someone I know is sexually harassed on campus.

True   **False**   **Unsure**

It's a good thing to know. We have more tips and information ahead. The more you know, the more help you can be to your friends.

11   If a student is raped, they are required to file a police report.

True   **False**   **Unsure**

The victim is not *required* to do anything. Of course, the victim *can* file a report when he or she is ready to do so.

12   I know the legal definition of "consent" in my state or jurisdiction.

True   **False**   **Unsure**

This is important to know. You can find more information about this and other important definitions in this chapter.

13   If two students are dating, it's not the school's problem if the relationship turns violent.

True   **False**   **Unsure**

Not true. The school is required to address the situation if they have any awareness of it, or could gain awareness through expected procedures.

14   Rape is the most common violent crime on American college campuses.

True   **False**   **Unsure**

True. Sadly, this and other statistics reveal that sexual violence is a serious problem on U.S. campuses.

15   If a student is accused of sexual assault, the school will put them on probation.

True   **False**   **Unsure**

This is false. The school must hear from both the accuser and the accused, gather evidence, and resolve the situation accordingly. Specific punishment, if any, is decided based on the individual case.

16   I am familiar with my school's emergency response procedure.

True   **False**   **Unsure**

This is important to know if an emergency does occur. Your school likely has a published procedure.

You probably found this set of questions a lot more difficult to answer. It's vital that you know the correct responses. This information can help to ensure your safety and well-being on campus, guarantee that your rights are protected, and help you understand what you should expect from your school.

The answers have been partly revealed above. We say "partly" because the answers are often not simple. They need to be fully explained for proper understanding. You will learn some of the answers to these questions as you complete this section. However, some of the answers will depend on your school and area of the country. For those answers, you will find a resource list for your campus at the end of this section to help you learn more.

Key Questions

1. What are my rights on campus?

2. What are the college's legal responsibilities regarding my safety and well-being?

3. What is sex discrimination and what constitutes sexual violence?

4. How do I best protect myself, respond to and report incidents, and use available campus resources?

CHAPTER PREVIEW

This chapter will make the point that how we get along with one another depends on respect, rights, and responsibility. Respecting others' rights and taking responsibility for our actions are pivotal to a healthy society.

©SnowWhiteimages/Shutterstock.com

Many cultures around the world have customs that promote respect for each other, especially with how we greet people. In North America we shake hands and look each other in the eyes. In eastern Asia, people often bow to each other. In southern Asia there is the greeting of "Namaste," which can be accompanied by the palms pressed together in front of the heart and a bowing of the head. The greeting and the gesture are said to represent several things. First, it signifies a deep recognition of the other person and yourself as equals.[1] Bringing the palms together over the heart also represents connecting to each other in friendship, respect and humility.

Most people would agree that it would be great if everyone followed the ideals of Namaste and respected one another to such a great degree. However, we know that things don't always work out that way and that society needs clear rules on how mutual respect can be maintained. Rights and responsibilities can be considered rules for how to maintain that respect. For example, the right to free speech ensures we respect others' points of view. The responsibility to report crimes ensures respect for the laws that protect our safety.

This chapter will cover topics that range between the abstract ideals of respect to the more concrete concepts of laws and rights. However, we hope you keep in mind the connection between those abstract and concrete ideas, just like the connection of the hands in Namaste.

SECTION 9-1: TITLE IX

What is Title IX?

If your school receives federal financial assistance from the United States Department of Education—which most colleges and universities in the U.S. do—then it is required to comply with several laws designed to protect students. The granddaddy of these laws is known as Title IX and it was originally enacted in 1972.

> No person in the United States shall, on the basis of sex, be excluded from participation in, be denied the benefits of, or be subjected to discrimination under any education program or activity receiving federal financial assistance.

Title IX is a federal civil rights law that protects people from sex discrimination in education programs and activities. It may come as a surprise to you to learn that, just a few short decades ago, women required higher grades than men to get into college. There was a limit to the number of women admitted to graduate schools. Many colleges and universities flat out refused to admit women, and no law existed that could force them to do so. College scholarships for female athletes were virtually non-existent, and financial aid was often withheld from women who were married, pregnant, or parents.

The Impact of Title IX

Medical school graduates[1]:
1970 – men 92% and women 8%
2013 – men 52% and women 48%

Nursing graduates[2]:
1972 – men 1% and women 99%
2012 – men 16% and women 84%

What Title IX Covers

Even if you have heard of it before, you might think Title IX applies mostly to college sports. But, in fact, Title IX is a wide- ranging piece of legislation. While inequities still exist, Title IX is helping to level the playing field—in athletics, academics, and many other areas. Check out the table to see some of the main areas addressed.

Some Areas Addressed by Title IX

- **Admission and recruitment**: Prior to Title IX, many colleges and universities used discriminatory recruitment and admission practices, such as setting gender quotas. This helped to exclude or severely restrict women's access to higher education. Reducing the barriers has allowed more women to pursue degrees, gain entry into non-traditional fields, and improve their earning potential.
- **Financial assistance**: A variety of tactics were once used to prevent women from receiving scholarships, loans, and other forms of financial aid. Today, the law requires a more equitable distribution, although certain scholarships are still legally permitted to be gender-specific. Athletic scholarships, which were rarely available to women, must now be made available to men's and women's athletic programs proportional to their rates of participation.
- **Academic programs**: Title IX has widened the scope of course offerings and programs available to all students. The law requires institutions to provide both genders with comparable levels of resources, support and promotional opportunities in academic programs. Men and women are now graduating from programs that once were inaccessible to them—and enjoying better career prospects and higher salaries as a result.
- **Career and vocational education**: Woodworking is for boys and sewing is for girls, right? Before Title IX, that outdated mentality ensured that students were restricted to training for jobs considered suitable for their sex. These days, a person's gender cannot be used to determine their career education options. So if a male student wants to pursue a credential in nursing and a female student wants to learn welding technology, that's their decision to make.
- **Sex-based harassment**: Sexual comments, jokes or gestures, unwelcome sexual advances, inappropriate touching—all used to be brushed off as "harmless." But these actions are all examples of sexual harassment. Under Title IX, schools are legally obligated to protect students from these and other forms of unwelcome sexual conduct, whether the perpetrator is a student, instructor, or other staff member.
- **Treatment of pregnant and parenting students**: Schools once had the right to expel pregnant students. Under Title IX, pregnant and parenting students must be given equal access to schools, programs and activities. Students cannot be forced to attend separate programs, nor may they be penalized for absences relating to their pregnancy. When they return to class following a medical leave, they must be given the opportunity to make up missed coursework.
- **Learning environment**: Gender stereotypes in classrooms, and in textbooks and other learning materials, are changing as a result of Title IX. All students have the right to expect a supportive educational environment, unbiased learning materials and the same level of assistance in class, regardless of their gender or the subject they're studying.

- **Grades**: Title IX law extends to discriminatory grading practices. Educational institutions are prohibited from grading students unfairly based on their gender. The law also protects students who feel they have been unfairly graded in retaliation for reporting or rejecting unwelcome sexual advances.
- **STEM careers**: Science, technology, engineering, and math have been heavily influenced by stereotypical mindsets. Men have traditionally been viewed as having more natural ability in these fields. That's discouraged women from pursuing STEM majors and prevented them from participating in the lucrative high- tech and engineering job sectors. Title IX requires that both genders receive equal access and support. Women are still underrepresented in these fields, but the tide is slowly turning.
- **Housing**: In the past, a lack of appropriate housing was another means by which colleges could limit the number of female students. Under Title IX, schools are permitted to provide separate, gender-based housing, but only if it is both proportionate in quantity to the number of students of each sex applying for the housing and comparable in quality and cost to the student. Schools are forbidden from applying different rules or regulations, imposing different fees or requirements, or offering different services or benefits related to housing.
- **Discipline**: Title IX forbids sex discrimination in disciplinary procedures and sanctions. Students in a similar situation must not be disciplined differently for the same offense based on their sex. Institutions must also ensure that a student's gender identity, or a refusal to conform to sexual stereotypes, is not a factor in disciplinary procedures.
- **Athletics and recreation**: Title IX prohibits sex discrimination in interscholastic, intercollegiate, club and intramural athletics. Schools must provide equal benefits and treatment overall—this includes such things as equipment, locker rooms, coaches, medical and training services, game facilities, travel, publicity, and practice time. Schools must effectively accommodate students' athletic interests and abilities, and provide both sexes with the opportunity to participate in sports.

In addition to all these areas, it's important to remember that Title IX applies equally to all students.

Some examples of students protected by Title IX
- Female, male, transgender, and gender non-conforming
- Straight, gay, lesbian, and bisexual
- Part-time and full-time students
- Students with and without disabilities
- Students of different races and national origins

Check out the video at Link 9-1 for a summary of what Title IX entails.

To learn more about the rights enshrined in Title IX, read the info sheet from the U.S. Department of Education Office for Civil Rights at Link 9-2.

What Happens if a School Does Not Comply with Title IX?

The consequences for schools that do not comply can be serious. If discrimination or sexual violence hinder a student's ability to continue their education and the school fails to respond appropriately, the school may be found to have violated that student's rights. According to the American Civil Liberties Union (ACLU), a school may be held legally responsible when it knows about and ignores sexual harassment or assault in its programs or activities. The school can be held responsible in court whether the harassment is committed by a faculty member, staff or a student. In some cases, the school may be ordered to pay damages to the victim.

The Department of Education requires your school to define sex discrimination and to publish a policy stating that the school does not discriminate on the basis of sex. The school is also required to designate a Title IX coordinator, and publish grievance procedures providing for the prompt and equitable resolution of sex discrimination complaints. These requirements apply to all forms of sexual harassment, including sexual violence.

Take a few minutes right now to briefly familiarize yourself with your school's non-discrimination policy and grievance procedures. You don't have to read them in depth, but it's a good idea to understand the basics and know where you can find this information if you need it.

Go online and use your school website's search tool to locate the school's non-discrimination notice or policy. Then look up its grievance and due process procedures.

Get to Know Your Title IX Coordinator

Your school is required to designate at least one employee to organize its Title IX responsibilities, administer the requirements and ensure the school complies. In most schools, this person is called the Title IX coordinator.

Title IX protects students, as well as employees and certain others, from all forms of sex discrimination in every aspect of the school's educational programs and activities, so the coordinator's role is extensive. They're involved at many levels, and deal with students, staff and people from various departments. They're often called on to investigate complaints or reports of sexual misconduct and other sex-based discriminatory practices.

They're also a great source of information, because educating students about their rights under Title IX is part of the job. So if you don't understand your school's non-discrimination policy, or don't know what sexual harassment means, ask your Title IX coordinator. If you have questions about gender equity in athletics, extracurricular activities, academics or any of the other areas covered by Title IX at your school, they can provide the answers. If you want information about your school's grievance procedures, or don't know how to file a complaint alleging a Title IX violation, the coordinator can provide consultation and information.

Bear in mind, however, that Title IX coordinators are not counselors. They are not permitted to take sides during investigations of Title IX complaints, and they cannot advocate on your behalf. Also, while they will deal with complaints as sensitively as possible, confidentiality cannot be guaranteed. State law, and the school's responsibility to provide a safe environment for everyone, will determine whether or not requests for confidentiality can be honored.

You should be able to find contact information for the Title IX coordinator on your school's website.

TITLE IX REFLECTION

What did you learn about Title IX? Did any of it surprise you? Explain.

Describe an example of a situation in which Title IX would apply and what a school should do to address it.

SECTION 9-2: CAMPUS SAVE ACT

Jeanne's Story

Photographs of Jeanne Clery portray a young blonde woman with a bright smile. At 19, she was a freshman student living on campus at Lehigh University, about 60 miles away from her family home. Her parents were pleased with her choice of Lehigh, a private, co-ed school in the historic city of Bethlehem, PA. It was small, close by and seemed like a safe choice for their only daughter.

On the morning of April 5, 1986, a few days after she had returned from spring break, Jeanne was asleep in her third-floor dorm when a stranger entered her room. Initially intent on theft, the intruder violently attacked Jeanne when she woke up during the robbery. Jeanne was beaten, tortured, raped, and strangled.

Her murderer, a 20-year-old sophomore, was a fellow student at Lehigh who lived off campus. Jeanne didn't know him. He had gained entry to the dorm through three doors, each equipped with automatic locks, that had been propped open by students for simple convenience. Jeanne's room was selected at random because it offered easy access: the door had been left ajar at the request of her roommate, who was out on a date and had misplaced her key.

Jeanne's devastated parents were shocked to learn later that the leafy campus their daughter had so loved, and which had seemed like such a safe place, had been the scene of 38 violent crimes, including rape, robbery, and assault, in the three- year period before her murder. There had also been 181 reports of her dorm's auto-locking doors being propped open.

The Clerys filed a civil suit against the university charging negligence and alleging, amongst other things, that the school had known about students' habit of propping doors open. An out-of-court settlement was reached in return for an undisclosed amount and a pledge from Lehigh to strengthen its security measures. Jeanne's parents went on to found the Clery Center for Security on Campus, a non-profit organization dedicated to safe campus communities. You can learn more about the Clery Center and its work at Link 9-3.

MINDSET 9-1
Access Policy

Do you know your school's access policy? If you found a door propped open at your college, what would you do? Record your answer in the space below.

The Clery Act and Campus SaVE

Prior to Jeanne's death, there were no laws requiring colleges to report crimes on campus to students, employees, potential students, or their parents. Thanks to Jeanne's parents' lobbying efforts, and with outrage growing over other non-reported incidents across the country, awareness of campus crime increased. In 1991, the federal government enacted the Jeanne Clery Disclosure of Campus Security Policy and Campus Crime Statistics Act—commonly known as the Clery Act.

The Clery Act requires all colleges and universities that receive federal financial aid funding to collect and disclose information about crime on and near their campuses. These schools are required to disclose their security policies, maintain a public crime log, publish annual security and fire safety reports, and provide timely warnings to students and employees about crimes posing a serious or ongoing threat to the campus community. They must devise emergency response and evacuation policies, and have procedures in place to handle reports of missing students.

The act requires schools to annually report statistics for various criminal offenses, including forcible and non-forcible sex offenses and aggravated assault. The crimes of domestic violence, dating violence and stalking were added in March 2013 with an amendment called the Campus Sexual Violence Elimination Act (known as Campus SaVE), in response to the need to address high rates of these crimes on college campuses. The U.S. Department of Education is required to collect and publish the crime statistics.

CRIME STATISTICS FOR YOUR SCHOOL

Visit the Department of Education's **Campus Security Statistics** website using Link 9-4. Click on "Get data for one institution/campus." Look up the information for your school and answer the questions below.

©arka38/Shutterstock.com

1 How many criminal offenses have taken place on campus in the last three years? What types of crimes were committed?

2   How many people have been referred for disciplinary action in the last three years? What laws did they violate?

3   How does this information make you feel about your safety on campus? Explain.

Know the Warning Signs

Statistics show how prevalent the problem of sexual violence is on campuses across the nation. Consider the facts in the following table.

U.S. Campus[1]

- Rape is the most common violent crime on American college campuses.
- One in four women will be the victim of sexual assault while in college.
- Every 21 hours there is a rape on an American college campus.
- College women are most vulnerable to rape during the first few weeks of their freshman and sophomore years.
- College rape victims receive external physical injuries in over 47% of all rapes.
- 43% of dating college women have experienced abusive dating behaviors including physical, sexual, tech, verbal, or controlling abuse.
- 57% of college students who report experiencing dating violence said it occurred in college.
- 63.3% of men at one university who self-reported acts qualifying as rape or attempted rape admitted to committing repeat rapes.
- More than 90% of sexual assault victims on college campuses do not report the assault.

For a closer look at the problem of campus sexual assault, read the personal stories of some real-life victims at Link 9-5. Then come back and answer the questions.

@Alena Hovorkova/Shutterstock.com

SEXUAL VIOLENCE

What have you learned about crime and sexual violence from this section so far? Are you surprised by what you've read? Explain in the box below.

Would you recognize the warning signs that someone was at risk of sexual violence? What if the potential victim was a friend of yours? What if the person at risk was you—would you be aware of the danger?

People who are planning to commit an assault often exhibit certain behaviors. By learning to identify those behaviors, you could help to prevent a sexual assault from occurring. Here's what to watch out for.[2]

A potential perpetrator is likely to:
- Zero in on a person they can easily influence, such as a student who is new on campus or someone who is drunk or high
- Encourage the intended victim to consume more alcohol or drugs in order to increase their vulnerability
- Use compliments and give the person their undivided attention to encourage a sense of ease and intimacy
- Disregard personal boundaries by standing too close or touching the person without permission
- Attempt to isolate their target by getting the person to leave the safety of the group—inviting them to "go somewhere quiet where we can talk," for example

Following an assault, a perpetrator will often:
- Attempt to confuse the victim by acting as if nothing is wrong
- Try to make it seem like the victim initiated the sexual activity
- Send follow-up messages ("U were HOT last night!") to make it seem like the activity was consensual
- Boast about the incident to friends
- Expect others to view this behavior as acceptable conduct

Sometimes people who witness these actions don't react because they're too embarrassed or afraid to interfere. Sometimes they don't know what to do, or they just don't believe it's happening. If you think a friend is being singled out and could be in danger of assault, but you're not sure, all you need to do is check with them. Just walk up and ask how they're doing. Then you can decide whether or not it's necessary to do anything further.

Let's say you sense your friend is in trouble, but you don't know how to intervene. In the next section, you'll get some advice on how to become an active bystander.

SECTION 9-3: BYSTANDER STRATEGIES

WHAT WOULD YOU DO?

Read the following scenarios and respond to the questions for each one.

Imagine you're going to a party! It's taking place at a friend's dorm on campus
Imagine yourself walking in and helping yourself to food and a drink. The music's great, the party
has a good vibe and you're feeling relaxed. You decide to find a comfortable place to sit down and do a
little people watching.

1. Over by the bar, you can see Megan. She's pretty drunk and is having trouble standing up. Megan
made it clear earlier in the evening that she wasn't interested in Scott. But Scott's been giving her drinks
all night and it looks like she's loosening up. She's not pushing him away any more when he tries to kiss
her. He grabs her around the waist and you hear him suggest they go find somewhere more private.
Megan doesn't look capable of resisting.

   What would you do in this situation? Write your response in the box below.

2. Near the door, you hear angry voices. It's James and Toya. They've been dating for a few months, but
it's a rocky relationship. It seems like they argue most of the time. Toya has confided to a friend that
James sometimes pushes her around. He even gave her a black eye once, but she lied and told people
she bumped into a door. She'd like to break up with James, but is afraid to. Now he seems mad about
something and wants to leave the party. Toya says she'd like to stay and talk to her friends, but he grips
her arm and starts pulling her out the door.

   What would you do in this situation? Write your response in the box below.

©arka38/Shutterstock.com

3   Sitting quietly in the corner is Joe. Joe lives with his partner Rob in an apartment near campus. Rob is about 10 years older than Joe and works at a restaurant in town. Rob resents the time Joe spends on his studies and gets jealous when Joe socializes with classmates. He tries to make Joe feel guilty about going to college and berates him for not contributing enough financially. At times he gets so angry that he lashes out. Joe checks the time, an anxious look on his face, and picks up his coat. He'd better get home before Rob returns from work or he'll have to deal with the usual inquisition about where he's been and who he's been talking to.

What would you do in this situation? Write your response in the box below.

4   You're having a conversation with Thomas when a text comes in on his phone. He glances down to see who it's from. Not again! Will this ever end? It's Cindy. They dated once, briefly. It didn't work out, but Cindy is not willing to let go. She bombards Thomas with calls and texts and turns up everywhere he goes. She lurks on social media, trying to get Thomas to talk to her and attempting to get information from his friends. Thomas couldn't prove it, but when someone slashed his car tires, he immediately suspected it was her. Thomas hits Delete and turns back to talk to you, but the text has clearly disturbed him. He confides the situation is getting worse and it seriously creeps him out.

What would you do in this situation? Write your response in the box below.

In June 2013, an unconscious young woman student at a Tennessee university was carried into a dorm room by several members of the university's football team. One of the men, who she had been dating, invited the others to rape her. A few feet away, in a nearby bunk, lay the man's roommate. He saw what was happening but pretended to be asleep, later testifying in court that he felt scared and uncomfortable and didn't know what to do.

Following the assault the woman was dumped, still unconscious and partially clothed, in the hall outside the dorm room. A number of people saw her there, including a friend of hers. Not one of them tried to help. Two other men eventually picked her up and carried her back into the dorm room and left her on the bed. Neither of them reported the incident or called for assistance.

While the attack was clearly witnessed by the roommate, and the woman's plight was observed by a number of people in the hallway, not one of these bystanders intervened. Why were they reluctant to assist a defenseless victim who was so obviously in need of help?

HOW TO BE AN ACTIVE BYSTANDER

Be honest. How would you have reacted in this case? Note your response below. Then watch the video at Link 9-6 for a good example of the difference between being a passive onlooker and an active bystander. After you watch the video, look back at your answer and think about how you might respond differently in future.

How to Be an Active Bystander

In the What Would You Do scenarios, you learned that you have a choice to make in situations where you can see that someone is vulnerable and in danger. You can elect to be a passive onlooker, remain silent and do nothing. Or you can choose to get involved and be an **active bystander**.

Active bystanders are people with the self-confidence to step up and take action to prevent or interrupt a sexual assault. Intervening could be as simple as offering to take a friend home if they've had too much to drink. In more serious situations, it might involve contacting the police or campus security.

Why get involved? For one thing, you'll experience the rewarding feeling of having assisted a person who's in trouble. Equally important, your decision to take action can influence others around you to get involved. So if you choose to be an active bystander, you'll not only be helping one individual one time—you'll also be inspiring others to have the courage to intervene, which will help to reduce the possibility of future acts of violence.

> *"Things are never quite as scary when you've got a best friend."*
>
> –BILL WATTERSON

If you encounter a situation in which you've determined that someone is at risk and you've decided you want to help, there are constructive things you can do to intervene. It's vital to remember that **active bystanders must always act in a safe and positive way**. At no time should you risk harm to yourself.

Bystander Options[1]

- If the situation is not volatile, you could step in and ask the person if they need help.
  Example: *"Hey, how are you doing? Is everything OK here?"*
- If the person is incapacitated, stay with them or arrange for their friends to take care of them.
  Example: *"You look pretty tired. Your friend says she'll take you home. I'll sit with you until she gets here."*
- If you know the aggressor, talk to them directly. Tell tell them you don't approve of what they're doing and ask them to leave the person alone.
  Example: *"What do you think you're doing? You're acting like a jerk. Cut it out and leave her/him alone."*
- If you don't know what to do or are not comfortable intervening, contact your resident assistant (RA) or campus public safety department.
  Check your school's website for information about local safety contacts.
- If the situation is an emergency, call 9-1-1.

"I swore never to be silent whenever and wherever human beings endure suffering and humiliation. We must always take sides. Neutrality helps the oppressor, never the victim. Silence encourages the tormentor, never the tormented."

–ELIE WIESEL

BYSTANDER STRATEGIES

Choose one of the two options below and complete the journal entry accordingly.

Option A - Talk to Someone
Together with one or two other people, think of some other situations in which people could be helped by bystanders. Discuss strategies that could be used to intervene in a safe and positive way. Record a summary of your discussion below.

OR

Option B - Web-based Research
Read stories from bystanders who have stepped in to help someone. Based on what you read, describe one effective strategy that you could use to intervene in a safe and positive way. Use the website at Link 9-7 as your resource.

SECTION 9-4: PERSONAL SAFETY

Prohibited Conduct

It's your right, and the right of your fellow students, to learn and study at your school in a safe environment without fear of harassment and sexual violence. By federal law, your school prohibits the offenses of sexual assault, dating violence, domestic violence, and stalking. Schools that receive federal financial assistance are required to provide specific definitions for these terms. They are also required to provide a definition for consent with regard to sexual activity.

IMPORTANT DEFINITIONS

Find the definitions that your school provides for the following terms. You can typically find them on your school's website by using the website's search tool. If that doesn't work, try to find the definitions in areas such as "policies and procedures," the student handbook, or the campus police/security department. If you are still having trouble, contact the campus Title IX coordinator for help. Find the definitions, read them, understand them, and copy them into the spaces provided.

Sexual assault is defined as...

Dating violence is defined as...

Domestic violence is defined as...

Stalking is defined as...

Myths about Sexual Assault[1]

If a victim doesn't scream and fight to rebuff an unwanted sexual encounter, is it considered rape? There are many myths and misunderstandings about rape and sexual assault. See how many of these you recognize. Read the myth and think about it before you go on to read the fact.

- **Myth**: Women who dress or act provocatively are "asking for it"
  Fact: This type of mentality tries to blame the victim. A person's dress or behavior is not an invitation to be sexually assaulted.
- **Myth**: People who get drunk or high are looking to have sex
  Fact: Being intoxicated can make a victim more vulnerable to being raped or assaulted. It doesn't mean they consent, or are even capable of consenting, to sexual activity.
- **Myth**: If a couple has already had consensual sex, there's no need to ask the next time
  Fact: Sex without consent, at any time and under any circumstances, is sexual assault.
- **Myth**: Men don't get raped
  Fact: It's estimated that about 10% rapes are committed against males. Few tend to be reported due to the stigma of having been forced into sex by a woman or another man.
- **Myth**: Sexual assault happens on impulse, when things go too far and get out of control
  Fact: Many rapes and sexual assaults are planned and carried out deliberately.
- **Myth**: People make accusations of rape when they're seeking revenge or regret having had sex
  Fact: Statistics show that false allegations of rape are extremely rare.
- **Myth**: It's not rape if the person doesn't fight back
  Fact: Victims often feel too threatened to defend themselves. Nonconsensual sexual intercourse is rape.
- **Myth**: Only gay men get raped
  Fact: Men of all sexual orientations are the victims of rape, and men who rape other men are often straight. Rape is an act of violence. It's about power and the need to dominate another person.

The Facts about Date Rape

Here's another common myth. Many people think rape* is something that only happens between strangers in a dark alley. But in fact, a large proportion of rapes are committed by assailants who know their victim. It's estimated that 90% of college women who are victims of rape or attempted rape know the person who attacked them. Usually the perpetrator is a classmate, friend, boyfriend, ex-boyfriend, or other acquaintance[2].

Acquaintance rape is nonconsensual sexual intercourse that happens between people who know each other—like classmates, neighbors or work colleagues, for example. Date rape is a term often used to describe a form of acquaintance rape that happens between people who are in a dating, romantic or potentially sexual relationship.

* Note that the legal definitions and terminology for rape, date rape, and other forms of sexual violence differ from state to state. For guidance on the laws in your jurisdiction, see the resource at Link 9-8 provided by the Rape, Abuse and Incest National Network (RAINN).[3]

In some states, the legal definition of date rape involves drugging the victim to make them more submissive. This can include plying the victim with excessive amounts of alcohol (the most common drug of all), or slipping a "date rape drug" such as GHB, Ketamine or Rohypnol ("roofies") into the victim's drink to render them unconscious, numb, or unable to move.

Date rape drugs are often colorless and have no discernible smell or taste, so the victim can't tell they're being drugged. Some of these drugs can affect the victim's memory, making it difficult for the person to recall the attack later. They can also have very serious side effects, such as causing problems breathing, seizures, coma and death. Both males and females can be the victims of date rape drugs.

The physical and emotional trauma caused by date rape is just as harmful as the damage inflicted on victims of rape by a stranger. But because of the circumstances, many date rape victims don't report the attack. They may feel shame or guilt and blame themselves for what happened. Perhaps they had too much to drink and ended up going back to their assailant's room. Perhaps they dressed provocatively or flirted outrageously. They may have consented to some sexual contact or have had sex with the perpetrator before. If they were drugged, they may be confused about what happened.

Within a relationship or in a dating situation, it can be especially difficult to accept that a crime has been committed. Often victims don't even realize that what happened to them is legally defined as date rape. However, no matter what the circumstances—no matter if the couple is on a first date or have been in a long-term dating relationship—if the sex was nonconsensual, **it was rape and it's a crime.**

What to Do

Sadly, victims of date rape sometimes face the additional burden of having to convince the authorities that an attack has happened. Memory lapses (potentially caused by alcohol or date rape drugs) and a lack of physical evidence can make it difficult to build a case. Following a rape, it's important that victims[4]:

- Call 911 if they are seriously injured or in immediate danger.
- Ensure they feel safe. They should contact someone they trust, tell them what happened and what they can do to help.
- Preserve the evidence. As difficult as it may be, victims should try to avoid bathing, shampooing or combing their hair, using the restroom or changing clothes prior to seeking medical help.
- Get medical attention. They should go to the hospital or call the National Sexual Assault Hotline at 800.656.HOPE (4673) for advice regarding local health facilities.
- Contact the police or campus law enforcement to report the rape—if they want to. The decision to report or not to report is completely up to the victim.
- Get help in healing. Following the trauma of a sexual assault, a survivor will need time to recover. The support of family and friends is important. It may also help to join a support group, consult a counselor or seek advice from the National Sexual Assault Hotline at 800.656.HOPE (4673).

Protecting Yourself

Ensuring your personal safety requires awareness and preparation. Everyone is vulnerable, but there are steps[5] you can take to reduce your risk of becoming a victim.

Reducing Your Risk

- Always be aware of your surroundings. Be aware of where you are and who is around you.
- Try to avoid isolated areas and stick to well-lit, well-traveled locations.
- When you go out, be sure to have your cell phone with you or money to make a phone call.
- Let someone know where you're going and when you'll be home. Be sure to let them know if your plan changes.
- Don't allow yourself to be left alone with someone you don't trust or don't know.
- Use the buddy system. At social gatherings, arrive and leave with a group of friends, and check up on each other during the event.
- Don't accept drinks from people you don't know or trust. Get your own drink and ask that it be opened or poured in front of you. Never leave it unattended.
- If you suspect that you or a friend has been drugged, call 9-1-1 immediately.
- Don't accept rides from casual acquaintances.
- Trust your intuition. If you feel unsafe in any situation, go with your instincts and leave.

If someone is pressuring you:

- Don't be intimidated. You should never feel obligated to do anything you don't want to do.
- Make up a reason to leave. You could tell the person you feel unwell, that you have somewhere else you need to be, or that you've arranged to meet up with family or friends.
- Arrange a code word with your friends or family, so that you can call and communicate your concern to them without the person you're with knowing. The person you call can come and get you or make up an excuse for you to leave.
- Try to think of an escape route. How can you get out of the room? Are there people around who could help you?

If someone is stalking you:

- Avoid all contact with the stalker.
- Tell your family, friends and others around you about what's going on.
- Keep a detailed log of all the incidents related to the stalking.
- Keep all evidence, such as texts, letters, packages and messages received from the stalker.
- Consider reporting the stalking to your local police.

Most schools have some sort of public safety office to provide information and services that help make the campus safe and secure. You may be able to find information about this on your school's website.

JOURNAL 9-2 What Would You Do....Now?

Think about the legal definitions for domestic violence, dating violence, sexual assault and stalking and the information you've read about protecting yourself and others. Consider your responses to the questions about the party. Would you still handle things the same way? What would you change, if anything? Record your answer below.

"It's a really screwed-up world, but it's not your fault. And what happened to you, it doesn't make you the monster."

–MARISKA HARGITAY

Reporting an Incident

If you have been sexually assaulted or the victim of other forms of sexual violence, remember, **it's not your fault**. You have not done anything wrong. The blame lies entirely with the perpetrator of the crime. Do seek medical attention and counseling, even if you decide not to report the incident.

The decision to notify campus authorities or file a complaint against the person(s) responsible is completely up to you. If you decide to report an offense, your school will inform you of the procedures victims should follow. You will be provided with information about the person or office you should contact, the importance of preserving evidence, and the school's responsibilities regarding judicial no-contact, restraining and legal protection orders. The school is required to provide you with written notice of your rights and options.

In cases of sexual assault, federal law safeguards certain basic rights for both the accused and the accuser:

Rights of the Accuser and the Accused

- Schools are required to inform victims about their options in notifying law enforcement
- Victims must be advised of the availability of counseling services, legal assistance and medical care
- Victims must be notified of options to change their academic and living situations
- Victims' confidentiality must be protected to the extent that it is permissible by law
- The accuser and the accused must be given the same opportunity to have advisers or others present at any disciplinary hearing
- Both parties must be informed of the outcome of any disciplinary proceeding simultaneously and in writing. A school cannot require a victim to keep the outcome confidential

Schools must ensure that their disciplinary procedures will provide a prompt, fair, and impartial investigation and resolution. As part of its sexual misconduct policy, a school is required to outline sanctions or protective measures that may be imposed following a final determination of rape, acquaintance rape, domestic violence, dating violence, sexual assault, or stalking. Some examples of sanctions include verbal warning, probation, suspension, and expulsion.

Take another look at the survey you completed at the beginning of this chapter. Are you confident that you know all the correct answers? Review this chapter and check your school's website and student handbook to ensure you have all the information you need. You can also contact your school's Title IX coordinator to discuss any questions.

On-Campus and Off-Campus Resources

Your school also requires you to be aware of the following resources.

- **The Consequences of College Drinking**: See Link 9-9 for the sobering statistics
- **Emergency Procedures**: Check your school's website for information on its emergency procedures.
- **Reporting a Crime**: Check your school's website for information on its crime reporting procedures.
- **Self-Defense**: See Link 9-10 for an article with several viewpoints on self-defense. If you are interested, your school or community is likely to have self-defense courses available.

What is Consent?

What's your understanding of "consent"? A group of students at the University of Florida set out to learn how their fellow students would respond to that question. They recorded a video in which students were asked to define consent, and whether they knew their school had a definition for it. The results were mixed. Most respondents were able to provide an adequate explanation for the meaning of consent. However, only one person was aware the school had its own definition.

What does it matter? you might be asking. In fact, it matters a lot. Not knowing how consent is defined in your state, and at your school, could have serious consequences. If you violate school policy or unwittingly break the law, you could find yourself unintentionally committing a sexual assault. On the flip side, if you've been victimized by someone who assumed their unwelcome actions were "harmless," you might realize there's a case to be made for a formal complaint.

The U.S. Department of Justice defines sexual assault as "any type of sexual contact or behavior that occurs *without the explicit consent of the recipient*." In other words, the participants must clearly and willingly indicate their agreement to engage in sexual activity. Non-consensual sexual contact is against the law.

@Alena Hovorkova/Shutterstock.com

CONSENT

Check out the video at Link 9-11. Then, in the box below, write a few words to describe your own understanding of consent.

Yes Means Yes or No Means No?

It would be great if consent was easily defined and the same interpretation applied across the country. Unfortunately, it's not that simple. Each state, and the District of Columbia, has its own laws regarding consent. As well, every school has its own definition for consent, which is based not only on state legal requirements but on factors such as the school's size, its students and its past experiences. So it's important to understand not only your state's laws, but how consent is defined at your school.

As a general starting point, the White House Task Force to Protect Students from Sexual Assault suggests a school's definition of consent should include the following[5]:

What is Consent?

- Consent must be informed, voluntary, and mutual
- Consent is not a single, one-time agreement. It must be ongoing throughout a sexual activity and can be withdrawn at any time
- There is no consent when force, coercion, intimidation or threats are used
- Silence or absence of resistance does not imply consent
- Past consent does not imply ongoing future consent with that person nor consent to that same sexual activity with another person
- A person who is incapacitated cannot consent; this includes impairment due to alcohol or drug consumption, or being asleep or unconscious

In many states, consent is defined on the basis of "No means No." Essentially that means a person is responsible for verbally saying "No," or for physically indicating that they do not consent to sex, clearly and definitively.

Think about that for a minute. If a person is intoxicated or drugged, they may not be capable of saying No. If they feel threatened or intimidated, they may be too scared to say No. Not having the ability to say No doesn't necessarily mean a person consents to having sex. But under these circumstances, a victim who makes an accusation of sexual assault could have difficulty proving their case.

The State of California recently adopted an affirmative consent standard. Often referred to as "Yes means Yes," affirmative consent means both participants must agree—mutually, consciously, and voluntarily—to engage in sexual activity. The onus is not on one person to say No, but rather on both people to clearly, emphatically, and continuously say Yes.

While it has its critics, affirmative consent is largely considered to be a step in the right direction. A number of other states are considering adopting it as law, and **many colleges and universities are already including affirmative consent language** in their student codes of conduct. Be sure to know what the rules are at your school.

For your school's definition of "consent," check the school's website, contact the Title IX coordinator, or refer to your state's definition of consent.

Still not entirely clear about what constitutes consent? Watch the video at Link 9-12 for a simple explanation.

Consent: Talk About It

Talking about consent may feel a little awkward at first if you're not used to discussing it. But there's nothing shameful or embarrassing about deciding to engage in sexual activity, or declining to engage in it. What's important is that you make your own decisions and are able to communicate easily and openly about them, and that you have respect for other people and the choices they make.

Having a conversation about consent helps you to:
- avoid ambiguity in your sexual interactions
- clearly express your interest, what you're comfortable with and how far you want to go
- plainly indicate when you're not interested
- recognize and acknowledge other people's boundaries
- ensure that your sexual activity is entirely mutual and consensual

Here are a few things to keep in mind:

Don't assume: Never assume consent is implied. Body language can be misinterpreted. Even if it seems like a person is flirting, it doesn't mean they're offering to have sex with you. So always ask. If the other person doesn't respond, or doesn't appear capable of consenting (if they're drunk, high or asleep, for instance), then it's *not* OK to proceed. It's also not OK to try to bully, charm or cajole them into it. Don't complain that if they really loved you, they would have sex with you. Don't threaten to go somewhere else to get what you want. Remember, consent needs to be clear, mutual and freely given.

Show some respect: If the other person isn't into it, or just isn't into you, respect their decision. Don't look at this as an opportunity to accuse them of being a prude, or attack them for their sexual orientation, or jeer at their choice to abstain from sex. People can have all sorts of reasons for not wanting to have sex. They don't owe you a reason or an explanation.

Establish the boundaries: If both of you consent to engage in sexual activity, talk with your partner about what you'd like to do. Specifically. Both of you need to be in agreement about what you're going to do. If you're not accustomed to having this kind of talk, practice. Think of some ways you can say things, like:
- "Can I kiss you?"
- "Have you ever...? Do you want to do it with me?"
- "What would you like to do with me?"
- "Is there anything you don't want to do?"
- "Are you comfortable with...?"
- "Would you like it if I....?"
- "Do you want to try...?"

Keep talking: Check with your partner every so often to ensure that both of you are still comfortable with what's happening. If you want to move on to a sexual act you haven't already discussed, talk about it first. If you feel like things are moving too fast, tell your partner you want to slow down. If you or your partner wants to stop, the person should say so. The activity must stop right away.

Saying No: If you don't want to engage in sexual contact with the other person, or you're being pushed to do something you haven't agreed to, you can say things like:

- "I'm not interested in having sex/doing that"
- "I'd like to be friends. Can we just hang out?"
- "Please give me some space. Don't get so close to me"
- "I'm not comfortable with that"
- "Stop touching me"
- "Don't do that"
- "I'm not ready for that yet"
- "Stop. I don't want to do that"
- "You're not listening. Please respect my decision"
- "I'm drunk"
- "I'm tired. I just want to go to sleep"
- "I'd like you to leave now"
- "Not now"
- "No"

Take a look at the statements you've just read under Saying No. Are you the person who's on the receiving end of these comments? If someone is saying things like this to you, back off. The other person clearly does not want to do this with you. If you attempt or commit a sexual act with someone who has not given consent, you could find yourself charged with sexual assault.

How to Have a Healthy Relationship

It's been said that friendships made at college can last a lifetime. Many students will also experience their first serious romantic relationship while at college. Whether it lasts forever or just a few semesters, a healthy relationship can be a source of happiness, excitement, security, and support while you're at college—and evoke warm memories long after your school days are over.

Sometimes, when you're caught up in the exhilaration of a new romantic attachment, you may not realize that everything isn't as right as it should be. How do you know if your situation is beneficial or harmful? Here are some of the main qualities of a healthy relationship:

- Your partner is your best friend. You genuinely enjoy spending time together and like a lot of the same activities. Friendship provides the bond that comes with having mutual interests. Without it, when the initial attraction that brought you together begins to fade, there will be nothing left to build on.

- You communicate openly, honestly and respectfully. Good communication is a key ingredient of any successful relationship. You may not agree about everything, but when conflict arises, you're able to deal with it in a positive way.
- You both value the relationship and want the same things out of it. Differing expectations—about the amount of time you spend together, the things you do, your hopes and prospects for the future—can be a source of tension and disappointment.
- You feel safe, secure, and at ease in each other's company. Fear, violence, intimidation, possessiveness, and humiliation are signs of a destructive relationship.
- You have an equal partnership. You make important decisions together and negotiate and compromise in a respectful way. One partner doesn't try to manipulate or control the other.
- You're great when you're together *and* when you're apart. Mutual respect, trust, and honesty are the cornerstones of a solid relationship. But being together 24/7 doesn't necessarily result in a stronger connection. In a healthy relationship, you are considerate and supportive of each other's needs to take time for activities, family or friends outside of the relationship.

While most students experience healthy, fulfilling relationships at college, dating violence is on the rise. According to a survey conducted by Knowledge Networks[6], many college students do not know how to help their friends or themselves get out of abusive relationships.

Student Poll on Dating Abuse

Students say...	Percent
"dating abuse is difficult to identify"	57
"I don't know how to help someone who's a victim"	58
"I don't know how to get help on campus if I were a victim"	38

Whether it involves you or a friend of yours, there are signs you can look for that indicate the relative safety or risk of a relationship. Take the quiz to learn how to spot the signs of abuse.

A HEALTHY OR HARMFUL RELATIONSHIP?

Decide whether each statement is sign of a healthy or harmful relationship. Then check your answers.

1. Your partner understands and doesn't mind when you spend time apart.

2. Your partner makes jokes about your looks and laughs about it with friends.

3. Other people think your partner has a violent temper, but you know it's just bad behavior—your partner would never hurt you.

4. Your partner insists that you spend all your time together, even though that means less time for family and friends.

5. You and your partner listen to each other's opinions and respect them, but you don't always agree about everything.

6. When you're apart, your partner calls repeatedly to check up on you.

7. Your partner tells you how to act, how to style your hair and what clothes you should wear.

8. You sometimes have to hide or explain away bruises inflicted on you by your partner.

9. It's OK to say "No" if you don't want to have sex and your partner will respect your wishes.

10. If your partner does something wrong, you feel it's your duty to make excuses and cover for it.

11. You've stopped pursuing hobbies and activities you used to enjoy, because your partner says it's more important that you both share all the same interests.

12. You feel you're loved and valued, because your partner gets jealous when others pay attention to you.

Answer: Numbers 1, 5 and 9 are signs of a healthy relationship. All the other statements indicate unhealthy, potentially abusive relationships.

©arka38/Shutterstock.com

"Friends can help each other. A true friend is someone who lets you have total freedom to be yourself—and especially to feel. Or, not feel. Whatever you happen to be feeling at the moment is fine with them. That's what real love amounts to—letting a person be what he really is."

–JIM MORRISON

Know the Signs and Get Help

Violence in a relationship often starts with emotional and verbal abuse—threats and oppressive behavior, sarcastic comments, degrading jokes, and insults. An abuser will use domination and intimidation tactics in an attempt to gain greater control in the relationship and isolate their partner from other people. By making false accusations and unreasonable demands, the abuser makes their partner feel guilty for not being "perfect enough," causing them to become more passive and eager to please. The belittling remarks and harsh treatment gradually erode the victim's self-confidence and make them feel worthless.

This pattern of behavior typically escalates, and the abuse becomes more frequent and increasingly severe. By the time a situation has progressed to physical violence, the victim could be in danger of serious injury—or worse.

If you or someone you know is in an abusive relationship, it's important to get help. Talk to your campus counseling center for support and advice. Check your school's website for information on counseling services.

CHAPTER 9 QUIZ

Rights, Respect, and Responsibility

Select the best answer for each of the following questions.

1. Title IX is
   a. a status award for colleges.
   b. a grant to help create more women's sports teams.
   c. a law to protect against discrimination in education.
   d. something that requires schools to reveal their security policies and crime statistics.
   e. none of the above.

2. Which of the following is FALSE regarding Title IX?
   a. It only applies in interactions between a school employee and a student.
   b. It applies to all students, including part-time students.
   c. When in violation of Title IX, a school may have to pay damages.
   d. The school must attempt to resolve situations even when the police are already involved.
   e. All of the above are true.

3. The Clery Act is
   a. a status award for colleges.
   b. a grant to help create more women's sports teams.
   c. a law to protect against discrimination in education.
   d. something that requires schools to reveal their security policies and crime statistics.
   e. none of the above.

4. By definition, sexual assault includes all of the following, EXCEPT
   a. attempted rape.
   b. unwanted sexual touching.
   c. coercing someone into having sex.
   d. having sex with someone too intoxicated to consent.
   e. All of the above are considered sexual assault.

5. One in every _____ women will be the victim of sexual assault while in college.
   a. four
   b. seven
   c. ten
   d. fifteen
   e. twenty

6. Which of the following is NOT a good option for a bystander of sexual assault?
   a. If the person is incapacitated, stay with them or arrange for their friends to take care of them.
   b. If you don't know what to do or are not comfortable intervening, do nothing.
   c. If the situation is not volatile, you could step in and ask the person if they need help.
   d. If you know the aggressor, tell them you don't approve and ask them to leave the person alone.
   e. All of the above are good options.

7 Which of the following should you NOT do if someone is stalking you?
a. Avoid all contact with the stalker.
b. Tell your family, friends, and others around you about what's going on.
c. Consider reporting the stalking to your local police.
d. Throw away or delete things like letters or messages from the stalker.
e. All of the above are things you should do if someone is stalking you.

8 Federal law safeguards certain basic rights of the people accused of sexual crimes and of the people making the accusation. Which of the following is NOT one of those rights?
a. Schools are required to inform victims about their options in notifying law enforcement.
b. Victims must be advised of the availability of counseling services, legal assistance and medical care.
c. Accusers and the accused must be able to have advisers present at disciplinary hearings.
d. Only the victim should be informed of the outcome of the disciplinary proceedings.
e. All of the above are correct.

CHAPTER 9 FEEDBACK

Congratulations, you've completed Chapter 9! To conclude your learning in this chapter, consider and note the following:

What parts of this chapter were most helpful to you?

How would you improve this chapter?

ENDNOTES

CHAPTER 1

Section 1

1. Viktor Frankl. (2013, February 11). In Wikipedia, The Free Encyclopedia. Retrieved 23:42, February 18, 2013, from http://en.wikipedia.org/w/index.php?title=Viktor_Frankl&oldid=5376302826
2. Bronk, K. C., Hill, P. L., Lapsley, D. K., Talib, T. L., & Finch, H. (2009) Purpose, hope, and life satisfaction in three age groups. *The Journal of Positive Psychology, 4*(6) 500-510 DOI:10.1080/17439760903271439
3. Debats, D. L. (1998). Measurement of personal meaning: The psychometric properties of the life regard index. In P. T. P. Wong & P.S. Fry (Eds.), *The human quest for meaning: A handbook of psychological research and clinical applications* (pp. 237–259). Mahwah, NJ: Lawrence Erlbaum Associates, Inc.
4. Rush University Medical Center (2012, May 7). Greater purpose in life may protect against harmful changes in the brain associated with Alzheimer's disease. *ScienceDaily*. Retrieved February 12, 2013, from http://www.sciencedaily.com /releases/2012/05/120507164326.htm
5. Protects against heart disease. Koizumi, M., Ito, H., Kaneko, Y., & Motohashi, Y. (2008) Effect of having a sense of purpose in life on the risk of death from cardiovascular diseases. *Journal of Epidemiology, 18*(5) 191-6.
6. Damon, W., Menon, J., & Bronk, K. C. (2003): The Development of Purpose During Adolescence, *Applied Developmental Science, 7*(3) 119-128. DOI:10.1207/S1532480XADS0703_2

CHAPTER 2

Section 1

1. Dweck, C. S. (1986). Motivational processes affecting learning. *American Psychologist 41* (10): 1040–1048. doi:10.1037/0003-066X.41.10.1040
2. Silverman, S. C., & Northcutt, F. *How to Survive Your Freshman Year.* Print. p. 591

3. Postsecondary Institutions and Price of Attendance in 2013-14; Degrees and Other Awards Conferred: 2012-13; and 12-Month Enrollment: 2012-13: First Look, National Center for Education Statistics accessed from http://nces.ed.gov/pubsearch/pubsinfo.asp?pubid=2014066rev

4. Adapted from 'What Does a Typical College Class Schedule Look Like?.' 2011. 7 May. 2014 http://www.campusexplorer.com/college-advice-tips/8BB2B355/What-Does-a-Typical-College-Class-Schedule-Look-Like

5. Adapted from Mullendore, R.H. and Hatch C. (2000). Helping your first-year college student succeed: A guide for parents. Columbia, S.C.: OCM and Texas A&M University.

Section 2

1. http://www.scientificamerican.com/article/a-learning-secret-don-t-take-notes-with-a-laptop/

2. https://www.altoona.psu.edu/fts/docs/SeatingPositionGrades.pdf

3. Adapted from *The 15 Habits of Top College Students*. 8 May, 2014. http://www.washcoll.edu/live/files/3704-the-15-habits-of-top-college-studentspdf

Section 3

1. Bernstein, M. W., & Kaufman, Y. Northcutt, F., & Silverman, S. C. special editors. *How to Survive Your Freshman Year*. Atlanta, GA: Hundreds of Heads, 2008. Print.

2. Reading Major Profiles - Exploring College Majors - BigFuture. 2012. retrieved 14 May, 2014. https://bigfuture.collegeboard.org/explore-careers/college-majors/reading-major-profiles

Section 4

1. Bernstein, M. W., & Kaufman, Y. Northcutt, F., & Silverman, S. C. special editors. *How to Survive Your Freshman Year*. Atlanta, GA: Hundreds of Heads, 2008. Print.

2. How to Pick Extracurricular Activities in College. 2010. Retrieved May 14, 2014 from http://www.universitylanguage.com/blog/27/extracurricular-activities-in-college/

Section 5

1. Blind spot - *Merriam-Webster Online*. 2006. Retrieved May 21, 2014 from http://www.merriam-webster.com/dictionary/blind%20spot

2. Bernstein, M. W., & Kaufman, Y. Northcutt, F., & Silverman, S. C. special editors. *How to Survive Your Freshman Year*. (5th Edition) Atlanta: Hundreds of Heads, 2013. Print.

CHAPTER 3

Section 3

1. Work Stress On The Rise - *Huffington Post*. 2013. Retrieved on Apr. 25, 2014 from http://www.huffingtonpost.com/2013/04/10/work-stress-jobs-americans_n_3053428.html

2. Earnings and unemployment rates by educational attainment (2015) U.S. Bureau of Labor Statistics. Retrieved on August 25, 2015 from http://www.bls.gov/emp/ep_chart_001.htm
3. Charting the Projections: 2012-22. *Occupational Outlook Quarterly*. U.S. Department of Labor http://www.bls.gov/careeroutlook/2013/winter/winter2013ooq.pdf
4. Can Money Buy You Happiness? (2014) *Wall Street Journal*. Retrieved from http://online.wsj.com/articles/can-money-buy-happiness-heres-what-science-has-to-say-1415569538?mod=trending_now_3 Nov 12, 2014

Section 4

1. Make the Case: College Ready AND Career Ready. 25 Apr. 2014 retrieved from http://www.future-readyproject.org/sites/frp/files/Flex-CollegeReady&CareerReady.pdf
2. 10 Dying U.S. Industries: IBISWorld - *Huffington Post*. 2011. Retrieved on Apr. 25, 2014 from http://www.huffingtonpost.com/2011/04/02/uss-most-endangered-industries_n_842787.html
3. http://business.time.com/2012/09/24/how-different-generations-of-americans-try-to-find-work
4. 5 Businesses That Technology Has Dramatically Changed ... 2011. Retrieved on Apr. 25, 2014 from http://www.businessinsurance.org/5-businesses-that-technology-has-dramatically-changed/
5. http://jobs.aol.com/articles/2011/10/07/9-skilled-occupations-being-killed-by-technology
6. http://jobs.aol.com/articles/2011/10/07/9-skilled-occupations-being-killed-by-technology

CHAPTER 4

Section 1

1. www.youtube.com/watch?v=54aFTZ9POw4
2. jamesclear.com/goals-systems
3. http://www.dailygood.org/story/684/this-coach-improved-every-tiny-thing-by-1-and-here-s-what-happened-james-clear/
4. http://www.loveatfirstfight.com/relationship-advice/communication-skills/decision-making/
5. Goal - *Merriam-Webster Online*. 2005. 6 Jun. 2014 retrieved from http://www.merriam-webster.com/dictionary/goal
6. Plan - *Merriam-Webster Online*. 2005. 6 Jun. 2014 retrieved from http://www.merriam-webster.com/dictionary/plan

Section 2

1. Nemes, C. (1996). *Young Thomas Edison: Great Inventor*. Mahwah, NJ: Troll Associates.
2. SMART criteria - Wikipedia, the free encyclopedia. 2006. 7 Jun. 2014 http://en.wikipedia.org/wiki/SMART_criteria

Section 3

1. http://www.goal-setting-for-success.com/short-term-goal.html

Section 4

1. Sisyphus - Wikipedia, the free encyclopedia. 2003. 7 Jun. 2014 http://en.wikipedia.org/wiki/Sisyphus

CHAPTER 5

Section 1

1. Dweck, C. (2005). *Mindset: The New Psychology of Success.* Teaching a growth. 12 Jun. 2014 http://mindsetonline.com
2. The Duckworth Lab - University of Pennsylvania. 2013. 12 Jun. 2014 https://sites.sas.upenn.edu/duckworth
3. Kendra Cherry. What Is the Difference Between Extrinsic and Intrinsic ...? 2013. 28 May. 2014 http://psychology.about.com/od/motivation/f/difference-between-extrinsic-and-intrinsic-motivation.htm
4. Marinak, B. A., & Gambrell, L. B. 'Intrinsic Motivation and Rewards: What Sustains Young Children's Engagement with Text?' *Literacy Research and Instruction 47,* 2008, 9-26.
5. Mark R. Lepper, David Greene and Richard Nisbet, 'Undermining Children's Intrinsic Interest with Extrinsic Reward; A Test of 'Overjustification' Hypothesis,' *Journal of Personality and Social Psychology 28,* 1973, 129Ð37.
6. Wigfield, A., Guthrie, J. T., Tonks, S., & Perencevich, K. C. (2004). Children's motivation for reading: Domain specificity and instructional influences. *Journal of Educational Research, 97,* 299-309.

Section 2

1. Dictionary.com, 'critical thinking,' in *Dictionary.com,* Unabridged. Source location: Random House, Inc. http://dictionary.reference.com/browse/critical thinking. Accessed: 22 June 2013.
2. UNESCO.org - International Day for Tolerance - Declaration of Principles on Tolerance, Article 4, 3

Section 3

1. Schraw, Gregory (1998). Promoting general metacognitive awareness. *Instructional Science 26:* 113-125. doi:10.1023/A:1003044231033.

Section 4A

1. Schacter, J. (1999) The impact of Education Technology on Student Achievement. Milken Exchange. Retrieved from http://www2.gsu.edu/~wwwche/Milken%20report.pdf June 12, 2014.
2. Review of Learning 2.0 Practices. Christine Redecker. 2009 retrieved from http://ftp.jrc.es/EURdoc/JRC49108.pdf
3. Adapted from 5 Tech Skills Every Job Seeker Needs. Sara Angeles. *Business News Daily.* April 24, 2015. http://www.businessnewsdaily.com/6316-tech-skills-job-seeker.html and The Tech Skills Employers Want. Chad Brooks. Business News Daily. July 15, 2013. http://www.businessnewsdaily.com/6316-tech-skills-job-seeker.html

4. IDC Press Release Oct. 29, 2014. http://www.idc.com/getdoc.jsp?containerId=prUS25224914

5. 6 Reasons your phone bill keeps rising. Kim Peterson. *CBS Moneywatch*. Retrieved from http://www.cbsnews.com/news/6-reasons-your-phone-bill-keeps-rising/ Dec 29, 2014

6. http://www.pcblawfirm.com/articles/legal-issues-photographing-people/

Section 4B

1. Herbert, W. (2014) Ink of Paper: Some Notes on Note-taking. *Association for Psychological Science*. http://www.psychologicalscience.org/index.php/news/were-only-human/ink-on-paper-some-notes-on-note-taking.html Taken May 8, 2014.

2. Mueller, P., and Oppenheimer, D. (2014) The Pen Is Mightier Than the Keyboard: Advantages of Longhand Over Laptop Note Taking. *Psychological Science*. doi: 10.1177/0956797614524581

3. Well Cast. http://www.watchwellcast.com/

Section 4E

1. Halpern, D. F., Hansen, C., Riefer, D. (1990) Analogies as an aid to understanding and memory. *Journal of Educational Psychology, 82*(2) 298-305. doi:10.1037/0022-0663.82.2.298

2. Fenker, D., and Schutze, H. (2008) Learning By Surprise. *Scientific American*. Retrieved from http://www.scientificamerican.com/article/learning-by-surprise/ on July 2, 2014.

3. Mather, M., and Sutherland, M. (20012) The selective effects of emotional arousal on memory. *Psychological Science Agenda*. Retrieved from http://www.apa.org/science/about/psa/2012/02/emotional-arousal.aspx on July 2, 2014.

4. Xue, G., Mei, L., Chen, C., Lu, Z., Poldrack, R., Dong, Q. (2011). Spaced Learning Enhances Subsequent Recognition Memory by Reducing Neural Repetition Suppression. *Journal of Cognitive Neuroscience, 23*(7), 1624-1633. http://dx.doi.org/10.1162/jocn.2010.21532

Section 4G

1. adapted from http://www.macewan.ca/web/services/ims/client/upload/10%20tips%20for%20Writing%20Multiple%20Choice%20Exams%20-%20Web.pdf, http://www.socialpsychology.org/testtips.htm

2. *Journal of Personality and Social Psychology*, Vol. 88, 725-735

3. Adapted from *U.S News*. Top 10 Tips for Taking Essay Tests. http://www.usnews.com/education/blogs/professors-guide/2009/11/18/top-10-tips-for-taking-essay-tests retrieved Jan 5 2015

CHAPTER 6

Section 1

1. http://www.forbes.com/sites/jacquelynsmith/2013/03/11/10-nonverbal-cues-that-convey-confidence-at-work/

Section 2

1. People Problems Cost Calculator, *Satisfaction@Work*, accessed from https://www.satisfactionatwork.com/resources/people-problems-cost-calculator
2. The Negative Impact of Ineffective Teamwork in Companies, *Inside Business 360*, accessed from http://www.insidebusiness360.com/index.php/the-negative-impact-of-ineffective-teamwork-in-companies-15568/
3. Adapted from Building a Sense of Teamwork Among Staff Members, *American Management Association®*, accessed from http://www.amanet.org/training/articles/Building-a-Sense-of-Teamwork-Among-Staff-Members.aspx and Benefits of Teamwork, Wikipedia accessed from http://en.wikipedia.org/wiki/Teamwork#Benefits
4. Adapted from Characteristics of Good and Poor Collaborators, accessed from http://core.ecu.edu/engl/kaind/4530/ftp/hgood.htm
5. Adapted from Resolving Conflicts on the Team by Marty Brounstein from *Managing Teams For Dummies*. http://www.dummies.com/how-to/content/resolving-conflicts-on-the-team.html
6. Adapted from Resolving Conflicts on the Team, *For Dummies*, accessed from http://www.dummies.com/how-to/content/resolving-conflicts-on-the-team.html and 6 Ways to Effectively Deal with Team Conflict, Dale Carnegie Training, accessed from http://blog.dalecarnegie.com/leadership/6-ways-to-effectively-deal-with-team-conflict/

Section 3

1. Adapted from Seven Qualities of a Good Leader, Groco CPAs and Advisors, accessed from http://www.groco.com/readingroom/bus_goodleader.aspx and Top 10 Qualities that Make a Great Leader, *Forbes*, accessed from http://www.forbes.com/sites/tanyaprive/2012/12/19/top-10-qualities-that-make-a-great-leader/http://en.wikipedia.org/wiki/Teamwork#Benefits
2. Adapted from The Effects of Poor Leadership, *eHow*, accessed from http://www.ehow.com/info_8649813_effects-bad-leadership.html and Good Leaders are Invaluable to a Company. Bad Leaders will Destroy It, *Forbes*, accessed from http://www.forbes.com/sites/amyanderson/2013/01/14/good-leaders-are-invaluable-to-a-company-bad-leaders-will-destroy-it/
3. FAQs, Nelson Mandela Foundation, accessed from https://www.nelsonmandela.org/content/page/faqs and Nelson Mandela, Wikipedia, accessed from http://en.wikipedia.org/wiki/Nelson_Mandela
4. Tuckman's Stages of Group Development, Wikipedia, accessed from http://en.wikipedia.org/wiki/Tuckman's_stages_of_group_development and What to Know about Group Dynamics, United Nations Environment Programme, accessed from http://www.unep.org/ieacp/iea/training/guide/default.aspx?id=1202

CHAPTER 7

Introduction

1. 2013 http://www.imdb.com/title/tt2234155/1

Section 1

1. Stanford University Career Center. Retrieved from https://studentaffairs.stanford.edu/cdc/jobs/internships#layout July 2014
2. Gustavus Adolphus Career Center. Retrieved from https://gustavus.edu/servantleadership/careercenter/intern/ July 2014
3. http://money.usnews.com/money/careers/slideshows/10-tips-to-get-the-most-out-of-your-internship
4. Nina Friend. The Online Advice You Need to Crush Your Internship. July 11, 2014. *Huffington Post.* Retrieved from http://www.huffingtonpost.com/2014/07/11/advice-to-crush-your-internship_n_5568495.html on February 12, 2015
5. GetEducated.com. Retrieved from http://www.geteducated.com/cutting-online-university-cost/145-online-life-experience-degree July 2014

Section 2

1. Adapted from 'Sample Workplace Expectations,' College of Charleston Career Center. Retrieved on February 16, 2015 from http://careercenter.cofc.edu/employers/workplace-expectations.php
2. Alexander Kjerulf, 2007. Top 10 Reasons Why Happiness at Work is the Ultimate Productivity Booster. Retrieved on Feb 17, 2015 from http://positivesharing.com/2007/03/top-10-reasons-why-happiness-at-work-is-the-ultimate-productivity-booster/

Section 3

1. Kaplan Test Prep Survey: More College Admissions Officers Checking Applicants' Digital Trails, But Most Students Unconcerned. Press Release by Kaplan Test Prep Online Pressroom. Retrieved on Feb 18, 2015 from http://press.kaptest.com/press-releases/kaplan-test-prep-survey-more-college-admissions-officers-checking-applicants-digital-trails-but-most-students-unconcerned
2. Ibid.
3. Susie Poppick for Money Magazine. Sept. 5, 2014. 10 Social Media Blunders That Cost a Millennial a Job — or Worse. http://time.com/money/3019899/10-facebook-twitter-mistakes-lost-job-millennials-viral/
4. Elaine Burke for Silicon Republic. 30 May, 2013. 1 in 10 young people losing out on jobs because of pics and comments on social media. https://www.siliconrepublic.com/careers/1-in-10-young-people-losing-out-on-jobs-because-of-pics-and-comments-on-social-media
5. About LinkedIn. LinkedIn.com. Retrieved 2015-02-03 from https://press.linkedin.com/about-linkedin
6. Mel Carson for Entrepreneur. Dec 9, 2014. 5 Twitter Tips that Will Enhance Your Personal Brand. Retrieved Feb 20, 2015 from http://www.entrepreneur.com/article/240642.6
7. Ashley Zeckman for Search Engine Watch. May 20, 2014. Google Search Engine Market Share Nears 68%. Retrieved on Feb20, 2015 from http://searchenginewatch.com/sew/study/2345837/google-search-engine-market-share-nears-68
8. Horwitz, Josh. (2013-07-10) Semiocast: Pinterest now has 70 million users and is steadily gaining momentum outside the *US. The Next Web.* Retrieved on 2014-02-25 from http://thenextweb.com/

socialmedia/2013/07/10/semiocast-pinterest-now-has-70-million-users-and-is-steadily-gaining-momentum-outside-the-us/

9. Emily Driscoll (June 3, 2013) What Your Social Media Reputation Says to Employers. *FoxBusiness*. Retrieved on Feb 24, 2015 from http://www.foxbusiness.com/personal-finance/2013/06/03/what-your-social-media-reputation-says-to-employers/

Section 4

1. Retrieved from http://www.rinkworks.com/said/resume.shtml on February 25, 2015.
2. Williams, J. R. (1998). Guidelines for the use of multimedia in instruction, Proceedings of the Human Factors and Ergonomics Society 42nd Annual Meeting, 1447–1451.

Summary

2. Susan Adams (Sept. 9, 2012). The 10 Best Websites for Your Career. *Forbes*. Retrieved on April 21, 2016 from http://www.forbes.com/sites/susanadams/2012/09/14/the-10-best-websites-for-your-career/#2f95faba5330

CHAPTER 8

Introduction

1. Shawn Achor: The Secret to Better Work. 2011. Retrieved from https://www.youtube.com/watch?v=fLJsdqxnZb0
2. Daniele Quercia. Happy Maps. Nov 2014, TED@BCG Berlin. Retrieved from http://www.ted.com/talks/daniele_quercia_happy_maps/transcript?language=en

Section 1

1. The 2014 Consumer Financial Literacy Survey by Harris Poll. The National Foundation for Credit Counseling (NFCC). Retrieved on Mar 17, 2015 from http://www.nfcc.org/NewsRoom/FinancialLiteracy/files2013/NFCC_2014FinancialLiteracySurvey_datasheet_and_key_findings_031314%20FINAL.pdf
2. Table 331.30. Average amount of grant and scholarship aid and average net price for first-time, full-time students receiving Title IV aid, and percentage distribution of students, by control and level of institution and income level: 2009-10, 2010-11, and 2011-12. Digest of Education Statistics. National Center for Education Statistics. Retrieved on April 2, 2015 from https://nces.ed.gov/programs/digest/d13/tables/dt13_331.30.asp

Section 2

1. Martin Lindstrom (2011). Monkey See, Monkey Buy. *Time*. Retrieved on April 10, 2015 from http://ideas.time.com/2011/10/28/monkey-see-monkey-buy/
2. Prelec, D. and Simester, D. (2001). Always Leave Home Without It: A Further Investigation of the Credit-Card Effect on Willingness to Pay. *Marketing Letters 12* (1) 5-12. 10.1023/A:1008196717017
3. Sandy M. Fernández (2013). *7 Reasons We Overspend*. *Daily Worth*. Retrieved on April 13, 2015 from https://www.dailyworth.com/posts/2022-7-reasons-we-overspend-and-how-to-overcome-them
4. U.S. Federal Reserve-FRED Database - Retrieved April 2015 from http://research.stlouisfed.org//fred2/series/CMDEBT?cid=97
5. Dealing with Change. APS Healthcare University of Washington. Retrieved on April 2015 from http://www.washington.edu/admin/hr/benefits/publications/carelink/tipsheets/dealing-with-change.pdf

Section 3

1. Camille Peri. 10 Things to Hate About Sleep Loss. *WebMD* Feature. Retrieved on April 16 from http://www.webmd.com/sleep-disorders/excessive-sleepiness-10/10-results-sleep-loss
2. U.S. Department of Agriculture, http://www.choosemyplate.gov
3. The Challenges and Failures of Nutrition Studies. *Unite for Sight*. Retrieved April 2015 from http://www.uniteforsight.org/global-health-university/nutrition-study
4. U.S. Department of Agriculture, http://www.choosemyplate.gov
5. Darryl E. Owens, Sleep's Impact on Learning A to Zzzzz, *San Diego Union Tribune*, October 2, 2000.
6. From http://www.thirdage.com/cgi-bin/NewsPrint.cgi, 2002.
7. Francesco Cappuccio, Warwick Medical School, Researchers Say Lack of Sleep Doubles Risk of Death . . . But So Can Too Much Sleep, http://www2warwick.ac.uk, 2008.7
8. Denise Mann (Jan 2013). Alcohol and a Good Night's Sleep Don't Mix. *WebMD News*. Retrieved April 2015 from http://www.webmd.com/sleep-disorders/news/20130118/alcohol-sleep

Section 4

1. Eric Jaffe (April 2013). Why Wait? The Science Behind Procrastination. Observer. Retrieved April 2015 from http://www.psychologicalscience.org/index.php/publications/observer/2013/april-13/why-wait-the-science-behind-procrastination.html
2. Ibid.
3. Ibid.

CHAPTER 9

Introduction

1. The Meaning of Namaste. Rita Geno for *Yoga Journal*. Oct 3, 2014. Retrieved from http://www.yogajournal.com/article/beginners/the-meaning-of-quot-namaste-quot/ on Mar. 6, 2015.

Section 1

1. Association of American Medical Colleges (2014). Retrieved from https://www.aamc.org/download/321532/data/2013factstable27-2.pdf
2. National League for Nursing (2014). Retrieved from http://www.nln.org/researchgrants/slides/pdf/AS1112_F32.pdf

Section 2

1. https://www.clevelandrapecrisis.org/resources/statistics/sexual-violence-on-college-campuses, http://www.loveisrespect.org/resources/dating-violence-statistics/, http://nsvrc.org/sites/default/files/publications_nsvrc_factsheet_media-packet_statistics-about-sexual-violence_0.pdf
2. Adapted from http://apps.carleton.edu/dos/sexual_misconduct/get_involved/green_dot/signs/

Section 3

1. Tips in this section and Protect Yourself are adapted from: https://www.rainn.org

Section 4

1. Adapted from: U.S. Department of Justice Office of Community Oriented Policing Services. Acquaintance Rape of College Students. http://www.cops.usdoj.gov/pdf/e03021472.pdf. Retrieved 23 July 2015. Bentley University. Sexual Assault Prevention. http://www.bentley.edu/campus-life/sexual-assault-prevention Retrieved 9 July 2015. National Union of Students. I Heart Consent. http://www.nusconnect.org.uk/. Retrieved 22 June 2015.
2. Source: U.S. Department of Justice Office of Community Oriented Policing Services. Acquaintance Rape of College Students. http://www.cops.usdoj.gov/pdf/e03021472.pdf. Retrieved 23 July 2015.
3. Sources: https://rainn.org/get-information/sexual-assault-recovery/tips-for-after-an-attack and http://www.aftersilence.org/date-rape.php
4. Adapted from: https://www.rainn.org
5. Adapted from NotAlone.gov. White House Task Force to Protect Students from Sexual Assault. https://www.notalone.gov/assets/definitions-of-prohibited-conduct.pdf Accessed 3 July 2015.
6. Source: http://www.breakthecycle.org/dating-violence-research/college-dating-violence-and-abuse-poll